Jabber™ Programming

Jabber™ Programming

Stephen Lee and Terence Smelser

M&T Books
An imprint of Hungry Minds, Inc.

Best-Selling Books • Digital Downloads • e-Books • Answer Networks •
e-Newsletters • Branded Web Sites • e-Learning

New York, NY ◆ Cleveland, OH ◆ Indianapolis, IN

Jabber™ Programming

Published by
M&T Books
An imprint of Hungry Minds, Inc.
909 Third Avenue
New York, NY 10022
www.hungryminds.com

Library of Congress Control Number: 2002100105

ISBN: 0-7645-4934-0

Printed in the United States of America

10 9 8 7 6 5 4 3 2 1

1B/QY/QT/QS/NY

Distributed in the United States by Hungry Minds, Inc.

Distributed by CDG Books Canada Inc. for Canada; by
Transworld Publishers Limited in the United Kingdom; by
IDG Norge Books for Norway; by IDG Sweden Books for
Sweden; by IDG Books Australia Publishing Corporation
Pty. Ltd. for Australia and New Zealand; by TransQuest
Publishers Pte Ltd. for Singapore, Malaysia, Thailand,
Indonesia, and Hong Kong; by Gotop Information Inc. for
Taiwan; by ICG Muse, Inc. for Japan; by Intersoft for
South Africa; by Eyrolles for France; by International
Thomson Publishing for Germany, Austria, and
Switzerland; by Distribuidora Cuspide for Argentina; by
LR International for Brazil; by Galileo Libros for Chile;
by Ediciones ZETA S.C.R. Ltda. for Peru; by WS
Computer Publishing Corporation, Inc., for the
Philippines; by Contemporanea de Ediciones for
Venezuela; by Express Computer Distributors for the
Caribbean and West Indies; by Micronesia Media
Distributor, Inc. for Micronesia; by Chips Computadoras
S.A. de C.V. for Mexico; by Editorial Norma de Panama
S.A. for Panama; by American Bookshops for Finland.

For general information on Hungry Minds' products and
services please contact our Customer Care department
within the U.S. at 800-762-2974, outside the U.S. at 317-
572-3993 or fax 317-572-4002.

For sales inquiries and reseller information, including
discounts, premium and bulk quantity sales, and foreign-
language translations, please contact our Customer Care
department at 800-434-3422, fax 317-572-4002 or write to
Hungry Minds, Inc., Attn: Customer Care Department,
10475 Crosspoint Boulevard, Indianapolis, IN 46256.

For information on licensing foreign or domestic rights,
please contact our Sub-Rights Customer Care department
at 212-884-5000.

For information on using Hungry Minds' products and
services in the classroom or for ordering examination
copies, please contact our Educational Sales department at
800-434-2086 or fax 317-572-4005.

For press review copies, author interviews, or other
publicity information, please contact our Public Relations
department at 317-572-3168 or fax 317-572-4168.

For authorization to photocopy items for corporate,
personal, or educational use, please contact Copyright
Clearance Center, 222 Rosewood Drive, Danvers, MA
01923, or fax 978-750-4470.

 Hungry Minds™ is a trademark of Hungry Minds, Inc.   is a trademark of Hungry Minds, Inc.

Credits

Executive Editor
Chris Webb

Project Editor
Eric Newman

Technical Editor
William Pepper

Copy Editor
William A. Barton

Editorial Manager
Mary Beth Wakefield

Vice President and Executive Group Publisher
Richard Swadley

Vice President and Executive Publisher
Bob Ipsen

Vice President and Publisher
Joseph B. Wikert

Editorial Director
Mary Bednarek

Media Development Specialist
Travis Silvers

Permissions Editor
Laura Moss

Media Development Manager
Laura Carpenter VanWinkle

Project Coordinator
Nancee Reeves

Proofreader
Anne Owen

Indexer
Johnna VanHoose Dinse

Cover Image
© Noma/Images.com

About the Authors

Stephen Lee is a programmer/analyst with more than 16 years of experience. His background includes developing commercial applications for the auto industry in C and Basic. Stephen started with Visual Basic during the release of Version 2 and has continued to use it for projects ever since. He became involved with Jabber in October 2000 and has since written many clients and add-ons, as well as doing custom Jabber server development. You can download a free version of one of his clients at `http://www.myjabber.net`. He continually strives to have the best Jabber client available for the Windows platform and has upgraded it regularly since its release in December 2000.

Terence Smelser is a computer hobbyist whose interest in computers goes back to the late 1970s — starting with an old military ballistics computer — and has grown from there. His experience includes work with operating systems, starting with MS-DOS and progressing to early versions of Windows, OS/2, and modern Windows NT/2000 systems, plus Linux/Unix systems. He became involved in Jabber in November 2000 while looking for an internal communications platform for his then-current employer. Finding the first version of Stephen's Jabber client on the Web, he made a few suggestions and is now a partner in sltsCommunications and a co-developer of custom servers and chat clients. He does most of the writing for the company's Web sites and the technical writing for its products. His efforts have taken the company's Jabber client, myJabber, to the forefront of the Jabber community.

Dedicated to all the myJabber users and the original myJabber team. Without you guys, we wouldn't be where we are today!

Preface

When Hungry Minds approached me about doing this book, I was rather excited to think that Jabber had reached the point of having such a huge audience interested in its technology. Terry and I thought long and hard about it and decided that we'd give it a go. We both hope that we've done justice to the amazing world of Jabber.

The primary goal of this book is to teach you to use Visual Basic to create a basic instant messaging client based on the Jabber protocol. You learn how to write code that enables you to log in to a Jabber server, send basic messages, create a chat form, and create a group chat form. You will see examples of basic XML, which is the structure you use to send messages via the Jabber server. You learn the basic fundamentals of the `matrix.dll` COM object for accessing the Jabber server, which enables you to add to the code that we present with this book and create your own custom messaging client.

After an introduction to and overview of Jabber and the Jabber protocol, we show you how to install your own Jabber server for testing. (This step isn't required, but it makes testing your client and seeing how the Jabber protocol works easier.)

To gain the maximum experience from this book, we recommend that for the Jabber server installation (not required) you have a general knowledge of the Linux OS. A working knowledge of Visual Basic is expected throughout the book. An understanding of COM objects is recommended, as well as an understanding of XML.

To be specific, you should:

♦ Be able to install software and libraries on a Linux server

♦ Be able to write basic applications using the Visual Basic IDE

♦ Have an understanding of what a COM object is

♦ Have a basic understanding of XML

How This Book Is Organized

Many ways to organize this material are possible, but we settled on a scheme that divides the book into three main parts. In addition, we include a few appendixes that provide supplemental information you may find helpful.

Part I: What Is Jabber?

The chapters in this part look at the Jabber protocol and various parts of the Jabber server, discuss how and where to find a Jabber client, and, finally, show you how to get online by using the myJabber Personal Communicator.

Part II: Your Test Server

The focus of this part is on getting a test Jabber server up and running under Red Hat Linux (although you should not have any problems using any flavor of Linux to set up the server). This part includes instructions for getting the components from the Internet, setting up the core Jabber server, installing the Conferencing module, and, finally, setting up the AIM, ICQ, MSN Messenger, and Yahoo! transports.

Part III: Creating Your Own Instant Messaging Client

Part III leads you through the development of your own instant messaging client, written in Visual Basic and using the Matrix COM Library. We show you how to create a roster list, add and remove contacts, and send messages and chats, as well as participate in group chats.

Appendixes and CD-ROM

Finally, the appendixes present additional information on topics that we cover in the book. The CD-ROM contains the myJabber Personal Communicator as well as clients for the Linux and Macintosh platforms. It also contains the code for the Jabber server and other utilities and documentation that are helpful in working with Jabber.

Conventions Used in This Book

Each chapter in this book begins with a heads-up of the topics that we cover in the chapter and ends with a summary of what you should have learned by reading the chapter.

Throughout this book, you will find text that highlights special or important information. Keep an eye out for the following items:

NOTE The information in a Note is an aside to the main point.

TIP Tips provide tidbits that we picked up along the way and want to share with you.

CROSS-REFERENCE Cross-references indicate where in the book you can find more information on the topic at hand.

ON THE CD-ROM A specialized kind of cross-reference, this item indicates relevant content that you can find on the accompanying CD-ROM.

In addition to the preceding items, the following formatting and typographical conventions are used throughout the book:

♦   Code examples appear in a `fixed width font`.

- Other code elements, such as data structures and variable names, appear in `fixed width`.

- File, function, and macro names, as well as World Wide Web addresses (URLs), also appear in `fixed width`.

- Keyboard shortcuts are indicated with the following syntax: Ctrl+C.

- Menu commands are indicated in hierarchical order, with each menu command separated by an arrow. For example, File ⇨ Open means to click the File command on the menu bar, then select Open.

Contacting the Authors

We invite your feedback. One of the challenges we faced as we sat down to write this book was to make sure that the material was current and to explain each area in enough detail. If you think we don't cover the material you're looking for or if the coverage isn't detailed enough, let us know. Of course, if you think the book is fantastic, we'd also like to hear from you.

Feel free to send us specific questions about any of the material that we cover. We promise to do our best to answer. Please keep in mind that we both do have full-time jobs, so we can't guarantee an immediate reply. You can e-mail us at the following addresses:

```
srlee@sltscommunications.net
tsmelser@sltscommunications.net
```

We also invite you to visit our Web site at `www.openim.myjabber.org`, which contains all the source code listings that we use in the book. On the Web site, you also find updates to the relevant sections within the book, along with corrections to any errors that may have accidentally found their way into the material. We hope you enjoy the book and find it useful.

Acknowledgments

Stephen Lee:

My journey into the world of Jabber has been a very interesting one; I've met lots of interesting people and learned lots of new programming techniques along the way.

I want to thank many people, but I'm keeping it brief as I don't want to sound like an Academy Award winner.

First, I want to thank the original myJabber team. This group of people gave their spare time to help new users, test new versions, and give me huge amounts of feedback to get myJabber where it is today. The group included Terry Smelser (nightbreed), Mickey Cunningham (keno), Justin Bygrove (jbygrove), and Susan Kirkpatrick (kitykity). Thanks, guys! I just can't say it enough.

Shuyler Heath probably doesn't even remember talking to me. Shuyler was in the middle of upgrading the MSN transport to the new 1.2 versions when I started bugging him with questions about the transports. He always answered my questions promptly and never made me feel that I was wasting his time.

Numerous people in the jdev conference room have lent a hand when they could or offered advice when we were having problems setting up our original Jabber server. Special thanks to temas, who spends hours in the room and hours coding the Jabber core components.

I must thank Jeremie Miller. Without Jeremie's hard work creating the Jabber protocol, I'd never have had the opportunity to write the myJabber client or this book.

I also must thank all the folks at Hungry Minds for their commitment to and patience with me during this project. I know I was a pain at times, but we finally did it. Special thanks to Eric Newman and Chris Webb.

I want to say thank you to my technical editor, Bill Pepper. He made a lot of great additions to the content that helped make this book even better. He was also very kind whenever he found some lame bug I'd left in the code. Thanks, Billy!

And, finally, I want to thank my wife, Debbie, and my son, Christopher. Their patience with me while I worked on this book and the last year of myJabber development is more than I could have ever asked for. I love you both.

If I've forgotten some people, please don't feel offended. Thanks to all the people I missed!

Terence Smelser:

My story is a bit different from Steve's, but I have many of the same people to thank.

One of the first people I want to thank is Stephen Lee, my partner. His patience with my strange hours and half-baked ideas could earn him sainthood (but this is extremely unlikely). I've learned a lot from him during the year that we've worked together, and I hope that I've been able to teach him a few things as well.

Next, I must thank my friend Chris McDonald for showing me this project to begin with. (I promise to get you for it, Chris, if it's the last thing I do!) We spent many a happy hour working on this stuff together and learned from each other constantly.

My deepest appreciation goes to Jeremie Miller for his hard work in the beginnings and the work that he continues today. Also to the entire bunch at Jabber.org and the amazing people in the jdev room — I've learned more from you guys than you could know.

Most important, I, too, must thank my family for understanding my drive to do something like this. So to my wife, Helen; my daughter, Killie; and my sons, Alex and Aaron, goes all my love and my thanks for putting up with one more of Dad's "crazy ideas."

Contents

Part III: Creating Your Own Instant Messaging Client

Jabber™ Programming

Part I

What Is Jabber?

In This Part

Chapter 1

An Overview of Jabber and the Jabber Protocol

In This Chapter

♦ What is Jabber?

♦ Where did Jabber start?

♦ What can you, the developer, do with Jabber?

♦ The Jabber server under Linux

Welcome to Jabber programming.

This book shows you how to develop your very own Jabber client, based on the Jabber protocol. For whatever your purpose — fun, corporate development, or just a project for school — we provide the information that you need.

ON THE CD-ROM The CD-ROM that accompanies this book includes an electronic version of the book, source code, and all the tools you need to develop and use a working client application.

What Is Jabber?

Jabber is a very flexible, multi-protocol, multi-use, highly scalable, XML-based communications and presence-management platform. It's designed for everyone, at every level of experience. From the weekend chatter to the corporate power user, Jabber can allow you to dispense with several resource-stealing instant messaging (IM) clients and make your desktop and system neater and less cluttered. Jabber is more efficient in its use of your system resources; all of your IM resources can be in one neat package as opposed to being in several. And, in most cases, Jabber enjoys a more stable connection than other messaging platforms.

The unique presence-management system in Jabber, by far the most advanced of its kind, allows you to manage who can see you and who can't in ways that other chat platforms don't. For instance, when using AIM, we need know only your screen name to see that you are online. You would have to be aware of this and intentionally block us, assuming you knew our screen names. A Jabber user can control presence with very little effort. Another user, regardless of external platform, must *subscribe* to your presence. You have the choice of rejecting or accepting the subscription at the time it is submitted. Other applications of this system are yet to be discovered. Jabber is a work in progress; the community learns and creates applications of the protocol/platform on an almost daily basis.

Jabber continues to be developed in the open-source community, by people just like you, by professionals, hobbyists, and others with an interest in and commitment to open development.

The first application of Jabber technology is an instant messaging system focused on privacy, security, ease of use, access from anywhere using any device, and interoperability with IM-, phone-, and Web-based services. Jabber is quickly becoming a standard component of Internet infrastructure as public and corporate awareness of the usefulness of instant communications grows.

The Jabber IM system is very different from existing instant messaging services in several significant ways:

♦ Jabber is based on the Extensible Markup Language (XML), the universal format for structured documents and data on the Web. (See `http://www.w3.org/XML/`.) This provides an amazing amount of flexibility as to what the Jabber server itself can do.

♦ Jabber uses a worldwide distributed network, utilizing many interconnected servers. This almost ensures uptime in the network and gives users many optionsfor connecting to the network. For example, if one server is down for any reason, it is a simple matter to move to a new one.

♦ The Jabber code is open source.

♦ Jabber has a modular, extensible architecture, allowing the easy creation and integration of new features, especially those that address specific needs. Each new feature is added as a module instead of being added to the core server, so the server maintains its stability while still allowing for new features to be added. (Changes to the server itself are rarely ever needed, but they have been known to happen: One server that we built for a customer was almost unrecognizable as a Jabber server at the time we built it, but some of its features are now quite common.)

For the most part, the worldwide Jabber network itself is operated by people in the open-source community — people like you who have a need for or a drive to build a server and a network of users or to provide internal communications in a business or organization. Many servers started out as developers' testing platforms and have grown into publicly used servers, connecting the user to his or her various communications platforms. myJabber.org is a perfect example; for the longest time, the only users of the server were the authors of this book. Now, we rarely see fewer than 100 users online at any given time, and new signups are in the neighborhood of seventy-five a day. Even given the enormous, inestimable size of the Internet, these are significant numbers for us.

Jabber is built on client-server architecture and not a client-to-client architecture, as are some instant messaging systems. All messages and data sent from one client to another must first go through the Jabber server. Although any client is free to negotiate a direct connection to another client, those connections are for application-specific use only. In some specific instances, this is even encouraged — such as in file transfers — but the negotiations for these instances are first made by the server. This keeps the "flow of traffic" in a nice, organized stream and allows for various security protocols like SSL and PGP to be implemented.

Jabber has its own unique IM protocols built right in, enabling person-to-person instant messaging and "group conferencing" on many of the world's operational Jabber servers. In addition to these capabilities, Jabber enables the use of the AIM, Yahoo!, ICQ, and MSN Messenger networks so popular with many Internet users today. Jabber can also communicate with the old mainstay Internet Relay Chat (IRC), making it a very versatile and useful tool.

Where Did Jabber Start?

Jabber started in 1998 with a young man, Jeremie Miller, in the U.S. Midwest. Jeremie wanted to design a way to bring all his IM clients under control and place them in one easy-to-use piece of software. Saying, "I don't do GUI stuff very well," Jeremie determined that what he could do was design a protocol and the back-end server for his idea and then talk someone else into designing the client's user interface. Jabber today easily encompasses dozens of working client models, and the server has been customized by individuals all around the world for their own use. All this work has been done within the open-source community by people of all skill levels — hobbyists, professionals, and people who once were one or the other but now find themselves to be both. We were once hobbyists ourselves, and now our interests and work have brought us to a professional level of use and development.

What Can You, the Developer, Do with Jabber?

What are Jabber's capabilities? This question is hard to answer. Jabber's capabilities are limited only by the imagination and talents of the thousands of open-source designers and developers working with the protocol worldwide. This is tempered by the needs and imaginations of hundreds of thousands of users. Our users have asked us for certain functions, and we have tried to meet these requests whenever possible. Some of the requests were, frankly, quite impossible — some wanted us to model our client directly after their favorite chat client, and others have ask for things that just have not been developed at the server level yet. The way you handle this is completely up to you. You may wish to develop a client and build a large network of users as we have. Or perhaps your intention is to design a dedicated client to be used only by your company or organization.

Currently, Jabber is used as an instant messaging and conferencing platform by many large corporations, Internet service providers, special-interest groups, governments, and individuals all around the world. Some of the functions of these clients are very limited, and were designed or changed by development teams to do only what the organization wanted them to do. We have designed several that do just exactly that. Some will allow connections to only a specified server, others to a specified network. Others are fully functional but have had the "branding" changed so that they appear to belong to one organization.

Jabber clients have been developed to work with almost every known operating system, including but not limited to Windows (9x, NT4, 2000, ME, and XP), Linux (Jabber works with many of the most popular flavors of Linux, and users design patches for others all the time), Solaris, Macintosh, BeOS, AIX, and HPUX. People write for the platforms they use on a daily basis, so the operating system you can run a client from is limited only by the number of systems in existence.

Jabber is quite capable of working within existing wireless networks as well, sending text messages to wireless pagers and phones and receiving messages back from wireless-capable handheld devices, such as PDAs and BlackBerry devices. A few clients have even been written for the WinCE/Pocket PC platform and other PDA environments, such as the Palm OS. As the numbers of wireless devices grow, so do the operating systems and the numbers of users. The clients for these devices are still waiting to be designed.

Other new ideas and applications come out all the time. Maybe you've had a great idea about how you would use this unique protocol but were unsure how to make it work. Perhaps you have had a specific need in wireless communications — for example, being able to stay in real-time contact with a sales force that is in the field. This force could be carrying an existing wireless device; you need only make your server and/or client able to talk to it. Some of these devices used to require proprietary software, but now, with a little ingenuity (and a great protocol to apply it to), you can converse with this sales force from your desk, using the same software with which you hold online staff meetings and chat with your best friend or your mother. Whatever your need, look at the Jabber protocol closely and don't think "chat" — think "communications and presence." Jabber may be the platform for you.

The Jabber Server Under Linux

The core Jabber server was built to operate in the Linux environment. So far we have seen it built in almost every known flavor of Linux, including Slackware, Red Hat, Mandrake, SUSE, Debian, and Turbo, just to name a few. We have even seen it run in Yellow Dog Linux, which was written for the Macintosh hardware architecture. It has been built in the various flavors of BSD (developed as a variant of Unix at the University of California at Berkley) and has been adapted to the Mac OS X server, a variant of the BSD operating system. (Yes, Apple based OS X on BSD.) Jabber runs in Sun Microsystems' Solaris (most known versions) and in other Unix distributions used all over the world. Jabber servers have even been built on Windows NT4 Server and Windows 2000 Advanced Server, and we have no doubt that it will run on WinXP

Advanced Server as well. The Jabber server itself is written in the C programming language and can be adapted to any operating system that can work with C. If we didn't mention your favorite OS, don't despair; with a little adaptation Jabber will most likely compile and run in whatever you need it to.

Some of the readers of this book may be fairly new to the Linux operating system, some even extremely new, and one or two of you may have never heard of it before. Don't let this bother you in the slightest. As you become familiar with Jabber development, you'll find that almost everyone you run into in the Jabber community has a Linux/Unix box or two running for one reason or another; most of us have our own Jabber servers, even if they run only in a private LAN. Linux people are a proud bunch and are always willing to talk about their favorite flavors of the OS. Most are always willing to help someone new get started with Linux; keeping this in mind, you should have no shortage of help getting started. The Jabber server that we will build later in this book will be with the Red Hat flavor of Linux, a very powerful variant and as such, really quite common in the community. Consider Linux as a common ground in the Jabber community; even our Mac developers are pretty heavy into OS X and other Mac variants of Linux.

What's the best way to really get involved in this project and the open-source community — and, specifically, in the Jabber community? There are many ways to be involved if that is what you wish to do. Some of you may want only to develop your client and get it running in their private or corporate LAN. Others will jump into the community with both feet and become a part of us. We encourage everyone to take part in some way. Developing Jabber clients is a reasonably simple process, but everything is easier with some help.

The Jabber community has dozens of mailing lists filled with information about the many various parts of development. These lists are available to the Jabber enthusiast at `http://mailman.jabber.org/listinfo/`. Messages fill these lists daily and without a doubt are one of the top methods of communication for developers in the Jabber community. The lists and the messages they transport are a perfect form of "permanent" records for questions and answers concerning any part of the development of your server or your client and for previews of new ideas that people are working on. For more up-to-the-moment, "I need information now" support, visit the Jabber developer's conference room on the Jabber.org server (`jdev@conference.jabber.org`) — you will find most of the Jabber developers hanging out there. Stop in and say hello — they're a friendly bunch. Some of these folks are veteran members and a few are even founding members of our community. In other words, they know Jabber. Don't be afraid to ask any of these people questions — that is what they are there for, and often, a new person shows up and asks "What if we were to . . . ?" If you could, you'd see stunned looks on the other side of the keyboards — sometimes suggestions are made that we have never thought of. You can see how well the interaction of people can work; we learn from one another, sometimes without meaning to.

Summary

We have taken a brief look at the humble beginnings of Jabber and what it is, a look at its creator and the original thoughts behind the server. We have really only partly touched on the capabilities of Jabber, because these grow almost exponentially as more and more people become involved in the project. As we move on in this book, we will discover how many of these items come together into what we believe to be the most powerful communications platform in existence. We will further explore the things that you can do with Jabber, help you set up a server, and take a quick look at some of the available Jabber clients to be found in the community.

Chapter 2

A Sampling of Jabber Clients

In This Chapter

- Windows clients
- Macintosh clients
- Linux clients
- Java clients
- Other clients

Several fine examples of Jabber clients are available, written for all the popular platforms. In this chapter, we show you as many of these as we can and explain some features of each. In the open-source community, almost everything you see or experience is constantly under development. The clients that we describe here are certainly no exception, so be aware that what you see here may differ from the product that you download.

Windows Clients

The following clients are just some of those available for the Windows platform:

- myJabber
- Rival Messenger
- WinJab
- Jabber Instant Messenger

myJabber

At the top of the list of Windows clients is myJabber. Some may accuse us of being biased (and they'd be right), but this client we know inside and out, as we've been part of its development from the very beginning. Originally created out of curiosity and our personal interest in new software and communications developments, myJabber has grown in functionality *and* popularity at a steady rate.

myJabber has retained its basic form throughout its life, but some basic changes to the overall design have occurred, starting with the first beta of version 2. The client offers two views of itself, one of which is a small, "classic" IM version, as shown in Figure 2-1.

Figure 2-1: The "classic" view of myJabber

This compact client is very versatile yet can be resized to any dimension that works for your desktop. It loses none of its features in this mode; it merely hides some of them and makes them accessible through the use of expandable tool bars.

Figure 2-2 shows the other, expanded view of myJabber.

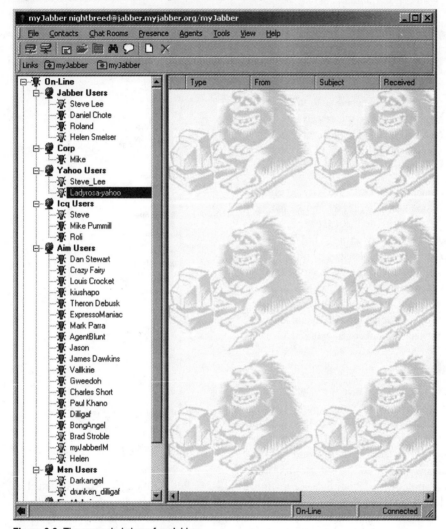

Figure 2-2: The expanded view of myJabber

The full-sized version gives the user access to a functional message window *and* the full toolbar. Overall configuration occurs via a tidy preferences window that you access from the Tools menu. The client exhibits some leading edge features such as "true" emoticons — ☺ as opposed to :-) — and the use of rich text (i.e., variable colors and fonts) in its chat and group chat windows. The browse feature enables you to cruise though the listed public conference rooms of any online conference server. myJabber is the flagship client for sltsCommunications (our company) and is being developed in Visual Basic by our programmers. myJabber supports Secure Socket Layers (SSL) for added security in corporate environments or for those concerned with privacy online.

Rival Messenger

Rival Messenger was originally the work of Daniel Chote of Hastings, New Zealand. In early November 2001, he approached sltsCommunications and asked us to take over the project's development. We viewed Rival Messenger as a good, solid project that needed only our "special" creative touches, and so we were more than happy to comply.

Rival Messenger is a classic "IM"-styled client, designed to look and function much like the popular ICQ client. As do most Jabber clients, it features interconnectivity with ICQ, AIM, MSN Messenger, and Yahoo! Messenger, plus it allows the use of the Jabber community's unique group chat and person-to-person chats. Figure 2-3 shows Rival Messenger's main window. Rival Messenger is being developed in Visual Basic and supports Secure Socket Layers (SSL).

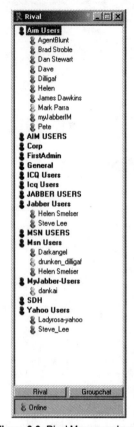

Figure 2-3: Rival Messenger's main window

WinJab

WinJab was one of the first Jabber clients released for public use for Windows. Written by Peter Millard of Jabber.com, it's a stable addition to the growing number of clients available to the general public. WinJab is a bit different from the first two clients we looked at, as it uses an "all-in-one" presentation of the Jabber data, very similar to IRC in looks. Of course, you can detach all child windows — chat, group chat, debug, messages — simply by dragging them out of the main client window. The preferences window is straightforward and easy to use. You must set up the customizable sound cues yourself, as this program doesn't install with them enabled, but you have a lot of choice in how you use them. WinJab is being developed in Delphi and implements Secure Socket Layers (SSL).

Figure 2-4 shows WinJab's main window.

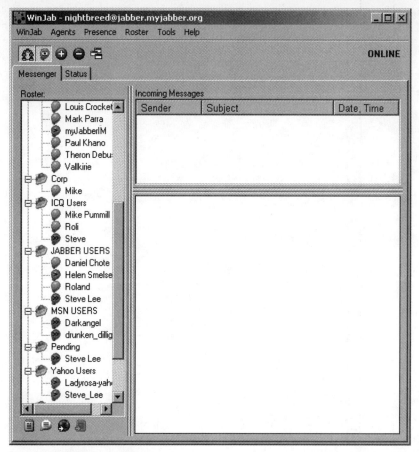

Figure 2-4: WinJab's main window

Jabber Instant Messenger

Jabber Instant Messenger — or JIM, as it seems to be known as in the community — is another client from the mind of Peter Millard of Jabber.com. This program is the flagship of the Jabber.com clients and is its commercial offering. JIM is built in classic IM style, reminiscent of AOL's instant messenger, AIM. Full featured and stable, with a working network browser and a familiar look to it, JIM is a popular choice in industry at this time. Jabber Instant Messenger is being developed in Delphi and implements Secure Socket Layers (SSL). Figure 2-5 shows Jabber Instant Messenger's main window.

Figure 2-5: Jabber Instant Messenger's main window

Jabber for Macintosh

The following clients are available for the Mac OS:

♦ Jabbernaut

♦ JabberFOX

Unfortunately, our friends using the Mac OS don't have a lot of choices. Nonetheless, two very nice applications can get you into the world of Jabber to look around and probably keep you hooked after you get there. Max Horn of Lahnstein, Germany, heads up both projects, with lots of assistance from members of the Jabber community and others. Not owning Macs ourselves makes giving you useful information a bit difficult, but we intend to do the best that we can.

Jabbernaut

Jabbernaut was written for the older Mac operating systems but runs very nicely on OS 9 using an iMac we have at work. Jabbernaut is very configurable and provides SSL support for the security minded. Its appearance really doesn't bring anything else to mind, so it's probably safe to say that it has its own unique look and fits very nicely on the Mac desktop. You can find more information on this great Macintosh app at www.jabbernaut.com/. It has a well-laid-out, easy-to-use roster, as you can see in Figure 2-6. Figure 2-7 shows Jabbernaut's preferences tab, and Figure 2-8 shows Jabbernaut sending an instant message. Jabbernaut is written in C++ using MacZoop.

JabberFOX

JabberFOX, or Jabber *For OS X*, is a relatively new app. Again, having limited access to a Mac that we can break if we choose, we can provide only a limited critique. Although we very briefly ran OS X on our iMac at work, it wasn't at a time that JabberFOX was public. (As soon as the IT people found out we had OS X on "their" network, that ended, so we've had little chance to work with it at all.)

JabberFOX is a good-looking client with all the standard features, plus it also uses SSL for added security. Figures 2-9 through 2-11 show JabberFOX. Mac users will notice the seamless integration

Figure 2-6: The roster view of Jabbernaut

into the OS. Something that we really like is the collapsible drawers in many of the features, like the group chat and preferences dialogs.

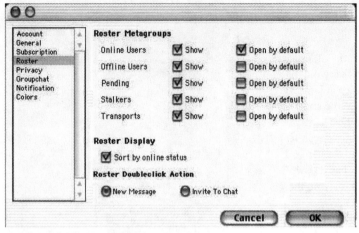

Figure 2-7: Jabbernaut's preferences tab

Figure 2-8: Jabbernaut sending an instant message

Figure 2-9: The JabberFOX roster

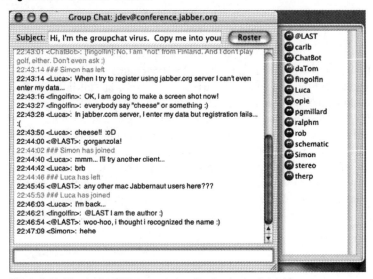

Figure 2-10: The JabberFOX group chat and roster drawer (*at right*)

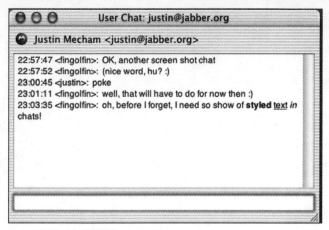

Figure 2-11: JabberFOX's person-to-person chat

Jabber for Linux

Here is where it all started. The incredible power and versatility of the Linux OS have led to many great things, and Jabber is one of them. Linux has a lot of Jabber clients, but we don't cover them all. Following are the three older and more stable offerings that we do cover:

♦ Jarl

♦ Gabber

♦ Konverse

Jarl

Jarl is a cross-platform Perl/Tk-based Jabber client, written by Ryan Eatmon. Ryan is a very experienced Perl programmer, and the fine quality of Jarl shows it. Jarl is an "all-in-one" client, meaning that one window contains everything. Supporting multiple profiles, SSL, and all known working transports, such as those for AIM, ICQ, MSN Messenger, and Yahoo! Messenger, Jarl is the Linux developer's dream. We can switch from login to login or server to server, SSL or no SSL. Jarl has many great features, some of which aren't even visible. But we will show you one of them in a moment. Figure 2-12 shows the logon screen for Jarl, and Figures 2-13 and 2-14 show additional views. From the screen in Figure 2-12, you can create new profiles or set the connection type. The menu is fully usable at this point, so you can access system preferences, add roster groups, and perform other administrative tasks even while offline.

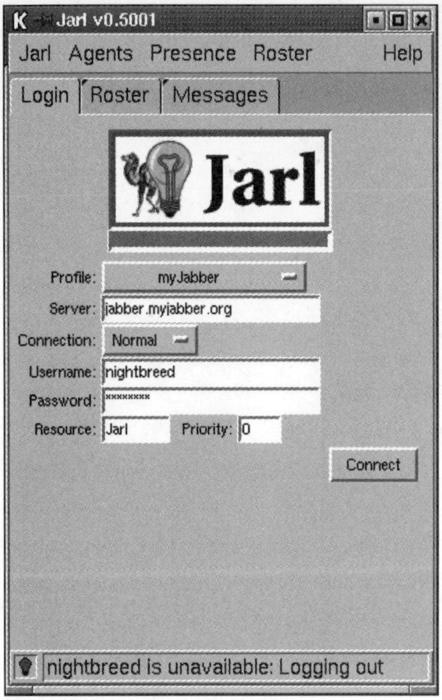

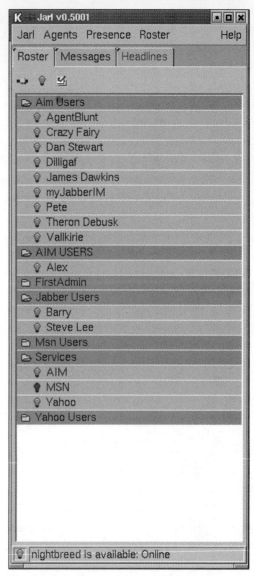

Figure 2-12: Jarl's logon window

Figure 2-13: Jarl's main window, showing the roster

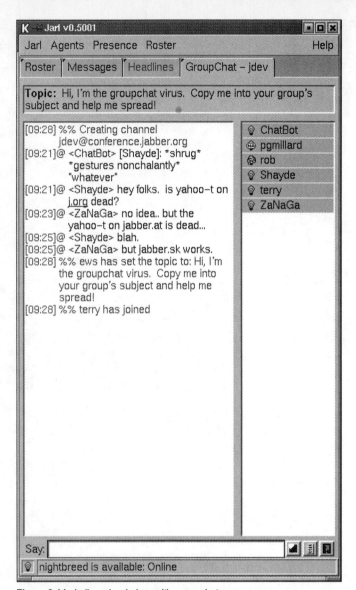

Figure 2-14: Jarl's main window, with group chat open

Jarl has a very convenient feature (one of the hidden ones mentioned earlier) — a second client! Jarl includes a command-line interface that enables you to use this second Jabber client, Jarl -cli, from a Telnet window (see Figure 2-15). For command-line enthusiasts, this is very handy! It can be used from anywhere you can get access to a shell account or even from a DOS or command prompt.

Figure 2-15: Jarl's command-line interface

Gabber

Gabber is an IM-style Jabber client for Xwindow, written for GNOME. (We've successfully run it under KDE and Enlightenment, too.) By "IM-style," we mean that it's very much like AIM and ICQ in that it uses its roster window as a main body and has discrete chat windows, preference windows, and conference windows. Supporting SSL and all other transports, it's a very compact and powerful Jabber client for Linux. Gabber was, in fact, one of the first clients released to the general public and has increased in popularity with Linux users worldwide. It comes in several languages and ships with one or two distributions of Linux. Gabber's main program is written in C++, while the user interface is written in Glade. See Figures 2-16 through 2-19.

This very sharp Jabber client is the brainchild of a two-man team, Julian "x-virge" Missig and Dave "DizzyD" Smith. More information is available at `http://gabber.sourceforge .net/index.php`.

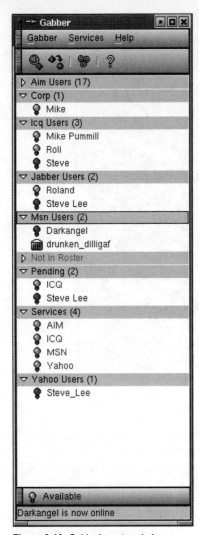

Figure 2-16: Gabber's roster window

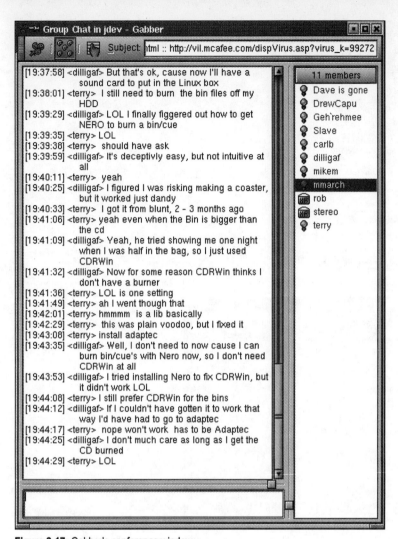

Figure 2-17: Gabber's conference window

Figure 2-18: Gabber's user-to-user chat

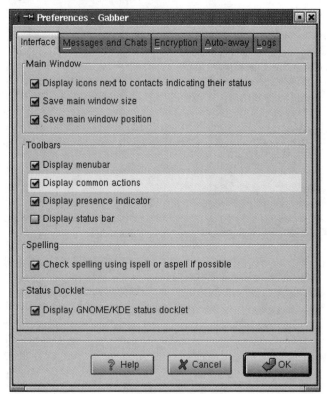

Figure 2-19: Gabber's Preferences dialog box

Konverse

Konverse is a very nice addition to the line of Linux Jabber clients. Konverse was written for KDE users and has a growing following. Konverse has had a few different people working on it and seems to have benefited from the consequent wide range of styles and programming ideas. The list currently includes Jerome Lalande, Ben Burton, and Seth Hartbecke. Konverse is written in C++, handles AIM, ICQ, MSN Messenger, and Yahoo! plus, of course, the Jabber protocols for group chat and person-to-person chats. It doesn't work with SSL support at this time, but we're certain that will be included soon. Figures 2-20 through 2-22 show you Konverse's sharp lines and well-thought-out UI. Konverse is very basic in its function and configuration and makes a great first Linux client for the KDE user.

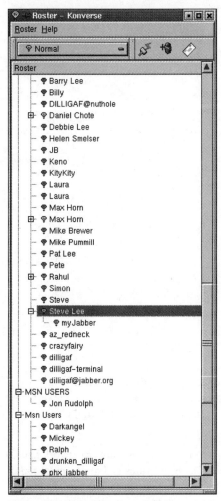

Figure 2-20: Konverse's roster window

Figure 2-21: Konverse's very basic preferences window

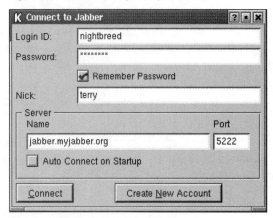

Figure 2-22: Konverse's logon dialog box

Java Clients

Quite a few Java-based clients are available, taking advantage of the very flexible Java programming language. Really far too many are out there to go into depth on any one of them, but we do want to say a few words about JabberApplet. In general, the flexibility of these clients (considering that most run right from a Web page) is tremendous.

JabberApplet is just that — a Java applet that enables you to contact the Jabber network and use the various transports right from a Web page. One of its restrictions is that you must run it from the same machine that the Jabber server is on. Built into a company's intranet, JabberApplet could prove a very low-cost solution to internal communications. Figures 2-23 through 2-25 show the user interface, and you can find more information at `http://jabberapplet.sourceforge.net/`.

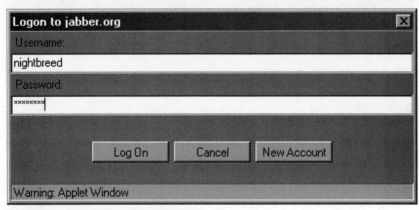

Figure 2-23: JabberApplet's Logon applet

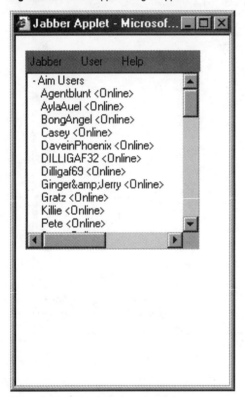

Figure 2-24: JabberApplet's roster applet

Figure 2-25: JabberApplet's group chat applet

Other Clients

Literally dozens of other clients are available for almost everything that you can think of, written in all kinds of programming languages. The list is just too vast to cover entirely and is growing every day as developers find that the dependable and stable Jabber protocol can do so many things that its possibilities are almost endless.

Here are just a few of the things we've noticed on the Jabber.org Web site:

♦ i3Connect (at `www.i3connect.com/`): Online games and chat.

♦ JabberCE (at `www.movsoftware.com/`): That's right, Jabber for your Pocket PC.

♦ SNAPchannels (at `www.snapchannels.net/`): For wireless devices such as the BlackBerry.

Summary

The world of Jabber has a lot to do and see. You can find a client for almost any operating system. Yes, Jabber even has a client for BeOS, but only one — so you could become the one to write its successor! You can find a client written in almost every programming language. Big mega corporations are now involved in Jabber's development, too — Microsoft is said to have something going based on the Jabber protocol, and IBM has thrown its Java runtime environment, known as SASH, into the mix and devised a client of its own.

We strongly encourage you to check out `www.jabber.org`. Take a look at the clients page to get an idea of what other developers have going on. Browse through the transports and see the many different directions this project is already taking. Then jump right in with your own ideas and help make it bigger and larger.

This chapter has presented only a sampling of the various platform-specific Jabber clients — there are many more than we can mention, and by the time this book is published there will be even more. We showed you some of the features of each and hope that you can use what you have read here for ideas as you build your own Jabber client. As we move on, we will give you a complete rundown of the setup and configuration of myJabber while pointing out some of the features you may wish to include in your own client.

Chapter 3

Getting Online with myJabber

In This Chapter

- Downloading myJabber
- Setting up myJabber for SSL
- Creating an account
- Configuring myJabber
- Searching for users
- Adding users
- Creating roster groups
- Chatting
- Conferencing

Now you have an idea of what Jabber is all about, and you've looked at some of the more popular Jabber clients. Now we want to get you online and talking with a Jabber client. To do so, we're going to use myJabber, the client that started our involvement in Jabber. In the following pages, we discuss every detail of the program and how it works to give you a "feel" for myJabber. You'll be able to see the choices we made in developing myJabber — the directions we took in our development and the way we handled the features we chose to include. As you build your own client, of course, you'll make your own choices.

What Is myJabber?

myJabber is your gateway to the world of dependable, easy-to-use instant messaging and group conferencing. Lightweight, configurable, and very user friendly, myJabber has quickly become the top choice of users everywhere.

Designed for both the individual and the corporate user, myJabber offers many features that users of instant messaging want. As part of the worldwide Jabber community, myJabber interacts with AIM, ICQ, MSN Messenger, Yahoo! Messenger, and IRC, plus it can speak to the unique Jabber group chat and person-to-person chat rooms. myJabber supports customizable sound cues and person-to-person file transfers, and it accepts "headline" broadcasts from MSN, Yahoo!, and Hotmail.

myJabber runs on Windows 95/98, NT, ME, 2000, and XP. You'll quickly discover that myJabber uses fewer system resources than other clients, sports a simple and friendly interface, and has fewer quirks to learn. Now, admittedly we are very biased in favor of our own product, but we constantly keep an eye on the competition for the latest changes and innovations within the Jabber community.

The myJabber home page (`www.myjabber.net`) offers the latest releases, Jabber community news, and other information from the worlds of computer and open-source development.

Downloading myJabber

Downloading myJabber is very simple, but actually, you already have a copy of it on the CD that comes with this book. myJabber is, however, a project in motion; we're constantly finding ways to make it better, mostly as a result of user input. The version on the CD may not be the most current one, so we're going to start by getting you the latest version from the Web site.

> **NOTE** The version that we're working with in this chapter is version 2.0.17, a testing version that was available only to development staff and beta testers. The version currently available for download will be very similar to it; you'll find very little difference in the two insofar as it affects what we're doing.

The download is available from `http://www.myjabber.net/myjabber.php`. This URL is that of our default download page, and you can find all the various components we provide here.

Simply click the link that reads `myJabFull2015` (approx. 3.12 MB), and Windows prepares the download for you. The next item that you see from Windows is shown in Figure 3-1.

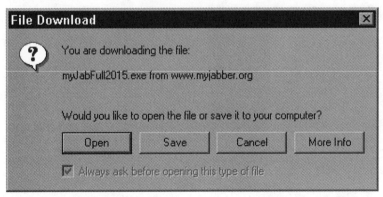

Figure 3-1: The File Download dialog box

Click Save and you see the next window, where you pick the location to copy the file to your hard drive. As you can see in Figure 3-2, we have a folder called \Chat Clients. To start the download, you'd double-click this folder to open it and choose Save on the dialog box. This action places the downloaded file in the \Chat Clients folder, where you can come back to it later. We suggest that you put your file where you can most easily find it, depending on how familiar you are with your drives and your computer.

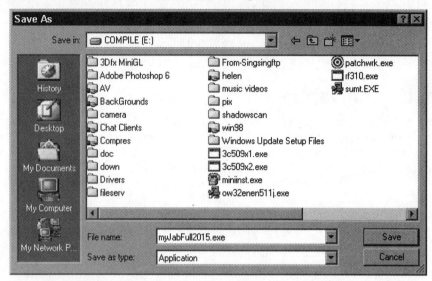

Figure 3-2: The Windows Save As dialog box, showing the possible destinations for the download

Leave unchecked the "Close this dialog box when download completes" check box on the final dialog box (see Figure 3-3). Doing so enables you to start the install directly from the desktop after the file has been downloaded.

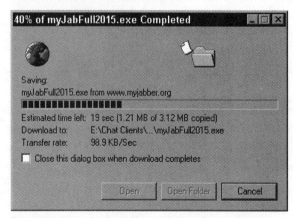

Figure 3-3: Leave the check box in this dialog box unchecked.

Installing myJabber

Find the downloaded file on your hard drive or, if you left the check box unchecked in Figure 3-3, click Open ("grayed out," or disabled, in the figure). This action starts the installation process by opening the Setup Wizard, as shown in Figure 3-4.

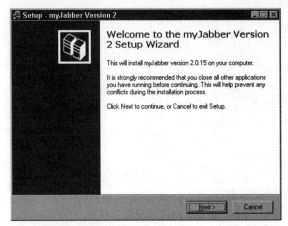

Figure 3-4: The Setup Wizard

This basic window shows the beginning of the installation process. Your options are clear here: Next or Cancel. You're here to install the software, so click Next.

Figure 3-5 shows the End User's Agreement. Anyone installing software almost always skips over such agreements, but remember that you're reading this book in preparation to write your own client for Jabber. We suggest, therefore, that you read the agreement; it's a bit different from the standard fare and can be used as a model for your own End User's Agreement, if and when you decide you need one. After you finish, click Yes to proceed or No to end the install.

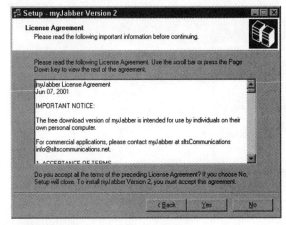

Figure 3-5: End User's License Agreement

Next, the Setup Wizard prompts you for a destination folder into which to install myJabber (see Figure 3-6). The default install path is C:\Program Files\myJabber, but you can choose your own path if you want. Notice that the installation of myJabber can take up more than 6 MB of hard-drive space. After you select your install folder, click Next.

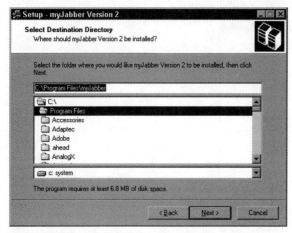

Figure 3-6: Choosing the folder in which to install myJabber

The Setup Wizard next asks whether you want it to create shortcuts to the program on the desktop and in the Quick Launch Bar to the right of your Start button (see Figure 3-7). The latter is an often-ignored feature of Windows and, in fact, one of its handiest. By default, myJabber creates only the desktop shortcut and creates a program group in the Start menu. The options you offer your users are up to you, of course. As you can see in the figure, we will be creating both the desktop and Quick Launch shortcuts. Make your choices and click Next.

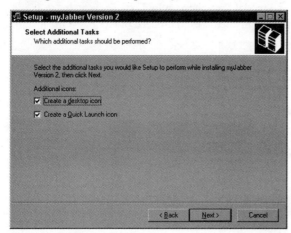

Figure 3-7: Additional tasks options

The next screen (see Figure 3-8) just confirms the choices that you've made. Here you see the install path and a list of additional tasks; if you see something that you don't like or want, you can click Back to change it. If everything's acceptable, click Install.

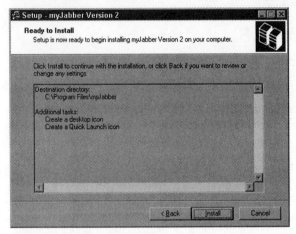

Figure 3-8: Confirming your options

You see the Setup Wizard install the program files and then finish by registering some files with the Windows Registry. These files are the data link libraries that make some of myJabber's features possible. After the wizard finishes, you see the last screen of the installation (see Figure 3-9). This screen announces the completion of the install and gives you one last choice. If you leave the check box checked (it is checked by default) and click Finish, myJabber loads, and you can move on to the task of setting up your account and configuring myJabber for the 'Net.

Figure 3-9: The final step in the myJabber installation

> **NOTE** On some rare occasions, the myJabber installation process requires that you reboot, and a dialog box offers you the options of doing so immediately or at a later time. The choice, of course, is yours, but if you're asked to restart, we advise against expecting optimal performance from myJabber until you've done so.

Setting up myJabber for SSL

Because of popular demand from users and prospective buyers alike, myJabber handles Secure Socket Layers (SSL) quite well. SSL is important in a lot of different environments; call centers and corporate offices, for example, need to protect corporate secrets and other information and thus require additional security for any kind of transmission of this type. You'll find that myJabber is up to the task! The entire Jabber protocol, in fact, itself is far more secure than that of any of the other chat programs in use today.

Adding SSL to myJabber is so incredibly simple that you could teach even the proverbial old dog to do it. Again, visit the myJabber Web site at www.myjabber.net/myjabber.php. At the bottom of this download page, you find an Add-Ons section, and in this section, you find Support for SSL. (The link itself is SSL DLL'S.) This link leads to a small Zip file (375 KB) containing two data link libraries (DLL files) that are going to do all the work for you. Download this Zip file to your hard drive and open it with your favorite compression program. Extract these files to the folder in which you installed myJabber. Figure 3-10 shows the files being extracted to the myJabber folder. (If you accepted the default choice, the location is C:\Program Files\myJabber.) That's it! SSL has been taken care of; the only thing left is to tell myJabber to use SSL whenever it logs on.

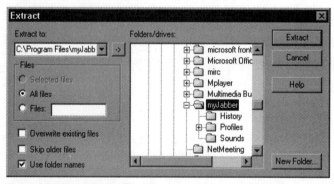

Figure 3-10: Extracting the SSL files to the myJabber install folder

Creating an Account

On clicking Finish on the previous installation screen (as we describe in the section "Installing myJabber"), you should see the Preferences dialog box, as shown in Figure 3-11. (If you needed to reboot, you see this dialog box the first time you run myJabber.) This dialog box is where you perform all the configurations in myJabber, including server and user information.

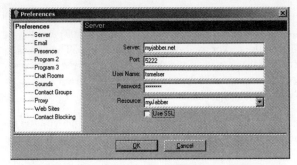

Figure 3-11: Creating an account in the Preferences dialog box

As shown in Figure 3-11, the first set of options in the Preferences dialog box falls under the Server category. This area is where you need to start. Here are six important options, only one of which you can skip (the Use SSL check box on the bottom). The following list describes these options, in order:

♦ **Server:** This text box specifies the server to which you want to log on. By default, it's set to myjabber.net.

♦ **Port:** This text box lists the port that you connect to. The default is 5222, but Jabber administrators can set their servers to work on any port they want to. If you're using SSL, you must set this port to 5223, as this port is the default for SSL in the land of Jabber.

♦ **Username:** This text box is where you type your username on the server. Pick something that you can remember!

♦ **Password:** Again, choose something that you can remember to type into this text box as your password and keep it safe. You know how important password security is.

♦ **Resource:** By default, this drop-down list box reads myJabber. It *must* say something — home, office, and school are all good choices for this option.

♦ **Use SSL (check box):** If you're using SSL, you must click this check box, regardless of what port you configure SSL to use on the server.

After you've made your selections and clicked OK, myJabber responds with the dialog box shown in Figure 3-12.

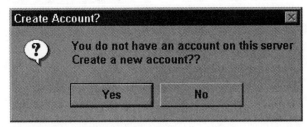

Figure 3-12: Create Account dialog box

Click Yes and you're connected! This process looks simple from here, but the server is now "working" for you in ways that you can't see. It's recorded your User Identity (UID) and the password for that identity in an XML file on the server, with your username on it. The server begins storing your contacts in its internal database, even if they're from another IM service such as AIM or MSN Messenger. This rather neat feature enables you to log on from any machine with a Jabber client and have your contact list ready to use.

Most Jabber servers, including ours, send out a welcome message the very first time you log in to it. Figure 3-13 shows the one we received while writing this section of the chapter. Just close this message after you've read it.

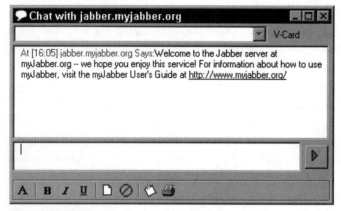

Figure 3-13: The myJabber server welcome message

Many Jabber servers send out what's known as the *Message of the Day*, or *MOTD*. Very few have handled it quite the way we do. Figure 3-14 shows a MOTD from November 2001.

Looks like a Web page, doesn't it? It should — it's a new posting on the myJabber home page. That's one of the differences in our MOTD; it shows you the latest posting on the myJabber site. The image you see in Figure 3-14 contains some of the news stories we post, bad grammar and all. In the beginning, this message popped up every time that you started the client; as you can imagine, that caused no end of complaints. After a while — and a support mailbox full of complaints and suggestions — we built a way that shows the MOTD only if you've not previously seen it. It's our way of keeping our users informed of the latest changes, new information, news, and the general gibberish that we post on the home page.

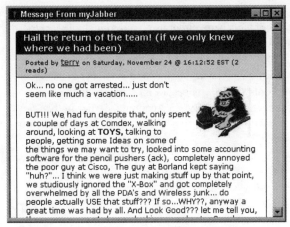

Figure 3-14: A myJabber Message of the Day

We've now shown you how to build a new account on the myJabber server and looked at some of the things you can expect to happen the first time you log in. Next, we get you talking with your contacts by configuring and setting up myJabber for your personal accounts.

Configuring myJabber

myJabber can be the most basic of programs to set up, but don't let that mislead you — it includes some very advanced features that can make it the most powerful communications tool you've ever used. In its basic form, you need only to create an account and start adding contacts. Many people like their lives and tools a bit more organized than that, however, so we've included many features that help you accomplish the task of organizing your contacts and the groups they occupy.

The running myJabber program offers two distinct views: the narrow "IM" style or a full-sized view that includes a message window. myJabber loads for the first time in the narrow IM style, but from that point on, it remembers which view it was in when you closed it and restores that view the next time. Figure 3-15 shows the narrow IM-style window.

In this chapter, however, we want you to work with the full-sized version. How do you get there? Look in the bottom left-hand corner of the smaller window. Click the blue arrow and myJabber expands to the full-sized version shown in Figure 3-16.

Figure 3-15: The narrow IM-style myJabber window

The full-sized view offers a lot of features, including a message window. You can set up server messages and private messages from your contacts here, either as an individual message or in a threaded format. We're going to work with the full-sized version because you can see all the menus up close and personal and don't need to know your way around to see what's happening.

We start with the Preferences dialog so that we can get you online and get some contacts in place. On the myJabber menu bar, select Tools ⇨ Preferences. (You saw this dialog box before, when we built your account in the section "Creating an Account," earlier in this chapter.) You see several more fields here, with some pretty neat stuff in them, as the following list shows:

- ◆ Server
- ◆ Email
- ◆ Presence
- ◆ Program 2
- ◆ Program 3
- ◆ Chat Rooms
- ◆ Sounds
- ◆ Contact Groups
- ◆ Proxy
- ◆ Web Sites
- ◆ Contact Blocking

Your first task is to add some of your contacts to the program, so you need to modify the roster list.

Click Contact Groups in the Preferences list of the Preferences dialog box so that it's highlighted. What you then see appear on the right side of the dialog box is an empty field and two buttons (Add and Delete). Click the Add button. You now see a small dialog box with a text box where you can add an item. This dialog box is where you populate the roster with all the different IM programs that you use. Figure 3-17 shows the addition of our Aim Users Group.

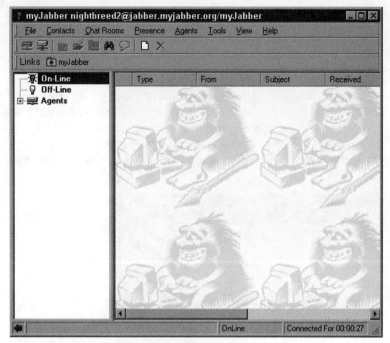

Figure 3-16: myJabber, the full-sized version

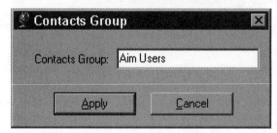

Figure 3-17: Adding a contacts group to the Contacts Group dialog box.

The options here are as follows:

♦ Jabber users

♦ AIM users

♦ ICQ users

♦ MSN Messenger users

♦ Yahoo! Messenger users

Other options may include: Work, School, Family, Tech Support, and Finances — only your needs limits this list.

> **NOTE** Yes, you want to add a group for Jabber users. Remember that you're going to write a Jabber client and you want to get your friends, family, business contacts, postman, canary, and anyone else you can think of using Jabber so that they can become your built-in "beta testing" group when the time comes.

You can correct mistakes or remove unneeded groups (you might create a group for use during a short-term project and then want to delete it after the project is complete) simply by clicking the name of the group in the Contact Groups list of the Preference dialog box to highlight it and then by clicking the Delete button. This step is very important in keeping your contacts organized and neat. Refer to Figure 3-18 for a look at the Contact Groups. The myJabber software is also going to do things with these groups to keep your offline contacts in order for you.

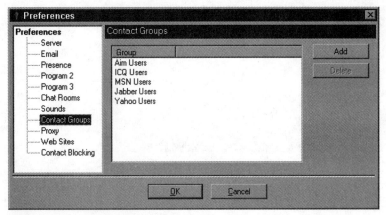

Figure 3-18: The completed list of Contact Groups

Setting up MSN

We've reached the moment that you've been waiting for — the time to get your other IM services online and add some people. myJabber (and any other client) is just like the client it's replacing in that you must first log in to the service. To demonstrate, we work with the MSN Messenger service in this section. MSN is a bit different from AIM and ICQ in that the MSN server stores your contact list for you remotely and force-feeds it to a client that doesn't have the list recorded. It works the same way with Jabber clients. On the left side of the myJabber client is the roster list, seen in Figure 3-19. In this list, you see the item Agents. Click the plus sign (+) next to the item to expand the list. The items that appear in this "grouping" are the services or agents offered by the server you're logged in to. These services include (in no specific order):

♦ Jabber User Directory (JUD)

♦ Public chat rooms

♦ AIM transport

♦ Yahoo! transport

♦ ICQ transport

♦ MSN transport

You notice in Figure 3-19 and in your online myJabber client that the top two services, Jabber User Directory and Public Chat Rooms, are already online. The small light bulb is bright green (or dark, since you're looking at it in black and white), which indicates online, and not white, which represents offline. These services are part of the Jabber server itself and should always appear as online.

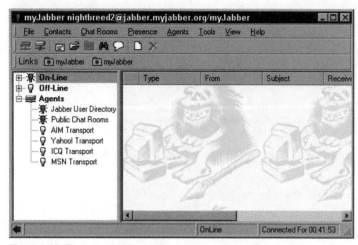

Figure 3-19: The expanded Agents list

Right-click the white bulb icon for the MSN transport and choose Properties from the pop-up menu. What you're going to get next is a sign-in dialog box for the MSN network (see Figure 3-20). This type of screen is going to become very familiar to you in the next few moments.

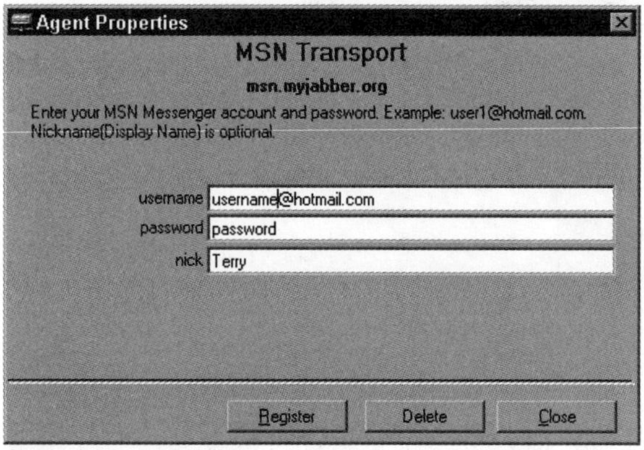

Figure 3-20: The MSN sign-in dialog

Enter your MSN username, your password, and the nickname that you want to use in your chat sessions. (MSN Messenger also uses this feature, as an option.) Click the Register button. A whole bunch of things should start happening in a few seconds: First, the light bulb icon next to MSN Transport in the Agents list turns bright green to indicate that it's online; next, you should get a subscription request dialog box from msn.myjabber.net. Click Yes. Now the fun begins. If you had people already registered in MSN Messenger, the MSN server is now going to force-feed them to the myJabber client. Depending on how many are in your roster, you may spend the next few moments clicking Yes or No to subscription requests. You may see the names of people you haven't spoken to in months or years popping up; the MSN servers aren't the neatest of housekeepers. Unfortunately, this situation is going to create a real mess in your roster, as myJabber currently doesn't know that these people belong to the MSN group. We help you clean that up before we move on to other services. Look at Figure 3-21 and you see these people listed by their Hotmail or MSN addresses but not in any particular group; they are just sort of taking up space in the general window. It takes a bit of effort, but this problem is easy to fix. You also notice that the Message window on the right-hand side is full of information about inbound subscription requests.

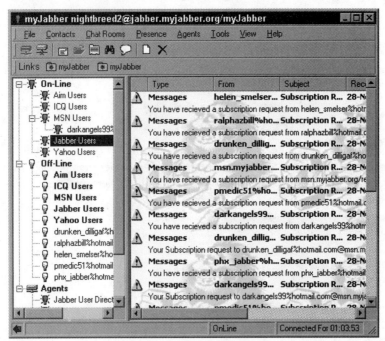

Figure 3-21: The subscribed MSN contacts are everywhere.

Contacts are going to appear in the roster in the online group if they're currently online and in the offline group if not. They're not going to appear in their MSN groups; this situation is just the nature of the beast, but you can clean it up very quickly. Right-click the name of someone who's online in the roster list and choose Properties from the bottom of the menu that appears. In the example in Figure 3-22, we picked our friend DarkAngel.

Figure 3-22: DarkAngel is online!

The Contact Properties dialog that appears contains the following fields:

♦ **User ID (UID):** This field contains the contact's username with the MSN Messenger service.

♦ **Nick Name:** This rather nice feature enables you to set the contact's name to anything that you want in the myJabber software.

♦ **Status:** This field shows the contact's current status: away, online, offline, or any of the custom away messages that can be set in many Jabber clients.

♦ **Contact Groups:** This list box contains the list of contact groups we built a few moments ago and that now comes into play.

Editing these messy contacts is a very simple task, and cleaning them up takes little time. First, click the MSN Users check box in the Contact Groups on the right side to select it. Now change the contact's Nick Name to whatever you want. (Notice that the nickname field currently contains the contact's UID.) Click the Update button. The contact should move to its proper location in the roster list. (If not, don't worry about it too much at this point; a quick refresh of the roster — by pressing F5 — after you finish cleans up the problem.) Pretty simple stuff, huh? We know, we know — you have 200 contacts in there and it's a real mess. In the end, it's worth it — trust us.

All finished? (The procedure gets easier after the first time through.) Press F5 to refresh your roster, and anything that didn't move to its group before should now go there. The online group opens displaying your contacts. Now how about that mess on the right-hand side of the client, in the message box? After you finish looking at it, right-click one of the items and choose Delete All Messages from the pop-up menu that appears. The message box will completely clear and is ready for new incoming messages.

Setting up ICQ

ICQ requires a fairly simple setup. In your roster list, open the Agents group and right-click the ICQ transport; choose Properties from the pop-up menu. Figure 3-23 shows the ICQ sign-in dialog.

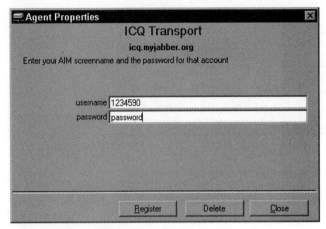

Figure 3-23: The ICQ Agent Properties dialog box

Type your ICQ UID number in the username box and your password in the password box and click Register. You should receive a subscription request from icq.myjabber.net, and the light bulb icon next to ICQ Transport turns green in the roster list. If it doesn't, first check to make sure you typed your UID and password correctly. If the light bulb icon turned green, you're online; the only thing left is to start adding your contacts. If you have only a few contacts in ICQ, the easiest thing to do is just add them manually (as opposed to importing them).

Choose Contacts ⇨ Add User from the menu bar. Figure 3-24 shows you the Add User dialog box that appears.

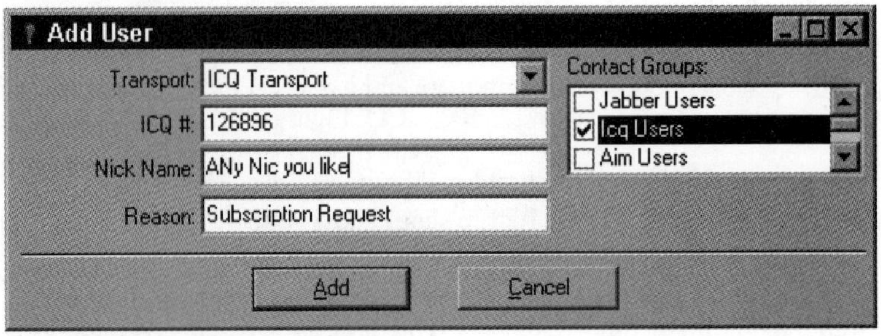

Figure 3-24: The Add User dialog box

The Add User dialog box offers the following options:

♦ **Transport:** This drop-down list box covers all the agents that the server lists. It will always default to Jabber User. Simply click the arrow on the right side and select the needed transport.

♦ **UID:** The label to the left of this field changes with the transport that you select, so if you select ICQ, as in this example, it reads ICQ #, as it does in the figure.

♦ **Nick Name:** This text box enables you to change the name of the user to one that you prefer, so if your contact is known as *dog breath* and you'd rather list him as Tom Hill, you can.

♦ **Reason:** This text box is by default set to Subscription Request.

♦ **Contact Groups:** Remember these groups? You defined them in the Preferences dialog in the section "Configuring myJabber."

So for ICQ, you click the arrow at the right side of the Transport drop-down list box and choose the ICQ transport. The next text box then changes to ICQ#. Enter the ICQ number that relates to your contact, enter a nickname for the contact, and mark the Icq User check box in the Contact Groups list box. Click the Add button. This contact now appears under the ICQ group in your roster list, either online or offline, depending on the contact's current status.

For those of you with a lot of contacts under ICQ, we have a special treat. Very early in the development of myJabber, we received many requests for an import tool for AIM and ICQ roster lists. In a very short amount of time, Steve came up with a way to import the ICQ contact list into myJabber. We never got around to finish an import tool for AIM, but we're working on it. And as you've seen, MSN and Yahoo! just don't need such a tool.

The ICQ import tool is an add-on to the main myJabber program, and you must download it separately. It's fairly small (approx. 275 KB) and is a quick download even on a slow connection. Go to www.myjabber.net/myjabber.php and scroll down the page to the Add-On section. Right there on top is the myJabber ICQ Contact Importer. Download this file and install it as you did myJabber.

> **CAUTION** The install path must match the path that you used to install myJabber. If you used the default path with myJabber, use the default path with the myJabber ICQ Contact Importer.

From the myJabber menu bar, select Tools ⇨ Import from ICQ. Figure 3-25 shows the resulting dialog box. This dialog box more than likely appears just as you see it here. (Remember that myJabber and the ICQ transport must be online.) You should need only to click the Apply button to access next dialog box, as seen in Figure 3-26.

Confirm ICQ Transport

Please make sure you have already logged into the transport before attempting to convert your current client list

Transport: ICQ Transport

Reason: Subscription Request

Apply   Cancel

Figure 3-25: The myJabber ICQ import tool confirms that the ICQ transport is active.

myJabber ICQ Importer

☐ Select All   Combo1

UIN	NickName

Import   Close

Figure 3-26: The myJabber import tool shows your ICQ contact list.

In the left-hand column, under the heading of UIN, you find the ICQ number of your contact, and on the right, you see the nickname that the contact registered. This dialog box is a tool to help you sort the list out and perhaps get rid of a few (or a lot of) contacts whom you haven't heard from in ages. Using this tool does involve a bit of mess, as you currently find no way to use the software to put your contacts in the correct Contact Groups, so you must sort them manually, as you do for MSN. Still, if you have a lot of contacts in ICQ, this tool offers you a faster method of getting them all into myJabber than typing all of your contacts in by hand.

NOTE We forced the import tool to come up blank for this screen shot, to safeguard the privacy of our friends and associates.

Setting up AIM

Setting up AIM involves much the same process as does setting up ICQ: Select the AIM transport in the Agents list, right-click it, and choose Properties from the pop-up list. Enter your screen name and password in the appropriate text boxes, click Register, and away you go. The light bulb icon turns green, you receive a subscription request from `aim.myjabber.net`, and you can start adding contacts. This process is very much like that of ICQ: On the menu bar, click Contacts ⇨ Add User. Select AIM Transport from the drop-down list box in the Add User dialog box and type the contact's screen name in the username box, click to mark the Aim Users check box in the Contact Groups, and click Add. Simple stuff, right? Go ahead and add your AIM contacts; we'll be right here whenever you get back.

Setting up Yahoo!

Yahoo! is very much like MSN in that it "force-feeds" your contacts to you after you connect. Yes, the process *can* become as messy as MSN's; whether it does or not depends on the size of your contact list. You register Yahoo! the same way you do all the others: Select the Yahoo! transport from your Agents list and right-click it, choosing Properties from the pop-up menu to open the Add User dialog box. Enter your Yahoo! username and password in the appropriate text boxes and click Register. The light bulb icon in the Agents list turns green, and you receive a subscription request from `yahoo.myjabber.net`. Click Yes, and the subscription requests from your existing contact list are inbound. The way these contacts are added to your roster, in just any old place they will fit, is another one of those messes that come under "the nature of the beast," but as you saw for the MSN transport, it's a relatively simple process to clean up.

Setting up Jabber

The last thing you need to look at is how to add Jabber contacts to your roster. Adding Jabber contacts involves only a small difference, and it serves a rather neat purpose. You enter the UID for a Jabber contact in the following manner: To access the myJabber server, the entry you type is `user@myjabber.net`. Why so much typing? Well, say you have a buddy who's running her own Jabber server and you want to add her to your roster. You use the entry `user@her.own.server.net`. This method, of course, works if your contact is using any server with the server-to-server feature enabled (most do). In the Add User dialog, specify a Nick Name, select Jabber Users in the Contact Groups list, and click Add.

We've now finished adding all your contacts to the myJabber program. Congratulations! If, like us, you're using all or many of these IM clients in one capacity or another, you've just rid yourself of the need for four pieces of software. myJabber can handle all these IM protocols for you — and in a neat, very configurable package. It's different from what you're used to and may not have some of the features that make the others such resource hogs. Yes, we hear you saying it now: "But I *liked* those features!" We understand. Really, we do, but hey — we're preparing you here to write your own Jabber client, so you can include those features in your Jabber client and get rid of the ones you never used. The sky's the limit here.

Additional Configuration Options

In this section, we're going to bore you to death with every tiny little detail that makes myJabber the program that it is. By doing so, we hope to provide you with some insight on Jabber clients and, at least, the features and functionality of a successful piece of software.

Menu items

Figure 3-27 shows the entire menu block at the top of the myJabber program. You can use it as an example, adding or removing items as your development progresses to suit your client's needs.

Figure 3-27: myJabber menu items

The current options on the menu bar, from left to right, are as follows:

- ◆ **File:** This menu is a standard Windows menu. The following program functions are available here:
  - • **Connect:** Connects the myJabber client to the server information set in the active profile.
  - • **Disconnect:** Disconnects the client from the server.
  - • **Exit:** Exits (closes) the myJabber program.

- ◆ **Contacts:** From here, you can manage information on your various contacts, as follows:
  - • **Add User:** Adds a contact to your roster. The keyboard shortcut is Ctrl+A.
  - • **Delete User:** Deletes a contact from your roster.
  - • **Block User:** Blocks the user from contacting you or from seeing your online status.
  - • **Search:** Enables you to search the Jabber Users Database (JUD) on the server or the global Jabber Users Database at Jabber.org, providing either local or global searches.
  - • **Message:** Sends a message to the highlighted contact. The keyboard shortcut is F2.
  - • **Chat:** Opens a chat with the highlighted contact. The keyboard shortcut is F3.
  - • **Send File:** Sends a file to the highlighted contact.
  - • **V-Card:** Opens the vCard for the highlighted contact.

- **Last Seen:** Allows you to determine the last time a contact was active.

- **Refresh:** Refreshes the roster in order to clean up or re-sort the roster after making changes to it. The keyboard shortcut is F5.

♦ **Chat Rooms:** This menu gives you access to the following conference features:

  - **Join:** Opens the Join Chat Room dialog box (see Figure 3-28). The keyboard shortcut is F4.

Figure 3-28: The Join Chat Room dialog box

This dialog box is designed to help you connect to a chat room on the Jabber server to which you're connected or, because of a unique feature of Jabber itself, on any other Jabber server running server-to-server connectivity. We cover using the conference servers in the section "Conferencing," later in this chapter.

- **Browse:** Enables you to browse through the various rooms on the conference server or any other servers offering server-to-server connectivity. Figure 3-29 shows the Browse Chat Rooms dialog box. This dialog box is very simple to use and is almost self-explanatory. We examine it in depth later on.

- **Favorites:** Lists your favorite conference (chat) rooms. This list comes with the "myJabber" room in it by default, and you can add to it by using one of two methods: First, if you're in a conference room, you can right-click the center of the room and choose Add to Favorites from the pop-up menu. Alternatively, you can add these rooms manually in the Groups area of the Preference dialog box.

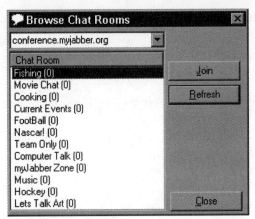

Figure 3-29: The myJabber Browse Chat Rooms dialog box

♦ **Presence:** This menu is where you set your status on the server It includes the following options:

• **Online:** Shows you as online and available.

• **Free for Chat:** Practically begs people to talk to you.

• **Away:** Shows the away message that you set in the Presence area of the Preferences dialog box. This setting is the default away setting.

• **Do Not Disturb:** Turns your light bulb icon (the one others see) bright red and warns people to leave you alone.

• **Extended Away:** Says, "I'm away for a while."

• **Custom:** Enables you to set a custom message ("At dinner — be right back"; "Off to the store for a bit"; "Goofing off") and a custom level or entry in the Custom dialog box.

♦ **Agents:** This menu enables you to manage your agents (or transports), as follows:

• **Log on:** Transport not connected? Highlight it in the Agents portion of the roster and click here.

• **Log Off:** Transport logged in but you don't want to talk to those contacts? Highlight it in the Agents portion of the roster and click here.

• **V-Card:** Opens the vCard for the transport.

• **Properties:** Shows you the Properties dialog box for the selected agent. You mainly use this item to register with the agent.

♦ **Tools:** This menu provides access to the various tools you use to configure and operate myJabber, as follows:

- **View history:** If you set the client to log your private and conference chats, enables you to access them. Opens a viewer and a Windows dialog box so that you can choose the conversation you want to view. You can save in Rich Text format only.

- **Send XML:** Enables server admins to send various commands to the server using XML. (This tool is for use only by server admins. If you don't have an admin account on the server, this menu item is completely useless to you. The commands you send can also be set in a hard coded form, needing only a click to request information from the server or to open a dialog to send messages to the server population. Keep these ideas in mind as you write your client.)

- **Server:** Opens into a submenu containing three more options, as follows:

- ◆ **Version:** Queries the server and returns the server version to the message window.

- ◆ **Time:** Queries the server and returns the machine time to the message window.

- ◆ **V-Card:** Displays the vCard for the server. You set this information in the `jabber.xml` file that you become familiar with in later chapters.

  - **Profiles:** Enables you to build separate logons for various servers, test accounts, and so on. This tool is a very powerful one for development users.

  - **Current Preferences:** Opens the Preferences dialog box, which is very complete in its design; you handle all client functions here. Because of the complexity of this dialog box, we cover it in its own section.

  - **V-Card:** Enables you to maintain your vCard. Everything here is quite self-explanatory.

  - **Change Password:** Enables you to change your password on the server to which you're connected.

  - **Import from ICQ:** The starting point for the ICQ import tool that we use in the section "Setting up ICQ," earlier in this chapter.

  - **MOTD:** Shows you the myJabber Web site's Message of the Day.

- ◆ **View:** This menu enables you to adjust the appearance of myJabber. All the following features display an **x** next to their name if they're enabled:

  - **Message Window:** Closes or opens the right-side message window.

  - **Main Tool Bar:** Enables or disables the main toolbar (the set of icons below the menu bar).

  - **Web Tool Bar:** Enables or disables the Web toolbar, located below your main toolbar in the client.

  - **Always on top:** If enabled, keeps the myJabber client on top of all other programs running onscreen.

- ◆ **Help:** This menu gives you access to the various Help resources for the myJabber communications platform, as follows:

- **On-Line Help:** Opens the Help documents at www.myjabber.net. As you develop your client, you may want to handle the Help feature differently, using the Windows Help format, HTML, or any of several ways to display your documentation to your users. The keyboard shortcut is F1.

- **myJabber Web Site:** Opens the home page at www.myjabber.net.

- **Email myJabber Team:** Opens a fresh e-mail in your default e-mail client to support@myjabber.org.

- **About:** Opens the stylish myJabber About dialog box, which displays version and contact information for myJabber.

Toolbar

myJabber's toolbar (see Figure 3-30) provides quick access to frequently used features.

Figure 3-30: The myJabber toolbar

From left to right, you find the following items on the toolbar:

- **Connect:** The connected network drive symbol ("grayed out" or disabled in the figure). Use this button to connect to the server.

- **Disconnect:** The disconnected network drive symbol. Use this button to disconnect.

- **New Message:** The letter. Use this button to open a message to the highlighted contact.

- **Send a file:** The open folder ("grayed out" or disabled in the figure). Use this button to send a file to the highlighted contact.

- **Show users V-Card:** The index card ("grayed out" or disabled in the figure). Highlight a user and click it to access that user's vCard.

- **Search:** The binoculars. Enables a search of the user database, which is very handy in corporate applications.

- **Chat:** The voice bubble. Opens a chat with the highlighted contact.

- **Add User:** The blank page. Opens the Add User dialog box.

- **Delete User:** The black **x** ("grayed out" or disabled in the figure). Deletes the highlighted contact.

These shortcuts for the items that you find in the menus come in very handy for experienced and new users alike.

Web toolbar

The Web toolbar, a neat little feature we added to myJabber and, subsequently, to all our custom applications, enables you to add links to some of your more frequently visited Web sites. By default, a link to the myJabber home page is already there. Figure 3-31 shows this feature up close and personal. We look at configuring this neat tool in the section "Preferences," later in this chapter.

Figure 3-31: The myJabber Web toolbar

Profile editor

One of the most powerful tools in myJabber is the profile editor, which enables you to set up different "profiles" for various servers or different user names on various servers. This allows you to switch between servers or user names as you need to because of a server's being down, your using a different name at home, or any of a dozen different reasons. Figure 3-32 shows the profile editor.

NOTE Opening the profile editor disconnects your Jabber session in preparation for switching servers or user IDs. In addition, all preferences that you set in the Preferences dialog box, while building a new or subsequent profile, remain with the new profile and don't affect any others.

To build a new profile, open the profile editor by selecting Tools ⇨ Profiles. Now click the Add button in the profile editor. A simple dialog box appears, asking you to enter a name for your new profile. Enter the name that you want for this profile in the text box provided and click the Apply button. Back in the profile editor, select (put a check mark by) the new profile in the Accounts Name list and make sure that the profile name highlights. Click Properties, and a familiar dialog box, the

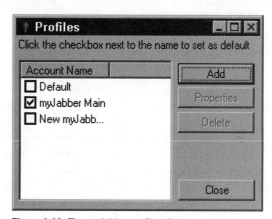

Figure 3-32: The myJabber profile editor

myJabber Preferences dialog box, opens to its Server tab. (See Figure 3-11.) Enter in the appropriate text boxes the name of the server you want to use and your username and password, remembering that *something* must appear in the Resources text box and making the settings changes you want for the rest of the preference settings in the dialog box. We discuss the use of this dialog box in more detail in the following section.

Preferences

This section is about the big one: the myJabber Preferences dialog box. We've showed you how to work in this dialog box a little bit, getting you online and building profiles, but now you're going to get into the real power behind myJabber — its configurability. myJabber offers a lot of features; some people find these features very useful while other people just ignore them. You may not incorporate some of these features into your own client, but we find some of them to be very useful. A brief listing of these features follows:

- Auto away
- Message logging
- Custom away and presence messages
- Fonts and colors
- E-mail notification
- Conference room management
- Customized sound cues
- Configurable contact groups
- Proxy server use
- Custom Web shortcuts
- Contact blocking

myJabber can do all these things, and the dialog box to get you to them is user-friendly and straightforward. On the myJabber menu bar, select Tools ⇨ Current Preferences. The by-now familiar Preference dialog box opens. So far, you've worked online with two of the items this tool offers, Server and Contact Groups. Now you get to look at the entire thing. We also cover the uses and configuration tips for each of these features. The following list again describes the options in the Preferences list at the left side of the dialog box, as well as the text box and other options that appear in the right side of the dialog box after you select one of the Preferences list options:

- **Server:** This option configures the dialog box to enable you to connect to a Jabber server, build profiles, or use Secure Socket Layers (SSL). It provides the following options:
  - **Server:** The DNS name of the chosen Jabber server. For internal use, you can set this to an IP address.
  - **Port:** The port number for the specified server. Standard is port 5222 for standard connections and port 5223 for Secure Socket Layers (SSL).
  - **User Name:** The username you will use on the specified server.
  - **Password:** The password for the specified account.

- **Resource:** A required entry, set by default to myJabber, but you can set it to anything you want. Suggestions include Home, Office, or School. These can tell a contact where you are, if you wish for people to know, or just the client that you are using

- **Use SSL:** A check box that, if you select it, enables the use of Secure Socket Layers (SSL) by myJabber This will automatically set the access port to 5223.

♦ **Email:** This option provides you with an e-mail *notification* client, not an e-mail client. It can show you the header of a new e-mail in the specified e-mail account and can even provide you with the content of the e-mail in plain text. You can read the message but can't reply to it. Future plans are to restrict this feature so that you can download only the header of the e-mail. This client works with POP3 accounts only. It doesn't work with HTTP-based e-mail (such as Hotmail or Yahoo!) or IMAP (Internet Message Access Protocol). The idea is for this feature to just notify you of new mail. Selecting this option in the Preferences dialog will show you the accounts you have included in your client configuration. To add to this list, click the Add button. This will open the Email Setup dialog you see in Figure 3-33. The Email Setup dialog box contains the following options:

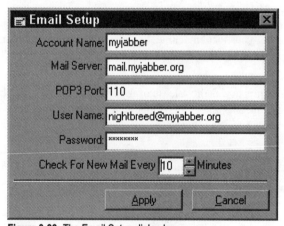

Figure 3-33: The Email Setup dialog box

- **Account Name:** Use this text box to give the account a friendly name to help organize your accounts. Whatever name you choose is only a label and has no bearing on the function of the client.

- **Server:** This text box is for the DNS name of your inbound POP3 mail server.

- **POP3 Port:** This text box is for the port on the mail server that responds to POP3 requests; as the standard on the Internet is port 110, myJabber defaults to this port.

- **User Name:** This text box is for the username for the desired account. This name can take several forms. If you don't know the format of this entry, check with your ISP's support staff.

- **Password:** This text box if for entering the e-mail password for your account, which may not necessarily be the same as your login authentication.

- **Check For New Mail Every *n* Minutes:** You can set this increment box so that your myJabber client looks in your mailbox at whatever interval you specify. A good round number to use here is ten minutes, as such an interval helps keep your connection alive on dial-up accounts with "no-activity" timeouts. You can enter the interval manually or use the scroll arrows to adjust it.

♦ **Presence:** This option opens a multipurpose dialog box that covers several functions. It was originally Program; we changed it to Presence as it addresses that function more than any other. This dialog box features the following options:

- **Message Logging:** Some people like to log their conversations with others; you often need to log business conferences and conversations as well. This saves your conversations to a text file in the myJabber install folder. Place a mark in this check box to do so.

- **Log Directory:** The default save path is C:\Program Files\myJabber\History. You can adjust this path to any folder on your local machine, however, or even to a network resource that you use for such things. A handy Browse button allows you to hunt down the folder.

- **Font:** One of our proudest moments was the release of the first version of myJabber that offered users their choice of fonts and colors. Open this by clicking the large blue "A" at the right end of the Font box. See Figure 3-34 for details.

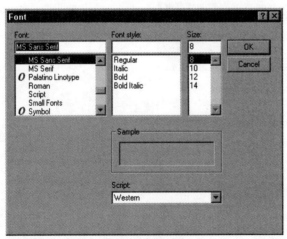

Figure 3-34: myJabber Font and Color dialog

Okay, you caught us: We didn't design this dialog box; it's been part of Windows all along. We just enabled myJabber to access and use it. We received a lot of positive comments on this addition to the program and are pleased that people enjoy it. The font and color selections you make are global and affect the overall client. You can set different fonts and colors for individual chats in each of those chats, at least for the present session.

- **Auto Away:** This option gives you a simple timer that tells myJabber to change your status to Away after so many minutes of nonactivity. You can set up to an hour delay in this timer. If you don't want myJabber to change your status for you and would rather do it manually (as we discuss in the section "Menu items," earlier in this chapter), simply blank this out.

- **Auto Away Message:** This option enables you to set the message that appears after the Auto Away timer changes your status to Away. You may edit this message to anything you want, but the option does come with a default generic Away message.

- **Show Auto Away Dialog:** This option makes the Auto Away dialog box appear in the center of your screen whenever myJabber marks you as Away. A single button in its center declares I'm Back. Clicking it, of course, returns your status to pnline. This feature is on by default; uncheck this box to turn it off.

♦ **Program 2:** This option opens a dialog box that provides a series of settings for the features in the program that are either on or off. With the use of simple check boxes, many powerful settings here can affect the looks and operation of the program. The dialog box contains the following settings:

- **Auto Connect at Start Up:** You open myJabber and, if it reads this setting as positive, it automatically logs on to the server configured in the Active profile.

- **Time Stamp Group Chat Messages:** This option places a time stamp, based on your computer's clock, on everything that you say or post in a group conference.

- **Time Stamp Chat Messages:** This option places a time stamp on anything that you say in a person-to-person chat.

- **CR Sends Message in Chat Window:** Set to on by default, this option enables you to send your message with a carriage return (a press of the Enter key) in a person-to-person or group chat. Switching it to off hides the carriage return in the text of your message and requires you to click the Send button.

- **Close Button Minimizes To System Tray:** Place a mark in this check box and the **x** in the top-right corner that normally closes a Windows program instead sends the client to the system tray (the depressed area of the Windows taskbar where the time appears). If you use this option, the only way to close the program is to select File ⇨ Exit from the menu bar.

- **Flash Caption on New Message in Group Chat or Chat Window:** The caption here is the light bulb icon in each of your open chat windows as represented in the Windows taskbar. If you turn on this feature, this icon will flash, giving you a visual alert that a new message has arrived in that window.

- **Visual Cue on New Message when Minimized:** The myJabber icon in the system tray flashes, signaling the arrival of a new message, if you minimized the program. (By default, myJabber minimizes to the system tray, thus not occupying any valuable taskbar real estate.)

- **Receive Messages in Chat Window:** This option is very handy for those folks using the ICQ transport. Put a mark in this check box, and anything that comes in as a message appears onscreen as a Chat window, including administrator messages from the server. Subscription requests still appear in the Message window.

- **Check for Product Updates:** This simple notification tool tells you when a new version of myJabber is available. It's not (at this time) a tool to automatically download updates of the program for you. It checks a page over at www.jabbercentral.com for any newly posted update.

- **Chat Instead of Message Window on Double-Click of Contact:** By default, the myJabber client opens a Message window to a contact whenever you double-click the contact's entry in the roster. If you prefer to use a Chat window by default, mark this check box.

◆ **Program 3:** This option is merely a continuation of Program 2. (We ran out of room.) Clicking on the entry on the left opens a dialog box containing the following options:

- **Turn Off Online Timer:** The online timer lives in the bottom right-hand side of the myJabber client. Its function is to track how long you're online. This feature drives some people stark raving mad. Put a mark in this check box to shut it off.

- **Group Messages in Message Window:** This option changes incoming messages in the right-side Message window from individual messages to "threaded" messages, similar to those of Usenet newsgroups and forums.

- **Show Contacts on Right Side:** Want to change things a bit? Perhaps you're left-handed? Maybe society just forces you to be different? Mark this check box and the roster moves to the *right* side of the Message window! You must restart myJabber for the change to take effect.

- **Turn Off Contact Tips:** This nice little feature shows you information about anything in the roster, just by pointing at it with the cursor. Unneeded or unwanted? Mark this check box to turn it off.

- **Disable User Online Pop-up:** If a user comes online, a bright-yellow panel with the notice *Username* has logged on appears in the bottom-right corner of your screen. Turn it off here.

- **Use Emoticons:** Emoticons! You know — smiley faces and the sort? myJabber comes with a limited number of them built right in, so that if you type :-) your contacts will see ☺ and if you type :-(your contacts will see ☹. See how many you can find! All the standards are there: smiley face, frowney face, winkey face, mad face, and so on. Our users have responded very favorably to this feature. You may want to consider something like it in your client.

- **Run Minimized:** If you mark this check box, myJabber minimizes itself after opening.

- **Auto Subscribe on Subscription Request:** A time and sanity saver if someone or, more specifically, a bunch of someones are subscribing to you. Instead of your needing to manually approve their subscriptions and then subscribe to them, this feature does it for you, automatically. Use with caution — you could wind up with someone in your roster whom you didn't want there.

- **Send Away Status in Chat Request:** This option replies to a chat request from one of your contacts and places your Away message in the body of the reply, in effect telling them, "No, I'm not ignoring you. I'm somewhere else" (or whatever) —unless, of course, you set your Away message to read "I'm ignoring you."

♦ **Chat Rooms:** Use this tool to manually configure conferences on both the server you're are logged in to and on any other server offering server-to-server connectivity (S2S). The main window provides a listing of the rooms configured in your client. Click Add to build more. Figure 3-35 shows the dialog box that opens; you use this box to build these rooms. The following options are available in the main window:

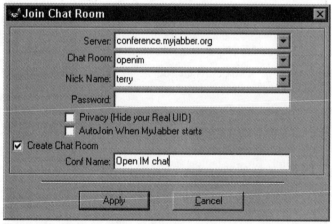

Figure 3-35: Conference room configuration and the dialog used to join a chat room

- **Server:** This option names the conference server that you want to join. All conference servers have unique DNS names. At myJabber, ours is called conference.myjabber.org. The one at Jabber.org is known as conference.jabber.org. Others leave conference off the name. Normally you need only check with the server admin for the server name.

- **Chat Room:** This text box is where you type the name of the conference room you want to add to your list.

- **Nick Name:** You type in this text box the name you want to go by in that conference room. Leaving this field blank causes the client to default to your username.

- **Password:** This text box is where you enter a password for the room itself. Public rooms don't have passwords, but if you're invited to use a private conference or you want to create one, you can't enter such a room without the correct password.

- **Privacy:** Marking this check box hides your "real" user ID from other users. If checked, this will hide your UID from other users.

- **Auto Join:** Marking this check box causes myJabber to automatically log in to this room after authentication to the main server.

- **Create Chat Room:** This option enables you to create a titled chat room on the conference server and works in conjunction with the next option. Enter in this text box the name of the room you are creating.

- **Conf Name:** An entry here places the conference name in the title bar of the conference room for everyone who enters to see. In the example chat room that we create in Figure 3-35, the name Open IM Chat appears in the title bar; without this entry, the title bar reads `Groupchat: openim@conference.myjabber.org`. The Create Chat Room check box must contain a mark for you to type anything here.

♦ **Sounds:** myJabber provides customizable sound cues that you can manage from this tool. You can add files to the Sounds folder under the main myJabber install folder. myJabber uses WAV files for sound. The following options are available:

- **Play Sounds:** This simple check box turns the sounds on and off. No mark in the check box means that no sounds are available.

- **Event:** Six events in myJabber have sound cues. Select the one you want to change or test in this block.

- **New Message:** Locate and specify the sound file that you want to play for the specified event here. You find a handy Browse button at the right end of the block.

- **Sample Sound:** This button plays the selected sound for testing purposes.

♦ **Contact Groups:** This option gives you a way of specifying and sorting your contacts. It provides the following options:

- **Add:** Clicking this button opens the Contacts Group dialog box. You add contacts by whatever group you want them to appear under. See Figure 3-36 for a look at this dialog box.

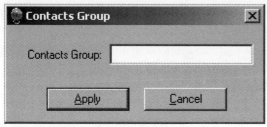

Figure 3-36: The Contacts Group dialog

- **Delete:** Highlight a contact group in the list on the right and click Delete. Doing so removes the group from your client and from the server's XML file in which it's stored.

◆ **Proxy:** Proxy servers enable members of a large or small LAN (local area network) to share a common connection to the Internet. They also provide security for that LAN by forming only one point that connects to the larger Internet. If you use proxy servers, client members must specify the proxy in various pieces of software that requires a connection to the Internet to function. Internet Explorer, Netscape, Opera, and various IM clients all use this gateway. myJabber offers support for Socks 4 and Socks 5. HTTPS is a project that we're still working on, as it requires interaction with a transport on the server. As yet, the transport is incomplete. Clicking this option in the Preferences list of the Preferences dialog box opens the proxy menu in the right side of the Preferences dialog containing the following options:

  - **Type:** This drop-down list box displays selections for the Socks 4 and 5 proxies or enables you to select None instead. If you're unsure of the proxy in use in your LAN, check with your system administrator. If you're on a simple dial-up or broadband connection in your home or office, most likely this option isn't a concern.

  - **Server:** This text box is where you enter the name of the proxy server itself inside the LAN in question. An example is `proxy.your.corp.net`. Check with your system administrator for this name if you're unsure what it is.

  - **Port:** This text box is where you type the number of the port that the proxy server uses to enable internal access to the Internet.

  - **User Name:** Some proxy servers require that you authenticate. This option is a security feature that some administrators use; the account name is most likely your LAN or NT login name. Enter this information in the box provided.

  - **Password:** This text box is where you enter the password to the account that you use to authenticate to the proxy.

NOTE The following two items are for advanced users behind firewalls or using NAT (Network Address Translations) for connectivity. They enable file transfers through the firewall or NAT device.

- **File Transfer Firewall IP:** You enter in this text box the IP address of the device that's handling NAT or of the firewall.

- **File Transfer Port:** The standard port number that you use for this text box is 5230; this port must be open through the firewall. If you're using a different port (ask the LAN people), you must specify it here.

♦ **Web Sites:** myJabber features a unique Web toolbar; selecting this option in the Preferences list changes the right side of the Preferences dialog box to enable you to configure it for your client. The myJabber site is already written into the code of the software itself, so you can use all three of these text box sets to enter information for new sites instead of needing to add myJabber here. Figure 3-37 shows you how we set up our Web toolbar in the Preferences dialog box. This version of the Preferences dialog box gives you the following options:

- **Site Name:** Just as it says, these text boxes are where you enter the names of the sites that you're listing in the Web toolbar.

- **URL:** These text boxes are where you enter the URLs or locations on the Web of the sites that you name in the Site Name text boxes. The `http://` prefix is hidden but already there for you, so you need add only the remainder of the location.

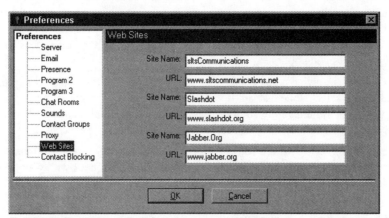

Figure 3-37: The Web toolbar configuration, as set up in the Preferences dialog box

♦ **Contact Blocking:** Yes, some people out there just refuse to leave you alone, even if you never want to hear from them again or have just never heard of them to begin with. And they keep sending you messages and chat requests. Enter their full UIDs in the block at the bottom and of the dialog box that appears after you select this option from the Preferences list of the Preferences dialog box and click Add. They're now blocked from sending you any kind of message or request.

> **NOTE** The "full UID" means something such as *user@myjabber.net* or, if the person's from another server, *user@jabber.org*.

That about covers the myJabber Preferences dialog box, and as you can see, myJabber is very configurable and quite powerful. (This discussion is only the beginning for us, however, as writing this book's given us new insights to what we've done and what we still can do with the powerful Jabber platform.)

Chatting

In this section, we finally get to the purpose of myJabber, chatting and conferencing. The basics of chatting are known to almost everyone today, and myJabber is a tool that everyone can use almost immediately. The Chat dialog box has some interesting features that we take a look at here.

Figure 3-38 shows the person-to-person Chat dialog box, and as you can see, Steve and I actually do speak to each other. Take a look in this section at some of the things that you can do from Chat.

Suppose you want to open a chat with one of your contacts. To do so the simplest way possible, just locate the person with whom you want to speak in the roster list of the main program and double-click the name. If you've set the client to open a Chat window by default, you get just that. Otherwise, you get a message dialog box. Alternatively, you can right-click the contact's name and choose Chat from the pop-up menu to open the Chat dialog box.

The title bar of the dialog box lists the contact's name, and just below that is a drop-down list box containing the contact's UID. At the top right, next to the UID, is a hyperlink to the contact's vCard. Clicking this link opens the vCard dialog box, as shown in Figure 3-39.

This dialog box displays personal information that the contact fills in and can include home and business addresses, Web sites, e-mail addresses, and other personal information — whatever the contact wants to reveal.

The Chat window is fully expandable, and you can even maximize it to the full screen. On the bottom of the Chat window is a row of icons (seen at the bottom of Figure 3-38) that give the Chat window its flexibility. The following list describes these icons:

- ◆ **A:** Opens the myJabber Font and Color manager. This manager affects the current chat only.
- ◆ **B:** (For Bold.) Sends your input in bold text.
- ◆ **I:** (For Italics.) Sends your input in italic text.
- ◆ **U:** (For Underline.) Sends underlined text.

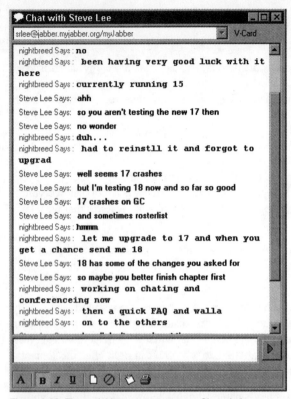

Figure 3-38: The myJabber person-to-person Chat window

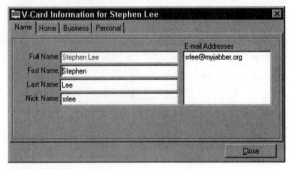

Figure 3-39: The contact's vCard dialog box

- ◆ **Blank Page:** Adds user to contacts. Click this icon and you open a form for subscription requests to the user.

- ◆ **Red Circle with the Bar:** Blocks contact. Clicking this icon prevents the user from contacting you in any way, so use with caution. You can remove blocked contacts in the Contact Blocking area of the Preferences dialog box.

♦ **Tilted Blank Page:** Clears the Chat window of all entries.

♦ **Printer:** Sends the chat to your default printer.

Conferencing

Conferencing enables users to participate in multi-user *chat rooms*. These rooms, or *conferences*, are either publicly accessible or private, password-protected rooms. Many corporate applications of this technology are possible. Used internally, Jabber conferences can help increase productivity and the timely flow of information throughout the workplace. You can set up your Help desk teams in a conference within your work environment, for example, and give those who may need help access to the teams. In so doing, you may shave significant time off the amount users lose while trying to contact Help on the phone. Say that Accounting has a quick question that only Shipping can answer, and Shipping is in another building. Or Sales needs to verify a technical question that a prospective customer poses and so needs to talk to Tech Support or Design. If your workplace is "wired" for Jabber, it can save you time and increase productivity in an endless number of ways. And it's totally secure because it uses the latest features of Secure Socket Layers (SSL).

Conferencing offers the same options as a person-to-person chat, with the following additions:

♦ **The Envelope:** Send a new message to a user by highlighting the user's name in the User List at the right and clicking this icon.

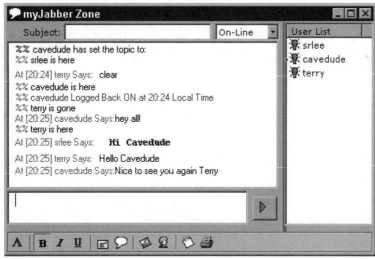

Figure 3-40: The myJabber Conference window

♦ **The Speech Bubble:** Highlight a contact in the User List at the right and click this icon to open a Chat dialog box. (You can also just right-click and open a chat with the user from the pop-up menu.)

♦ **Tilted Painting:** This icon adds the current chat room to your list of favorites. (You can also just right-click anywhere in the middle of the room and chose Add to Favorites from the pop-up menu.)

♦ **The Head:** Use this icon to invite a friend to the room; this invitation works only with other Jabber users, however, and not with anyone using transports. The Contacts dialog box that appears is very simple; just choose the person you want to invite from the list of contacts or type the person's UID in the text box at the bottom. The dialog box displays everyone on your roster who's online, but again, you can't invite contacts who are using a transport.

NOTE The known issue with "cross-platform" invites and chats is a limitation within the Jabber server and not the clients.

Summary

This chapter covers the configuration and use of the myJabber client. We hope all has gone well and that you're now enjoying the full use of all your IM contacts through the simple and powerful myJabber client. You find information about most configuration issues in this chapter. And you can direct all other questions to the support group at support@ myjabber.org.

Part II

Your Test Server

In This Part

Chapter 4

Installing the Core Jabber Server

In This Chapter

♦ Getting the components we need

♦ Getting started building your new server

♦ To CVS or not to CVS

♦ Using CVS

♦ Installing Jabber

♦ Editing the jabber.xml file

♦ Starting the server

♦ Finding missing libraries

♦ Adding SSL support

In this chapter, we show you how to install, configure, and run the basic Jabber server. If you want to install and use SSL (Secure Socket Layer) for added security, you must compile the SSL source first, before compiling the Jabber server. This order is *very* important. The configuration and setup of Jabber are slightly different if you use SSL. If you want to use SSL, skip to the final section of this chapter and use the information in Appendix E to compile and install the source for SSL before returning here to install the Jabber server.

Why would you need a test server? How do you go about finding and building this server? What is the best platform on which to build it? This chapter answers all these questions and more.

A *test server* (or *development server*) is exactly that — a place to test your new client and to develop the features you want it to have. These tasks go a lot more smoothly if you have a working server to bounce your client-in-progress off of.

Many server types are possible; each does a different job depending on one's needs. The following list describes a few of these types:

♦ **The all-purpose server:** This type is the basic server that we show you how to build. It enables the use of all the current transports to connect you to the various instant messaging networks in use today.

♦ **The mySQL-enabled server:** This server uses the mySQL database program to store its user data. It can also store specific information that relates to the purpose the server is filling, enabling users to access this data in real time, as they need it.

♦ **The closed-network chat server:** This server fills the role of person-to-person/group conferencing using the communication features built right into the basic server. You don't add transports, as the administrators or policymakers don't want or desire outside contact with the network.

These types of servers are only examples, of course. Only your imagination and needs limit the uses and modifications of the basic server package.

Getting the Components We Need

The first thing that you need, of course, is a computer running the Linux OS. The size and speed of this setup really don't matter that much for a development server, but we recommend at least a P1 166 MHz with 64 MB of RAM. We've run a production server for public or customer use with this configuration and had few, if any, problems with it. Of course, a large production server *should* be bigger and faster with much more RAM.

> **NOTE** We use Red Hat Linux 7.1 on all our production and development servers, so the examples that you see here are based on our knowledge of and experience with this particular Linux flavor. The server runs on almost any Linux flavor, including Slackware, Debian, Mandrake, Solaris, and BSD. Although we're sure that it runs on other Unix-based operating systems, finding examples is up to you.

We also need the server package. This package is available only in the TGZ or Tar.Gz format at the moment (or you can acquire it through CVS).

> **NOTE** *CVS (Concurrent Versions System)* is a version-control system, an important component of Source Configuration Management (SCM). By using it, you can record the history of source files and documents. For more information, see www.gnu.org/software/cvs/. We cover CVS later in this chapter.

Finally, we need the various transport packages. These packages are also available only in TGZ or Tar.Gz format (or you can acquire them through CVS). The transports include (but aren't limited to) those for AIM, ICQ, Yahoo!, MSN Messenger, and Conferencing. These transports are the ones that you work with and configure in this book.

Getting Started Building Your New Server

Now you have your computer up and running a recent version of your favorite Linux flavor. If you're installing the OS just to clean things up and get a fresh start, we can save you some trouble right here: Install *everything* — at least all the libraries that your OS supports and that are available on CD. That said, you need some software. (You can find all the server components in the \files folder on the CD that comes with this book).

To get the basic server package, download it from `http://download.jabber.org/dists/1.4/final/jabber-1.4.1.tar.gz`. We use `wget` in Linux to grab files from the Web. From the command prompt, type `wget http://download.jabber.org/dists/1.4/final/jabber-1.4.1.tar.gz` and follow the prompts. Download this software into your user directory.

Now you need the transports for your server. Although quite a few transports are actually available, all of which do different things, you need to concern yourself only with the following:

- ♦ **Conferencing:** A basic transport enabling group chat
- ♦ **JUD (Jabber User Directory):** A basic transport allowing searches of the local user database or the master database at Jabber.org
- ♦ **ICQ-Transport:** Provides interconnectivity with AOL's ICQ messenger
- ♦ **MSN-Transport:** Provides interconnectivity with Microsoft's MSN Messenger
- ♦ **Yahoo-Transport:** Provides interconnectivity with the Yahoo! Instant Messenger
- ♦ **AIMTransport:** Provides interconnectivity with AOL Instant Messenger (AIM)

You can find all these transports at `http://download.jabber.org/cvs/`. The links to each of the ones that you need follow:

- ♦ **Conferencing:** `http://download.jabber.org/cvs/conferencing.tgz`
- ♦ **JUD:** `http://download.jabber.org/cvs/jud.tgz`
- ♦ **ICQ:** `http://download.jabber.org/dists/1.4/final/`
- ♦ **MSN Messenger:** `www.jabber.org/?oid=274`
- ♦ **Yahoo! Messenger:** `http://download.jabber.org/cvs/yahoo-transport.tgz`
- ♦ **AIM:** `http://download.jabber.org/dists/transports/aim-transport/aim-transport-0.9.9.tar.gz`

ON THE CD-ROM You can also find these transports on this book's CD.

To CVS or Not to CVS

As we note earlier, CVS enables one to perform updates over the Web for many different software sources, including Jabber and its various components. We recommend its use. Using CVS gets you the latest versions of whatever you need and enables you to download them right into the directory you're currently in. Be aware, however, that sometimes the files in CVS are works in progress and you always want to consider them beta software. Tar-ball downloads are "normally" completed versions.

To use CVS, you must already have built the home directory for the Jabber server and set the permissions for that user/group. We cover this process in detail later in this chapter.

Jabber.org uses CVS, and you can find at that site almost anything you need for a Jabber server. CVS uses an authentication system that varies from server to server and can include private passwords known only to the principals of the project or can be anonymous or a variation of both. Jabber.org uses anonymous logins for its component storage; after you learn the system, it's a real time saver in building and maintaining the server.

To log in to the CVS server, enter this command:

```
cvs -d :pserver:anoncvs@jabber.org:/home/cvs login
```

The server asks for the password, of course, which in the case of Jabber.org is anoncvs (anonymous login).

This is the screen output from this request:

```
bash-2.04$ cvs -d :pserver:anoncvs@jabber.org:/home/cvs login
(Logging in to anoncvs@jabber.org)
CVS password:
bash-2.04$
```

Okay, you're in, so you can retrieve a component. As an example, use the following command to get, or "checkout," the ICQ-Transport:

```
cvs -d :pserver:anoncvs@jabber.org:/home/cvs -z3 checkout icq-transport
```

In your terminal session, the output from the CVS server is as follows:

```
bash-2.04$ cvs -d :pserver:anoncvs@jabber.org:/home/cvs -z3 checkout
icq-transport
cvs server: Updating irc-transport
cvs server: Updating irc-transport/debian
cvs server: Updating irc-transport/include
cvs server: Updating irc-transport/macros
cvs server: Updating irc-transport/src
cvs server: Updating irc-transport/src/gateway
cvs server: Updating irc-transport/src/misc
cvs server: Updating irc-transport/src/parser
cvs server: Updating irc-transport/src/transport
```

```
bash-2.04$
```

This is the method that you use for getting any of the parts and many of the library files that you need for the core Jabber server. As you build the server, knowing what files to request often proves difficult, as the software authors sometimes don't label things the way that you would. The contents of the /CVS directory are at `http://download.jabber.org/cvs/`. We use this directory listing as a reference to help us find the components we need. Many of the requested library files are also there.

You need to decide who's going to run the Jabber server. Certainly, it's you, but you should *never* run it as root. As an experienced Linux user, you know the security risks of running any external program as root. So set up a user just for the server. Common usernames that you can employ are admin, serveradmin, and so on. Throughout the remainder of this book, we use the username cavedude for the server admin and group.

We run our servers in the /usr/local directory in the subdirectories /jabber/jabber2.

How you get the final subdirectory here is up to you if you choose to use this location. But note that we refer to these directories throughout the rest of the book.

The commands may vary from one Linux flavor to the next, but the following procedure should work almost anywhere. To set up a user for the server, give it permissions, and move the Jabber server into place, follow these steps:

1. `su` to root and type the following command:

   ```
   /usr/sbin/adduser/ cavedude -p eddie -d /usr/local/jabber
   ```

   This command creates the user *cavedude*, gives him the password of `eddie`, sets his home directory to /usr/local/jabber, and creates the "jabber" directory in /usr/local.

2. Now you need to move the server into place. As shown in the following code, change directories to cavedude's home directory and `su` to him. (Better yet, log out of your current session and log back in as cavedude.)

   ```
   cd /usr/local/jabber
   ```

3. Now you want to get the server up here to /usr/local/jabber. If you haven't already downloaded it, do so now. If you downloaded it into your personal user space, the following command uncompresses it right to the current directory:

   ```
   tar xvfz /path/to/jabber-1.4.1.tar.gz
   ```

> **TIP** We downloaded the file into our user space located at /home/tsmelser. We often store libraries and source files in directories that we call "lib" or "files." The command to get the server source to where we wanted it was `tar xvfz /home/tsmelser/files/jabber-1.4.1.tar.gz`.

This procedure creates a directory called jabber-1.4.1 in the /usr/local/jabber directory. You can leave this directory name, or you can change it to whatever you want. Being lazy typists and knowing that we will type this folder name a lot, we always rename the server directory to something a bit easier or shorter. Take a look at the following command:

```
mv jjabber-1.4.1 jabber2
```

The "move" command is mv, but in this case, we're not naming a destination, so the command simply renames the directory to /jabber2. This directory is where it's all going to happen. For the sake of neatness and order, you should install all other files inside this directory (/jabber2). The main reason that we use /jabber2 is that, if you use CVS to get your server or to perform updates, that's the default directory. (Saves lazy folks such as we authors all that typing.)

Using CVS

You want to be in the /usr/local/jabber directory, as the "legal" server admin, when you issue the commands so that you build the /jabber2 directory in the right place and with the right permissions. (Why /jabber2? We don't know. That's just the way it's always been, at least since we've been involved in Jabber development.)

You can download the source for the server through CVS from the Jabber.org Web site by using the following command:

```
cvs -d :pserver:anoncvs@jabber.org:/home/cvs login
```

After the server ask you for the password, enter anoncvs. This command returns you to your shell prompt. You're logged in to the CVS server but still in your own shell. At this point, you're going to request the files that you want, so issue the following command:

```
cvs -d :pserver:anoncvs@jabber.org:/home/cvs -z3 checkout jabber2
```

Take a look at Figure 4-1, which shows the CVS login process.

TIP Depending on your Linux flavor and your configuration, often you need to install PTH (*Portable Threads*). You can find PTH at ftp://www.gnu.org/gnu/pth/pth-1.4.0.tar.gz. In addition, libpth is often missing, but you can find it at ftp://ftp.linux.com/pub/mirrors/debian/ pool/main/libp/libpth/libpth_1.3.7-3.1.tar.gz; this library is necessary for the next step. Read more about PTH and find the latest versions at www.gnu.org/software/pth/. This is the home site for PTH. PTH and other libraries can also be found using the search engine at www.tuxfinder.org.

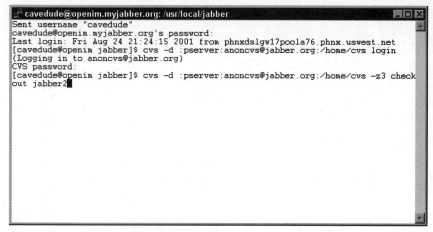

Figure 4-1: Downloading the Jabber server via CVS

Installing Jabber

Now you have the server on the Linux box in its own directory; it has a dedicated user, you've installed PTH if necessary, and you're ready to install Jabber. Just follow these steps:

1. Change to the /jabber2 directory with the following command:

```
cd jabber2
```

2. To configure the install, type the following command:

```
./configure
```

This process is a quick one that basically locates the libraries on the machine that the program needs. (At this point, you find out whether the PTH and libPTH libs are installed.) See Figure 4-2 for an example of the session output.

> **TIP** Even if you've installed a library, the OS may not know it's there, so the server `./configure` command can't find it. We've noticed this several times with PTH — it's a simple step that we keep forgetting, and it was very frustrating in the beginning before we caught on. It's an easy fix. PTH by default installs itself to a different path from that of many of the other libraries. You must edit the `/etc/ld.so.conf` file and add the path to the bottom of it. This path is normally /usr/local/lib. Save the file and, as root, run the command `/sbin/updatedb`; then run the command `/sbin/ldconfigure`. Now try the `./configure` command again. This process should get it running for you. Run these two commands any time that you add a library to Linux.

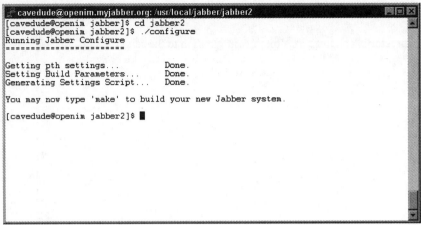

Figure 4-2: The configure command

3. At this point, you're ready to compile the Jabber server itself. Type make and hope for the best. Figure 4-3 shows the output of the make command. This process can take a while, depending on the machine and the amount of RAM, the size and speed of your hard drive, and so on. Unless you're a rocket scientist or a C programmer, you're unlikely to understand much of what you see onscreen. (We certainly don't.) You may notice the word WARNING appearing in the build output; pay little attention to it as whatever you're being warned about doesn't adversely affect the build or the server. The word ERROR, on the other hand, is followed by the termination of the build. (Not having a library installed or not having it in the path can cause this problem.)

```
cavedude@openim.myjabber.org: /usr/local/jabber/jabber2                    _ □ ×
make[2]: Entering directory `/usr/local/jabber/jabber2/jabberd/base'
make[2]: Nothing to be done for `all'.
make[2]: Leaving directory `/usr/local/jabber/jabber2/jabberd/base'
Making all in lib
make[2]: Entering directory `/usr/local/jabber/jabber2/jabberd/lib'
make[2]: Nothing to be done for `all'.
make[2]: Leaving directory `/usr/local/jabber/jabber2/jabberd/lib'
Making all
make[2]: Entering directory `/usr/local/jabber/jabber2/jabberd'
gcc -g -Wall -fPIC -I. -I.. -I/usr/local/include -DHOME="\"/usr/local/jabber/jab
ber2\"" -DCONFIGXML="\"jabber.xml\"" -o jabberd config.o mio.o mio_raw.o mio_xml
.o mio_ssl.o deliver.o heartbeat.o jabberd.o load.o xdb.o mtq.o static.o log.o l
ib/expat.o lib/genhash.o lib/hashtable.o lib/jid.o lib/jpacket.o lib/jutil.o lib
/karma.o lib/pool.o lib/pproxy.o lib/rate.o lib/sha.o lib/snprintf.o lib/socket.
o lib/str.o lib/xmlnode.o lib/xmlparse.o lib/xmlrole.o lib/xmltok.o lib/xstream.
o lib/xhash.o base/base_connect.o base/base_dynamic.o base/base_exec.o base/base
_stdout.o base/base_accept.o base/base_file.o base/base_format.o base/base_stder
r.o base/base_to.o -Wl,--export-dynamic -L/usr/local/lib -lpth -ldl -lresolv
make[2]: Leaving directory `/usr/local/jabber/jabber2/jabberd'
make[1]: Leaving directory `/usr/local/jabber/jabber2/jabberd'
make[1]: Entering directory `/usr/local/jabber/jabber2'
make[1]: Nothing to be done for `all-local'.
make[1]: Leaving directory `/usr/local/jabber/jabber2'
[cavedude@openim jabber2]$ ▮
```

Figure 4-3: The make command output

That's it! You've installed the server, but it's not quite ready to run. You don't use the make install command here, as this program is going to run right here in the /usr/local/jabber/ jabber2 directory. You must do a bit of configuration to the server's XML file, such as specifying a host name and some addresses. This step is the first of many and the first of many times you will visit this file. Let us save you a lot of time and profanity directed at your poor computer: Test *each* step that you do, making backups of the jabber.xml file as you go. Doing so really can save a lot of screaming. Trust us on this one.

Editing the XML File

Start up your favorite text editor. (And we suggest that you use something such as pico, joe, or vi and not one of the editors in KDE or GNOME; you need the capability to telnet or ssh to your server.). Then open the jabber.xml file in the jabber2 directory. We use joe, so the command is joe jabber.xml. Don't let what you see in the file daunt you; it's not as complex as it looks, and in fact, if you read the whole thing, you find most of the information that you need right there in the file. We work in a series of steps, starting at the top of the file and working our way down. How you do it is up to you, but try to develop a routine and stay with it. Doing so can prevent many mistakes.

> **NOTE** In XML, the symbols <!-- and --> describe a commented area. <!--Comments look like this and aren't read as part of the program or configuration.--> You see a lot of comments in the jabber.xml file, as it does a good job of documenting itself. Remember that, if you set any comments for yourself, work either inside an existing set of comments or start a new set *outside* an existing comment. XML doesn't like comments inside of comments; they cause the server to start to fail and are difficult to find.

In your editor, search for (or just scroll down to) the first section and find <host>. By default, <host> is set to localhost; you want to change this setting to *your.server.net*. In our case, of course, we set it to openim.myjabber.org. As shown in Figure 4-4, the line reads as follows:

```
<host><jabberd:cmdline
flag="h">openim.myjabber.org</jabberd:cmdline></host>
```

Figure 4-4: Edit the XML file and set the server name.

You can also set it to the local IP address of the machine in your network (if you're indeed running a network), as in the following example:

```
<host><jabberd:cmdline flag="h">10.0.0.5</jabberd:cmdline></host>
```

This command enables connections from within your local network and connections to the DNS name line server. Just make sure that these entries are on separate lines in this section. Be aware that the Jabber server treats each such entry as a separate server, so if you build an account on the local address and then "go live" on the Web, you're asked to build a new account.

Assigning a DNS name to the Jabber server is very important; the server can't run without a DNS name, as it needs to resolve to an IP address for the server-to-server (s2s) functions to work. The server-to-server features enable you to join a group conference on another server, contact a user on another server, or be contacted by a user on another server. As long as you know the JID (Jabber ID) of the person you're trying to talk to and place it in your roster, server to server enables this. Otherwise, everyone you know must reside on the same server.

> **NOTE** A hint on DNS names: They can prove a real hassle if you're on a dynamic or even static broadband — or even dial-up — account. (Yes, we've made Jabber servers work on dial-up.) With a static IP address, you still don't have a DNS name. Our solution to this problem was to use one of the many free dynamic DNS providers that you can find on the Web. Of course, `openim.myjabber.org` is on a fully qualified domain, so we don't have that issue in this case. We do have a fully functional Jabber server on a dynamic IP and an ADSL connection at home, so ways around the problem are available.

The next step is to put an end to a feature that just doesn't seem to work really well. The Jabber server is written to search for updates to itself and update accordingly. The server that it must speak to is rarely ever up or just plain refuses to recognize your server's request as a valid one. This situation can cause a variety of errors from your server that you just don't need and you can't do anything about anyway except shut it off.

As seen in Figure 4-5 (center), a line called `<update>` reads as follows:

```
    <update><jabberd:cmdline
flag="h">localhost</jabberd:cmdline></update>.
```

```
cavedude@openim.myjabber.org: /usr/local/jabber/jabber2                    _ □ ✕
 IW   jabber.xml              Row 215  Col 1        1:47  Ctrl-K H for help
      <write>tsmelser@openim.myjabber.org</write>
      <write>srlee@openim.myjabber.org</write>
      <write>cavedude@openim.myjabber.org</write>
      <reply>
        <subject>CaveDude Reply</subject>
        <body>This is a special administrative address.  Your message was rec
      </reply>
    </admin>
    <!-- The above  section (admin) has to be uncommented in the default
         xml file. This section is not needed for the server to run  TS
    -->

    <!--
    This is the resource that checks for updated versions
    of the Jabber server software. Note that you don't lose
    any functionality if you comment this out. Removing the
    <update/> config is especially a good strategy if your
    server is behind a firewall. If you want to use this
    feature, change 'localhost' to the hostname or IP address
    of your server, making sure that it is the same as your
    entry for <host/> above.
    -->
    <!--
    <update><jabberd:cmdline flag="h">localhost</jabberd:cmdline></update>
    -->

    <!-- The update section should be commented out as it has been causing
    problems for most admins and there are better ways of updating the server
    TS
    -->

    <!--
    This enables the server to automatically update the
    user directory when a vcard is edited.  The update is
    only sent to the first listed jud service below.  It is
    safe to remove this flag if you do not want any users
    automatically added to the directory
```

Figure 4-5: Edit the XML file to stop a problem before it starts.

Comment this out in the XML file (as shown in the following code example), and the problems it causes go away.

```
<!--
```

```
<update><jabberd:cmdline flag="h">localhost</jabberd:cmdline></update>.
-->
```

If you want to try to use this feature, change `localhost` to your server's name. Good luck.

The server is now ready to run, but a couple of optional settings make it more custom to you by adding server name, your greeting, the URL to your Web site, and so on as you see fit. See the section in Figure 4-6 under `The server vCard`.

Figure 4-6: Adding custom entries

Search the file for `The server vCard` and change the server information to suit your service, as follows:

```
<FN>The name of your server</FN>
<DESC>Keep this rather brief</DESC>
<URL>http://your.server.net</URL>
```

Check out the following example of the server's vCard configuration:

```
<vCard>
            <FN>Open-IM at myJabber</FN>
      <DESC>A Development Server</DESC>
      <URL>http://openim.myjabber.org/</URL>
   </vCard>
```

You can see from the example and in Figure 4-6 the settings that we used on `openim`. Your settings should be similar.

Now drop down a few lines to the welcome message. Change this to anything that you want or just comment it out. This message is a one-time thing, which appears only the first time that someone logs in to the server.

Now you can set up some administrators on the server. This feature again is strictly optional and is commented out by default in the `jabber.xml` file. The reason that you want this running is quite simple — it provides the specified users with information on the server and on new user signups, and more important, it gives administrators the capability to send global messages to the server population and set up a message of the day if they want.

Search for the entry `<admin>` and look at Figure 4-7.

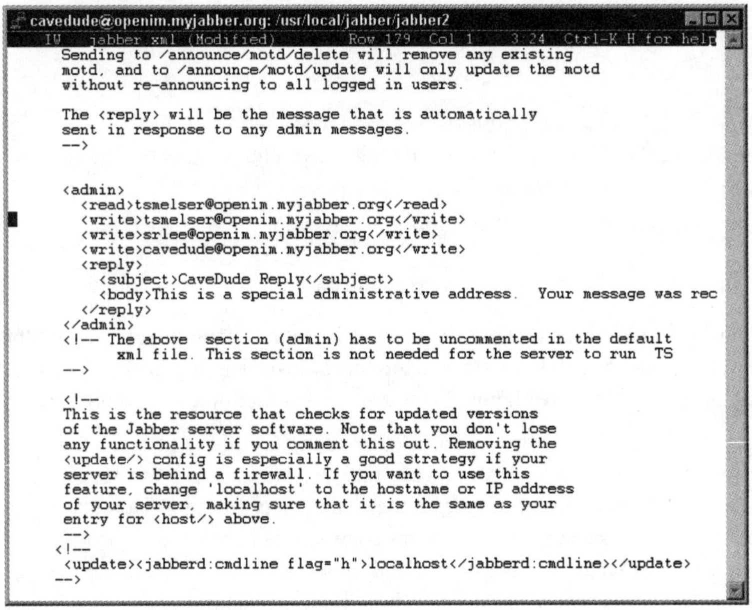

```
cavedude@openim.myjabber.org: /usr/local/jabber/jabber2
  IW   jabber.xml (Modified)       Row 179   Col 1    3:24   Ctrl-K H for help
        Sending to /announce/motd/delete will remove any existing
        motd, and to /announce/motd/update will only update the motd
        without re-announcing to all logged in users.

        The <reply> will be the message that is automatically
        sent in response to any admin messages.
        -->


        <admin>
          <read>tsmelser@openim.myjabber.org</read>
          <write>tsmelser@openim.myjabber.org</write>
          <write>srlee@openim.myjabber.org</write>
          <write>cavedude@openim.myjabber.org</write>
          <reply>
            <subject>CaveDude Reply</subject>
            <body>This is a special administrative address.  Your message was rec
          </reply>
        </admin>
        <!-- The above  section (admin) has to be uncommented in the default
              xml file. This section is not needed for the server to run  TS
        -->

        <!--
        This is the resource that checks for updated versions
        of the Jabber server software. Note that you don't lose
        any functionality if you comment this out. Removing the
        <update/> config is especially a good strategy if your
        server is behind a firewall. If you want to use this
        feature, change 'localhost' to the hostname or IP address
        of your server, making sure that it is the same as your
        entry for <host/> above.
        -->
       <!--
        <update><jabberd:cmdline flag="h">localhost</jabberd:cmdline></update>
       -->
```

Figure 4-7: Setting administrator accounts

As you can see, this process is pretty straightforward: Enter your JID in the `<read>` block (this one must have an entry), write yourself into the `<write>` block, and then duplicate the `<write>` block for any other JID that you want to have access to global messaging or MOTD (message of the day) posting.

When you're done, save the XML file.

Starting the Server

As an experienced Linux user, you may have your own way of starting the server. This method is ours. We want our server to run even if the session in which we started — a `telnet` or `ssh` session, for example — is disconnected. Often the server runs for a little while, and about the time that you start to trust that it's running, it shuts down without notice. Most flavors of Linux that we've dealt with provide a few solutions to this issue. Our favorite is one we learned about from a friend. It's the program called `screen`, which enables you to open a session "within" a session, run a process from there, and then detach that session and close the original session or move on to another project. It's quite simple to use and very reliable.

At the shell prompt, type the word `screen` and press Enter.

Most likely, you get a screen full of information about the screen program itself. Press Enter or the spacebar and you return to a command prompt "inside" a screen session. Now remember that this prompt is *not* the same place that you were a second ago. You are in a *new* shell session.

You're now ready to try to start the server. Always start the Jabber server in the /usr/local/jabber/jabber2 directory. It's just set up to run that way. The basic command to start the server is as follows:

```
./jabberd/jabberd
```

Of course, you may add a couple of options to the end of the base command, as follows:

- `-D` runs the server in debug mode; this option produces a *lot* of traffic in your session but can help locate errors. On a busy server such as the one at `jabber.myjabber.net`, it's also more mind-numbing than a lava lamp if you just need something to distract you.

- `&` forces the server to run in the background and "stay running." Many people use this option to run their servers. It may work and it may not. We prefer to run our servers in screen sessions so that after we disconnect from them, they stay running. This way is very reliable for running the server, and if you run commercial servers for paying customers, you usually find that having a server shut down and stay down while you're off at the pub doesn't go over well with the guys holding the checkbooks.

We use the command `./jabberd/jabberd &` from a secondary screen to enable us to use the command prompt again in that session. You normally see a line from the server saying that `jabberd` has started. You can safely press Enter again and you will be returned to a shell prompt.

If you want to make sure that the server is running, use the following command:

```
ps aux | grep jabberd
```

You can now see the running server. This command shows who's running the server; the pid file appears here also. (Handy if you're shutting down the server to add transports or work on it.) See Figure 4-8 for an example of this server output.

To detach the session, use this command:

```
screen -d
```

Congratulations — you're up and running with a very basic Jabber server. This server does person-to-person chats at this point.

```
  cavedude@openim.myjabber.org: /usr/local/jabber/jabber2                    _ □ ✕
[cavedude@openim jabber2]$ ./jabberd/jabberd &
[1] 16782
[cavedude@openim jabber2]$ ps aux | grep jabberd
cavedude 16782  0.8  1.3  2560 1308 pts/0     S     16:33   0:00 ./jabberd/jabberd
cavedude 16783  0.0  1.2  2416 1196 pts/0     S     16:33   0:00 ./jabberd/jabberd
cavedude 16785  1.0  0.6  1592  580 pts/0     S     16:33   0:00 grep jabberd
[cavedude@openim jabber2]$
[cavedude@openim jabber2]$
[cavedude@openim jabber2]$ screen -d




[remote detached]
[cavedude@openim jabber2]$ █
```

Figure 4-8: Starting the basic Jabber server

Here's the list of options and some other information about the screen program. We have screen in most of the flavors of Linux that we've worked with, but if you type screen and your computer gives you a "Have you lost your mind typing a command such as that?" message, you can always install it. Here's a link for the source code:

```
ftp://ftp.rge.com//pub/security/cerias/tools/unix/firewalls/screend/scre
end-980120.tar.gz
```

This program is also available in the rpm format at the following address:

```
ftp://ftp.grolier.fr/mirrors/ftp.pld.org.pl/PLD-
1.0/i386/PLD/RPMS/screen-3.9.10-4.i386.rpm
```

As noted earlier, screen is a utility that allows you to use multiple logins through one terminal session. This is very useful for running various servers to include, of course, the Jabber server we are working with here in this book. screen can allow you to start a process and then terminate your session with that process without terminating the process itself (this often happens in Linux).

Here's a listing of its use and options:

use:

```
screen [-opts] [cmd [args]]
```

or:

```
screen -r [host.tty]
```

Following are the various options that you can add to screen (and what they do; you can always get this list of options by typing the command screen --help):

◆ -a: Force all capabilities into each window's termcap.

◆ -A -[r|R]: Adapt all windows to the new display width and height.

◆ -c file: Read configuration file instead of .screenrc.

◆ -d (-r): Detach the elsewhere-running screen (and reattach it here).

◆ -dmS name: Start as daemon: Screen session in detached mode.

◆ -D (-r): Detach and logout remote (and reattach here).

◆ -D -RR: Do whatever's needed to get a screen session.

◆ -e xy: Change command characters.

◆ -f: Flow control on, -fn = off, -fa = auto.

◆ -h lines: Set the size of the scrollback history buffer.

◆ -i: Interrupt output sooner if flow control is on.

◆ -l: Login mode on (update /var/run/utmp), -ln = off.

◆ -list or -ls.: Do nothing; just list the SockDir.

◆ -L: Terminal's last character can be safely updated.

◆ -m: Ignore $STY variable; do create a new screen session.

◆ -O: Choose optimal output rather than exact vt100 emulation.

◆ -p window: Preselect the named window if it exists.

◆ -q: Quiet startup. Exits with nonzero return code if unsuccessful.

◆ -r: Reattach to a detached screen process.

- `-R`: Reattach if possible; otherwise, start a new session.

- `-s shell`: Use `shell` to execute rather than `$SHELL`.

- `-S sockname`: Name this session `<pid>.sockname` instead of `<pid>.<tty>.<host>`.

- `-t title`: Set title (window's name).

- `-T term`: Use `term` as `$TERM` for windows, rather than `screen`.

- `-v`: Print `Screen version 3.09.08 (FAU) 1-Sep-00`.

- `-wipe`: Do nothing; just clean up SockDir.

- `-x`: Attach to a not-detached `screen`. (Multi-display mode.)

Finding Missing Libraries

We've tried to help you avoid having to ask yourself whether you missed a library. It does happen, however. Be very mindful of your OS installation; we suggest a clean install before starting this project. Install everything in the Libraries directory — *everything*! You just never know. Literally, a page full of libraries can turn up missing while you're installing some of this stuff. So stack the deck in your favor, and if you can do a clean install of the Linux OS, include all the available libs. If you must work with a machine on which you can't or aren't going to reinstall the OS, prepare yourself to install libraries. If you have the install media for your OS, you can find a lot of them there and just install them all, right off the CD (or ftp, or whatever). One of the issues that you run into with libraries is that an installation file tells you that it can't install because it needs some `lib.so` and can't find it, and your search of the hard drives doesn't turn it up. So you get it off the Web and the file tells you that it can't install because it can't find some `lib.so`, and so on . . .

Okay, maybe this sort of thing happens only to us, but it's maddening at times. Several good file libraries are available on the Web; most provide advanced search features to enable you to get what you need and get on with your life. The old-fashioned gopher clients can also speed your way.

Some of the libraries that this server and its components request are Jabber specific and are available on the Jabber.org Web site or in CVS.

Following is a brief listing of some of our favorite sites:

- `www.freshmeat.net`
- `www.tuxfinder.org`
- `www.sourceforge.org`
- `http://download.jabber.com`

Adding SSL Support

The use of SSL (Secure Socket Layer) provides security in transmissions across the Web. The Web has a bad reputation for being insecure, and with the growing interest in more real-time communications at the corporate level, security has become a major issue. Jabber by its very nature is a secure platform; with the addition of SSL, it's becoming acceptable to many large corporate entities.

> **TIP** You can find a more complete description of the SSL protocol on the Web at `www.netscape.com/ eng/ssl3/draft302.txt`. Alternatively, just do a search on your favorite search engine for SSL.

Most of the recent servers that we've set up have been spec'd to run the SSL protocol for data security. A year or so ago, a close friend and accomplice of ours, Chris McDonald, had to set up SSL on a development server that he was hoping to convince his employers to use for internal communications in a major U.S. ISP. At that time, the documentation was *very* sparse, but we knew the server could do it; we knew our client would use it; and we knew that the software was available. We just didn't, however, quite know how. Needless to say, a lot of trial and error went into this, and quite frankly, it was mostly error. It was Chris who finally had a breakdown — oops, make that a breakthrough — and got the system to work. He wrote up some dandy instructions on this and, at our request, agreed to share them with you. You find them in Appendix E of this book, along with his writeup on how to get the Jabber server to use mySQL as a backend database for record storage. Both are great pieces of work and a testament to the determination and skill of the members of the Jabber community. We use excerpts from the SSL instructions in the rest of this chapter to help guide you through this amazingly simple task, but we highly suggest that you flip back to Appendix E and read the whole thing before going on.

In the very beginning of this chapter, we suggest that, if you want to set up your development server for SSL, you come here first and get an overview of the procedure. The Jabber daemon quite readily uses SSL to secure its communications, and setting it up is a simple matter. Our personal experience is that you're always better off installing the SSL portion of the server before you install the main server, especially with a fresh install. As we noted earlier in this chapter, SSL must be in place at the time that you compile the Jabber server for it to work. If you already have the Jabber server installed, you can probably reconfigure and then recompile it and have it work just fine.

What Else Do You Need?

Other than the core Jabber server components, you need only three other things: the source code for openSSL, the `ssl-keygen.sh script` (on the CD), and Chris McDonald's instructions. And, of course, a little guidance from us.

The source code is easy to find at www.openssl.org. Download the latest version that you find there to your personal user space. This is a system install, meaning that it's not a part of the Jabber server directory and installs to the default directory. Follow these steps:

1. By choice, we try to install software of this type from /usr/local/src, so su to root and change directory to /usr/local/src. Uncompress the files to this directory and issue the following command:

```
tar xvfz /path/to/openssl.tar.gz
```

2. Change directory to the /openssl directory by using the following command:

```
Cd openssl
./configure
make
make install
```

Now go back and install the Jabber server, but note that the configure command is slightly different. You must issue the following command to tell jabberd to build by using SSL:

```
./configure --enable-ssl

make
```

Now you need to test the Jabber server, so follow the instructions that we provide in the section on editing the jabber.xml file and start the server. (jabberd must be running for you to complete this task.)

Now you configure SSL by following these steps:

1. Generate your SSL Key.pem file.

2. Open your favorite text editor and create the following text file, called keygen.sh:

```
#!/bin/sh


######
#
# Generate a certificate and key with no passphrase.
#
######

# change to the correct path of your openssl command
OPENSSL=/usr/bin/openssl
#OPENSSL=/usr/bin/openssl


## This generates the cert and key
```

```
            $OPENSSL req -new -x509 -newkey rsa:1024 -keyout
privkey.pem -out key.pem
            ## This will remove the passphrase
            $OPENSSL rsa -in privkey.pem -out privkey.pem
            ## Put it all together
            cat privkey.pem >> key.pem
            ## Cleanup
            rm privkey.pem
```

3. Save this file and make it executable by using chmod.

4. Now execute keygen.sh by using the following command:

```
./keygen.sh
```

5. Complete the fields to fill out the form; after you finish, you have a file called key.pem in the directory from which you executed keygen.sh.

Now add SSL to the jabber.xml file by following these steps:

1. Find the commented SSL section of the jabber.xml file, in the <pthcsock> section and add the following values as necessary (one line for each IP address that your server may be listening on):

```
            <ssl port='5223'>127.0.0.1</ssl>
            <ssl port='5223'>192.168.1.100</ssl>
            <ssl port='5223'>xxx.xxx.xxx.xxx</ssl>
```

2. At the bottom of the jabber.xml file, you find an additional <ssl> section. Yours should look something like the following example after you finish:

```
            <ssl>
                    <key ip='127.0.0.1'>/usr/local/jabber-
1.4.1/key.pem</key>
                    <key ip='192.168.1.100'>/usr/local/jabber-
1.4.1/key.pem</key>
                    <key ip='xxx.xxx.xxx.xxx>/usr/local/jabber-
1.4.1/key.pem</key>
            </ssl>
```

NOTE The ip address *xxx.xxx.xxx.xxx* denotes the IP of your server; this value must be an IP address and not a DNS name.

3. Save the jabber.xml file and start the server.

If the server starts correctly, you can proceed with testing it by following these steps:

1. Open another terminal window and execute the following command:

    ```
    openssl s_client -connect 127.0.0.1:5223
    ```

2. Check Appendix E for the output from this command. If you get the three and a half pages of gibberish that we expect you to get, you're good to go!

The server functions in pretty much a normal manner — the SSL protocols are, for the most part, invisible to the users and to you from this point on.

Summary

In this chapter, we've shown you how to build and install a functioning, core-level Jabber server. Some of you have taken advantage of the SSL protocols and increased the security levels of your server.

We've gone over the ins and outs and the pain of Linux library files and discussed the easiest ways to handle them (fresh installs of the OS). We've also touched on the hazards of the mighty XML language, and you're now prepared to see plenty more of that in the coming chapters.

In Chapter 5, we begin the steps toward full functionality in the Jabber server. We work with the powerful Conference transport and set up the local and global user directories that enable users to search one another out on both the local server and on the global Jabber network.

Chapter 5

Installing Agents

In This Chapter

Installing the Conferencing transport

Editing the jabber.xml file for conferencing

In process or out of process?

Installing the various agents

A word about routers and firewalls

Jabber is a versatile communications platform in that it can interact with most all the big-name instant messenger networks already in use. It's easy to see the benefit of this compatibility. Our desktops used to be filled with chat windows from at least three different instant messengers. One we used for talking to just one person because it was the only IM client he wanted to run. The others were filled with the people we know from years of Internet and computer use. Getting anything done was almost impossible! Then along came Jabber, and we could now have all our instant messaging in one place — neat, stable, and manageable.

In Chapter 4, we showed you how to install and start the basic Jabber server. This server, as is, can conduct person-to-person chats and can handle server-to-server communications between people. Now we add the conferencing module to enable group chats on this server and on others.

Installing Conferencing

You can find the Conference transport at `http://download.jabber.org/cvs/conferencing.tgz`.

Or, as you can see in Figure 5-1, you can obtain it through CVS. (It's also on this book's CD-ROM.) Use the following command:

```
cvs -d :pserver:anoncvs@jabber.org:/home/cvs -z3 checkout conference
```

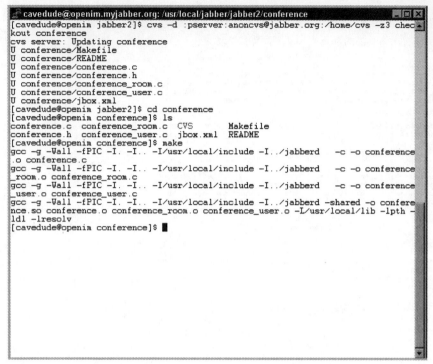

Figure 5-1: Downloading the Conference transport via CVS and then compiling

You also see the module compiling in Figure 5-1. There's no need to run `configure` — the module already has all that it needs and does not need references from the system, so just run `make`. This process is quick and produces only a few lines of feedback. As you can see, this build was successful. A sure sign of a good build is the appearance of the `conference.so` file in the /conference directory. Run the command `ls` in the /conference directory to check. The next step is to get the transport configured in the `jabber.xml` file and restart the server.

Editing the jabber.xml file for Conferencing

Return to the /usr/local/jabber/jabber2 directory and open `jabber.xml` in your favorite editor. Search for or scroll down to the `<browse>` section. (This area is going to become very familiar to you as you add more and more services to the server.)

In Figure 5-2 you can see the `<browse>` section with several services set up as examples. These services are commented out, and you work around them.

```
cavedude@openim.myjabber.org: /usr/local/jabber/jabber2          _ □ ✕
  IW   jabber.xml                Row 252  Col 2   10:09  Ctrl-K H for help
    -->

    <browse>

      <!--
      This is the default agent for the master Jabber User
      Directory, a.k.a. "JUD", which is located at jabber.org.
      You can add separate <service/> sections for additional
      directories, e.g., one for a company intranet.
      -->

      <service type="jud" jid="users.jabber.org" name="Jabber User Directory"
        <ns>jabber:iq:search</ns>
        <ns>jabber:iq:register</ns>
      </service>

      <!--
      The following services are examples only, you will need to
      create/modify them to get them working on your Jabber
      server. See the README files for each service and/or the
      server howto for further information/instructions.
      -->

      <!-- we're commenting these out, of course :) -->

      <conference type="private" jid="conference.localhost" name="Private Con

      <service type="aim" jid="aim.localhost" name="AIM Transport">
        <ns>jabber:iq:gateway</ns>
        <ns>jabber:iq:register</ns>
      </service>

      <service type="yahoo" jid="yahoo.localhost" name="Yahoo! Transport">
        <ns>jabber:iq:gateway</ns>
        <ns>jabber:iq:register</ns>
      </service>

      end of <service/> examples -->
```

Figure 5-2: Adding the Conference service to the jabber.xml file

The `<browse>` section of the `jabber.xml` file enables the various clients and your new one to "see" the services or agents that the server offers. The following bit of code is all that Conferencing needs to show up. You can see this in Figure 5-3. Observe the location where we placed this little bit of code — with all the prewritten examples, the `jabber.xml` file can become confusing. This entry, as is true of all the `<browse>` entries, must go inside the `<browse></browse>` section of the file.

```
<conference type="public" jid="conference.openim.myjabber.org"
name="Conferencing"/>
```

TIP Check your spelling and check it again — failing to do so is the most common error that people make while editing an XML file, which can't load if the server names don't resolve! Check it again.

```
 cavedude@openim.myjabber.org: /usr/local/jabber/jabber2            X
  IW   jabber.xml (Modified)       Row 243  Col 1   10:34  Ctrl-K H for help
    -->

    <browse>

      <!--
      This is the default agent for the master Jabber User
      Directory, a.k.a. "JUD", which is located at jabber.org.
      You can add separate <service/> sections for additional
      directories, e.g., one for a company intranet.
      -->

      <service type="jud" jid="users.jabber.org" name="Jabber User Directory"
        <ns>jabber:iq:search</ns>
        <ns>jabber:iq:register</ns>
      </service>

      <!-- For the sake of example I will start adding my services here and l
      the examples alone to be used as reference.
       -->
      <conference type="private" jid="conference.openim.myjabber.org"
      name="Conferencing"/>


      <!--
      The following services are examples only, you will need to
      create/modify them to get them working on your Jabber
      server. See the README files for each service and/or the
      server howto for further information/instructions.
      -->


      <!-- we're commenting these out, of course :)

      <conference type="private" jid="conference.localhost" name="Private Conf

      <service type="aim" jid="aim.localhost" name="AIM Transport">
        <ns>jabber:iq:gateway</ns>
        <ns>jabber:iq:register</ns>
```

Figure 5-3: Location of the Conference browse entry

Now you must tell the server how to run the conferencing module after it starts up. Find `<service id="s2s">` and scroll to the bottom of this entry. Here is the place that you start your service entries for the various agents and modules that you're going to work with in this server. If you look around a bit right here, you notice that you are well into the `service` area of the XML file. Scroll down a bit and you find the examples already built into the server. We choose to start above the examples so that you can have them for reference. Some server administrators just start editing these for their own use and uncomment them as they go. This practice is strictly a matter of personal preference.

Observe in Figure 5-4 the default `groupchat` service. This entry is an old conferencing module written for the 1.2.0 version and doesn't run well in the 1.4.1 version of the server. Regardless of where you place the `service` entries in your file, you need to comment out or just delete this entry.

Figure 5-4: The default examples in the service section

Your entry for the conference server should look like the following:

```
<service id ="conference.openim.myjabber.org">

<load><conference>./conference/conference.so</conference></load>
        <conference xmlns="jabber:config:conference">
        <public/>
                <vCard>
                <FN>Conference Server</FN>
                <DESC>This is your Conference Server</DESC>
                <URL>Http://openim.myjabber.org</URL>
                </vCard>
        <history>20</history>
        <notice>
        <join> just got here</join>
        <leave> has run away</leave>
        <rename> has changed names to </rename>
        </notice>
  </conference>
  </service>
```

This group of entries defines the module and the way that it acts as it's running. The following list defines each part of the entry to give you an understanding of how it works:

> `<service id>` identifies the module to the server and to DNS. Avoiding spelling errors and typos in this line is very important.

> `<load>` sets the path to the actual conference module itself (`conference.so`). If you build your server per our instructions so far, this path is correct.

`<conference xmlns>` is an XML namespace and defines to the server the configuration that it uses.

`<public/>` is an Open/Close statement that tells the Jabber server that this is a public server.

`<vCard>` is simply the identity of the service in a format the client can read and pass on to a user.

`<history>` is the number of lines in a conference that the module can store. Someone who logs in to a conference room sees these lines. In this case, it is set to 20 and this amount is more than enough.

`<notice>` is where you set all kind of neat custom responses (greetings, presence messages, departure messages) that you can set the conference server to do whenever someone enters or leaves a room.

`<join>` is the response whenever someone enters or joins a conference.

`<leave>` is the response whenever someone leaves a conference.

`<rename>` is the response whenever someone changes his or her nickname in a conference. You can set these responses to anything you want. Notice the space left at the beginning of the response. This space prevents the user's name from running into the response.

At the very bottom of the entry are three very important `close` entries. Their order is very important as they close `open` statements in sequence. Any other order causes the server itself to abort on startup. Figure 5-5 shows all these statements in correct order.

```
 cavedude@openim.myjabber.org: /usr/local/jabber/jabber2                    _ □ ×
   IU   jabber.xml (Modified)             Row 476  Col 10   6:15  Ctrl-K H for help
</service>

<service id ="conference.openim.myjabber.org">
        <load><conference>./conference/conference.so</conference></load>
        <conference xmlns="jabber:config:conference">
    <public/>
                <vCard>
                <FN>Conference Server</FN>
                <DESC>This is your Conference Server</DESC>
                <URL>Http://openim.myjabber.org</URL>
                </vCard>
    <history>20</history>
    <notice>
    <join> just got here</join>
    <leave> has run away</leave>
    <rename> has changed names to </rename>
        </notice>
</conference>
</service>



<!--
If you identified additional agents in the main <service/>
section (see examples above), you'll need to define each
of them here using a separate <service/> section for each
<agent/> you identified. Note that the <agent/> sections
determine what gets shown to clients that connect to your
server, whereas the following <service/> sections define
these services within the server itself. The following are
examples only, you will need to create/modify them to get
them working on your Jabber server. See the README files
for each agent and/or the server howto for further
information/instructions.
```

Figure 5-5: The service entry for conference module

The only thing left to do is start your conference module. This module runs *with* the main server and is almost never set up as a separate process.

Save the `jabber.xml` file and shut down the main server. You do so by first restoring the screen session in which you have the server running (by sending the command `screen -r`) and then finding the running `jabberd` processes by using the `ps aux` command. (Some of you may prefer the `hup` command, but this one always works for us.)

Send the command `ps aux | grep jabberd`. You get a reply from Linux similar to the following:

```
cavedude 22520  0.1  1.4  2604 1352 pts/0     S    18:53   0:00
./jabberd/jabberd
cavedude 22521  0.0  1.2  2452 1216 pts/0     S    18:53   0:00
./jabberd/jabberd
cavedude 22534  0.0  0.6  1592  580 pts/0     S    18:55   0:00 grep
jabberd
```

The number `22520` is your main server process `id` (pid), and `22521` is what we believe to be the server-to-server process. By stopping the main server, you terminate both these processes. Send the command `kill 22520` and watch the terminal for the response. See Figure 5-6, which shows the entire process.

Figure 5-6: Stopping and restarting the Jabber server

Sending the command `ps aux | grep jabberd` again shows only the `grep` command. Simply restart the server (by issuing the command `./jabberd/jabberd &`); as the Conference module is set up to run inside the main server, it's all running now, and a `ps aux | grep jabberd` doesn't show this process.

In Process or out of Process?

In process or out of process is a question of administrator's preference. You can run the additional agents, or "transports," that make Jabber so powerful internal to the Jabber server in the same process, much the same way that you run the conference module. Alternatively, you can run them as separate processes external to the main server but referring to the server for their information. A major disadvantage to running everything in the same process is that, if one of the subprocesses decides to crash, it could take the main server with it. This does not always happen, of course, but it happens often enough to be annoying. A disadvantage to running everything out of process is trying to start everything while users are logging in. Everything you're typing scrolls away from you and it's very difficult to keep track of what you typed and what process you just started. You can fix this problem with a simple shell script that we show you how to write in the section "Jabber Quick Start Shell Script," near the end of this chapter.

Installing the ICQ Agent

The ICQ agent (or transport) is as good a place to start as any, and installing and configuring the ICQ agent can be fairly simple to get done. Just follow these steps:

1. Move the source code into the /usr/local/jabber/jabber2 directory. We assume for the sake of demonstration that you have the source in your personal user directory. From the /jabber2 directory, issue the command (for `tar.gz` files) `tar xvfz /home/tsmelser/icq-transport-0.9.tar.gz` (in our case). This command extracts the source to the /jabber2 directory and places it in the subdirectory /icq-transport-0.9.

2. To save time and trouble later on in the install, issue the command `mv icq-transport-0.9 icq-transport`. This command renames the directory to /icq-transport, the name by which the `jabber.xml` file knows it; if you use CVS in the future, it just refreshes what you have and adds a new version if necessary. This step saves you many changes for your entries in the XML file later.

3. Change to the /icq-transport directory with `cd icq-transport`. Reading the documentation that you find in these files is always a good idea, so plow through the README and INSTALL and any other that you find.

4. To compile this agent, type `make` and let it run. (See Figure 5-7 for what we've done here.)

Figure 5-7: Compiling the ICQ transport

That's it! ICQ-Transport is installed. Now you need to write it into the `jabber.xml` file.

> **NOTE** Using the `make install` command while compiling the source for any of the Jabber components isn't necessary. You do *not* want any of these pieces of software installed globally, but only in the designated directory. Most of the components don't have a rule for `install` built into the `makefile` and simply return an error.

Editing the jabber.xml file for the ICQ transport

This procedure is going to become *very* familiar before you're done; soon, you're not going to need our help at all and can edit these entries on your own. Don't despair, however; we have included copies of the entire `jabber.xml` file, before and after, on the CD-ROM. To edit the file, follow these steps:

1. Open `jabber.xml` in your editor and add the service to the `browse` section of the file. Search for `<browse>` and put this one right under the entry that you made for `conference`. See Figure 5-8.

    ```
    <service type="icq" jid="icq.openim.myjabber.org" name="ICQ Transport">
            <ns>jabber:iq:gateway</ns>
            <ns>jabber:iq:register</ns>
            <ns>jabber:iq:search</ns>
    ```

```
    </service>
```

```
cavedude@openim.myjabber.org:/usr/local/jabber/jabber2                        _ □ ✕
[cavedude@openim jabber2]$ ps aux | grep jabberd
cavedude   504  0.0  1.6  3404 1596 pts/0    S    20:21    0:00 ./jabberd/jabberd
cavedude   505  0.0  1.2  2460 1212 pts/0    S    20:21    0:00 ./jabberd/jabberd
cavedude   506  0.0  1.0  2788 1004 pts/0    S    20:21    0:00 ./jabberd/jabberd
cavedude   570  0.0  0.6  1592  580 pts/0    S    22:57    0:00 grep jabberd
[cavedude@openim jabber2]$ kill 504
[cavedude@openim jabber2]$ 20010904T02:58:09: [alert] (-internal): Recieved Kill
.  Jabberd shutting down.
kill 506
[1]-  Done                      ./jabberd/jabberd
[cavedude@openim jabber2]$
[2]+  Done                      ./jabberd/jabberd -c icqtrans.xml
[cavedude@openim jabber2]$ ./jabberd/jabberd &
[1] 571
[cavedude@openim jabber2]$ ./jabberd/jabberd -c icqtrans.xml &
[2] 573
[cavedude@openim jabber2]$ ./jabberd/jabberd -c msntrans.xml &
[3] 574
[cavedude@openim jabber2]$ screen -d█
```

Figure 5-8: Adding the browse entry for the ICQ transport

Again, remember to check your typing and spelling carefully. A dropped comma or a space too many can cause the server to fail to start. (Another good reason to edit one item at a time.)

NOTE Including the `<ns>jabber:iq:search</ns>` line reportedly is an issue with some flavors of Linux. It works fine on Red Hat 7, for example, but doesn't work on Debian; we've had problems with it on Red Hat 7.1 on one machine but not on another. If you have issues where the ICQ transport doesn't start or run correctly, try removing the line. Remember to take `<search>Search for ICQ users</search>` out of the `service` entry. The reported error is 405 Not Allowed. This problem is sometimes a transport version issue.

2. Now you need to set up the service in the `jabber.xml` file. We're going to show you how to set up your server to run in the "out-of-process" mode because it's the best way to set up a server and builds a more durable server on which to write your client.

3. One of the tricks to getting the agent to run out of process is to build linkers between the main `jabber.xml` file and a smaller XML file just for the various transports. The linker goes in the `jabber.xml` file in the `service` area. See Figure 5-9 for the location. The entry is as follows:

```
<service id="icq_linker">
  <host>icq.openim.myjabber.org</host>
  <accept>
    <ip>205.150.219.39</ip>
    <port>7001</port>
    <secret>k7asfon</secret>
  </accept>
</service>
```

```
 cavedude@openim.myjabber.org: /usr/local/jabber/jabber2              _ □ ✕
   IW   jabber.xml              Row 484  Col 1      7:01  Ctrl-K H for help
          <penalty>-5</penalty>
          <restore>50</restore>
        </karma>
     </dialback>
  </service>

  <service id ="conference.openim.myjabber.org">
        <load><conference>./conference/conference.so</conference></load>
        <conference xmlns="jabber:config:conference">
        <public/>
                  <vCard>
                  <FN>Conference Server</FN>
                  <DESC>This is your Conference Server</DESC>
                  <URL>Http://openim.myjabber.org</URL>
                  </vCard>
        <history>20</history>
        <notice>
        <join> just got here</join>
        <leave> has run away</leave>
        <rename> has changed names to </rename>
        </notice>
  </conference>
  </service>

  <service id="icq_linker">
    <host>icq.openim.myjabber.org</host>
    <accept>
      <ip>205.150.219.39</ip>
      <port>7001</port>
      <secret>k7asfon</secret>
    </accept>
  </service>
```

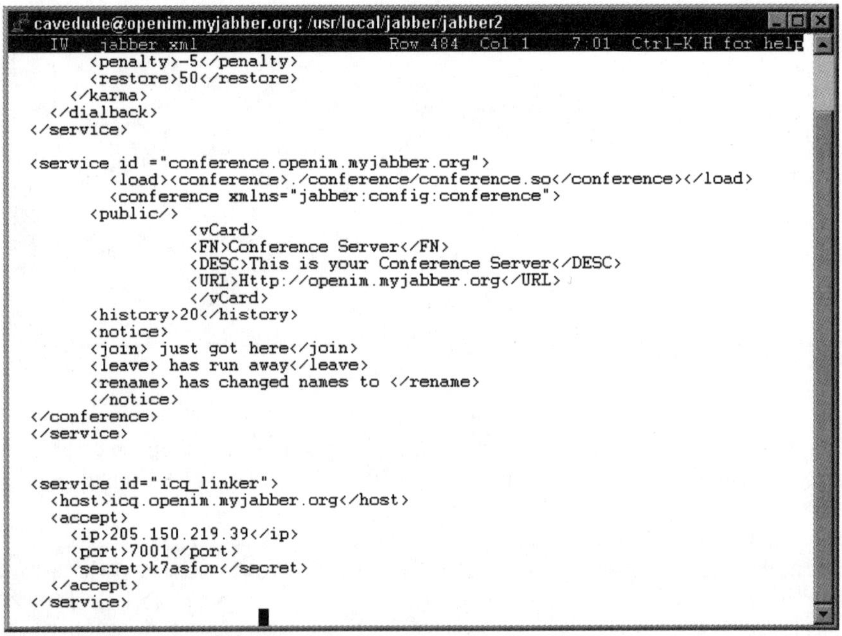

Figure 5-9: The ICQ linker

The following list describes these entries:

  `service id` is, of course, the name of the server and is how the XML file (and thus the server) refers to it.

  `host` is your transport name.

ip is the IP address of the server you're building. This entry is very important and must be accurate. It *must* match the ip in the icqtrans.xml file that you write next.

port is the port that the ICQ transport is going to use to talk though the server.

secret is the secret that the ICQ transport uses to authenticate itself after it connects to the Jabber server by making a TCP socket link to 205.150.219.39:7001. Every component that connects this way must authenticate — it does so by sending a <handshake/> that contains a message digest of this secret concatenated with another string from the stream header.

Writing the icqtrans.xml file

The icqtrans.xml file goes in the /jabber2 directory with the jabber.xml file. Simply open your editor with the command line for any file (for example, joe icqtrans.xml). This action opens an empty document called icqtrans.xml. Copy the following information into this file and save it, or just transfer the provided file from the CD to your /jabber2 directory and edit it for your host. This file and the <service> entry in the jabber.xml file refer to each other.

```xml
<jabber>

<service id="yahoo_linker">
  <uplink/>
  <connect>
    <ip>205.150.219.39</ip>
    <port>6001</port>
    <secret>k7asfon</secret>
  </connect>
</service>
<service id="icq.openim.myjabber.org">
  <icqtrans xmlns="jabber:config:icqtrans">
    <instructions>Please enter your ICQ number (in the "username"
field),nickname, and password.  Leave the "username" field blank  to
create a new ICQ number.</instructions>
<search>Search for ICQ users</search>
    <vCard>
      <FN>ICQ Transport</FN>
      <DESC>This is the ICQ Transport</DESC>
      <URL>http://openim.myjabber.org/</URL>
    </vCard>
    <prime>501</prime>
    <ports>
      <min>2000</min>
      <max>3000</max>
    </ports>
    <server>
      <ip>login.icq.com</ip>
    </server>
```

```
   </icqtrans>
   <load>
     <icqtrans>./icq-transport/icqtrans.so</icqtrans>
   </load>
  </service>
</jabber>
```

NOTE Remember to replace the host name with your own. We often fail to make that change because we are in a rush. Slow down and take your time. The server doesn't start, or at the very best, the transport doesn't respond correctly if you make this error. The rush isn't worth the headache that accompanies troubleshooting your own code.

After checking everything you've done for typos and saving it, you can start the transport. To do so, you must stop the main server and then restart it. (Any time you add code to the main server's XML file, the server must be restarted to use the new code.) The ICQ transport starts in a separate process.

1. Start by recovering the screen session with the following code:

   ```
   screen -r
   ```

2. Next, we find the process id number:

   ```
   ps aux | grep jabberd
   ```

3. Now we kill the main server:

   ```
   kill xxxxx (main server pid)
   ```

4. Restart the main server first:

   ```
   ./jabberd/jabberd &
   ```

5. Now we will start the ICQ transport. This is a very similar command to the main server's, and you can use it for all the transports you're running out of process.

   ```
   ./jabberd/jabberd -c icqtrans.xml
   ```

6. Now you need to detach the screen you're running by using the following command:

   ```
   screen -d
   ```

Look at Figure 5-10 for an example of what you should see after you complete this sequence.

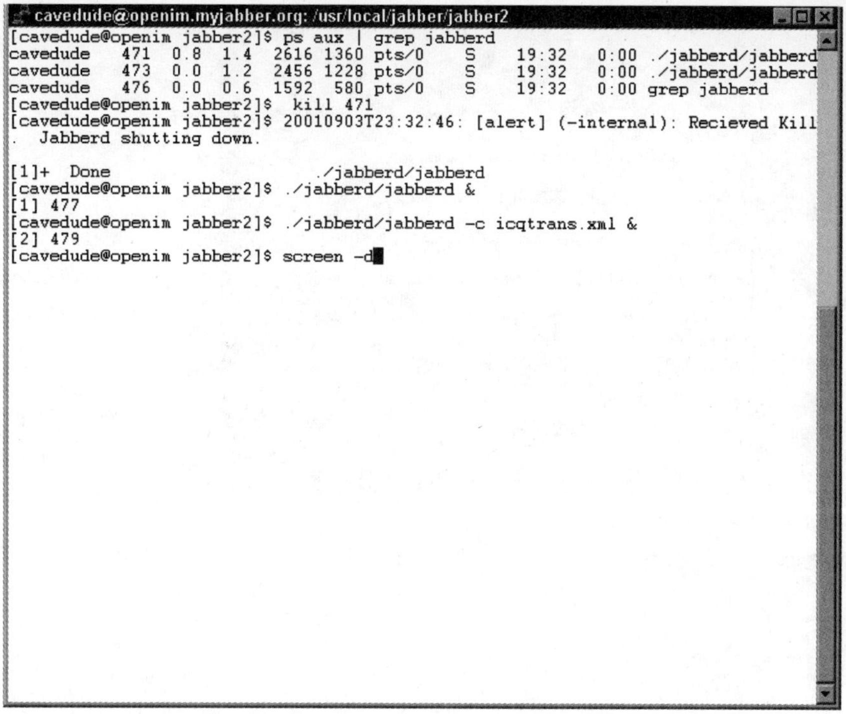

```
cavedude@openim.myjabber.org: /usr/local/jabber/jabber2              _ □ x
[cavedude@openim jabber2]$ ps aux | grep jabberd
cavedude   471  0.8  1.4  2616 1360 pts/0    S      19:32    0:00 ./jabberd/jabberd
cavedude   473  0.0  1.2  2456 1228 pts/0    S      19:32    0:00 ./jabberd/jabberd
cavedude   476  0.0  0.6  1592  580 pts/0    S      19:32    0:00 grep jabberd
[cavedude@openim jabber2]$ kill 471
[cavedude@openim jabber2]$ 20010903T23:32:46: [alert] (-internal): Recieved Kill
.  Jabberd shutting down.

[1]+  Done                  ./jabberd/jabberd
[cavedude@openim jabber2]$ ./jabberd/jabberd &
[1] 477
[cavedude@openim jabber2]$ ./jabberd/jabberd -c icqtrans.xml &
[2] 479
[cavedude@openim jabber2]$ screen -d█
```

Figure 5-10: Shutting down and restarting jabberd with the ICQ transport

Now for a quick test before moving on to the next transport. In Chapter 3, you download and install the Jabber client myJabber. You use this program as a testing platform for your new server. Open myJabber and from the menu bar, select Tools ⇨ Profiles. In the Profiles dialog box that appears, choose Add. myJabber asks you to name the profile; call it whatever you want. Highlight the new server in Profiles and click on Properties. The server name is, of course, the address of your server. Insert your user name and a password and click OK (see Figure 5-11).

Unless you've already logged in to your server, you get an error saying that you don't have an account and asking whether you'd like to create one. Click Yes. The client now logs on to the server and builds the account. Click the small + next to the word `Agents`; this action expands the Agents group and should show you the Conferencing transport and the ICQ transport. The Conferencing icon should appear in green, as it started with `jabberd` and is already online. ICQ, on the other hand, should have just a white bulb icon next to it. Right-click it and choose Properties from the pop-up menu (see Figure 5-12).

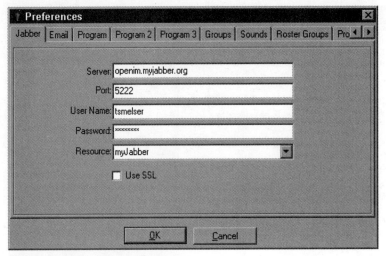

Figure 5-11: Logging in to your Jabber server

Figure 5-12: Logging in to the ICQ transport

Figure 5-13 shows the next dialog box, the ICQ logon. Fill in your user information and click Register. If you don't have an ICQ account, just leave the Username text box blank and fill in the rest. An ICQ user name will be assigned to you.

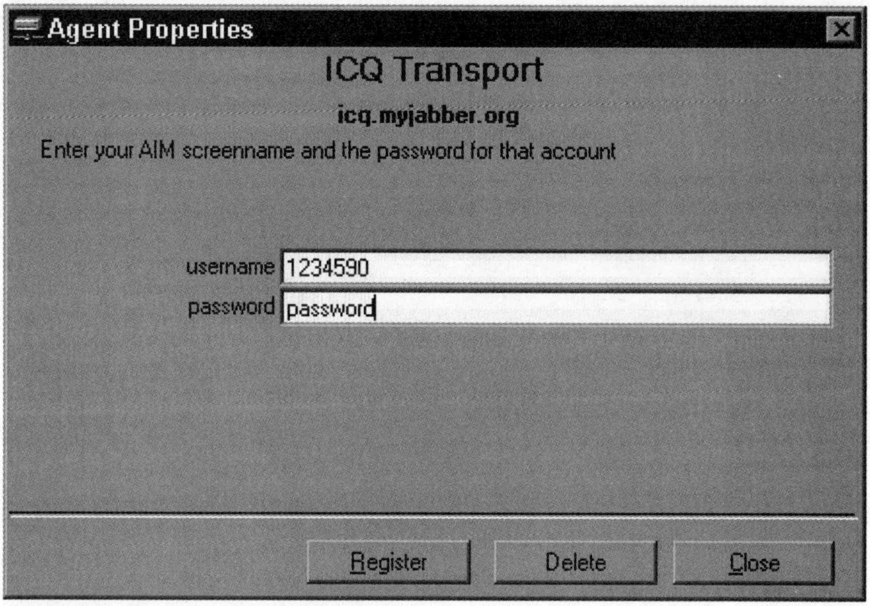

Figure 5-13: Registering with the ICQ transport

Give the ICQ servers a minute or two to respond for the first time; it can be a bit slow. You should get a subscription request back from `icq.`*`yourserver.net`*. Click Yes, and the little bulb should turn bright green to match Conferencing. If none of what we describe here happens in pretty much this order, check your `jabber.xml` and `icqtrans.xml` files for errors. If everything does happen in this order, congratulations — you have a running Jabber server with ICQ interoperability!

Installing the MSN Messenger Agent

Microsoft's MSN Instant Messenger is another of the popular IM clients that Jabber supports and is one of the easiest to set up. Its servers also actively store your contact list and can send it to you any time that you log in. This experience can be exciting with a Jabber client, as the first time you log in with one, it force-feeds you your entire contact list!

We've already gone over the various ways of getting the source information into your /jabber2 directory, but we want you to practice your CVS skills on this one. In the /jabber2 directory, type the following:

```
cvs -d :pserver:anoncvs@jabber.org:/home/cvs login
```

The CVS server asks for the anonymous password, which is as follows:

```
anoncvs
```

Now you request the files that you need by entering the following line:

```
cvs -d :pserver:anoncvs@jabber.org:/home/cvs -z3 checkout msn-transport
```

Even on a dial-up connection, this download finishes quickly. Following is what you will see as CVS downloads the code to your server machine:

```
cvs server: Updating msn-transport
U msn-transport/AUTHORS
U msn-transport/Makefile
U msn-transport/README
U msn-transport/chat.c
U msn-transport/cmd.c
U msn-transport/conf_room.c
U msn-transport/conf_sb.c
U msn-transport/iq.c
U msn-transport/md5.c
U msn-transport/md5.h
U msn-transport/message.c
U msn-transport/msntrans.c
U msn-transport/msntrans.h
U msn-transport/muser.c
U msn-transport/ns.c
U msn-transport/parser.c
U msn-transport/presence.c
U msn-transport/receive.c
U msn-transport/register.c
U msn-transport/session.c
U msn-transport/stream.c
U msn-transport/subscribe.c
U msn-transport/utils.c
```

Preceding are all the files you need for the MSN transport, now neatly placed in the /msn-transport directory. Figure 5-14 shows this process in the server itself.

Compiling the source for the MSN transport

The process for compiling the source for the MSN transport becomes painfully familiar to you as you go, but we promise that Yahoo! and AIM are a bit different. cd into the /msn-transport directory and type make. As the transport compiles, watch for errors (although the build most likely stops if it hits a big snag). On the completion of a successful build, you find the msn-transport.so file in the directory. Figure 5-15 shows the transport compiling.

```
cavedude@openim.myjabber.org: /usr/local/jabber/jabber2
[cavedude@openim jabber2]$ cvs -d :pserver:anoncvs@jabber.org:/home/cvs login
(Logging in to anoncvs@jabber.org)
CVS password:
[cavedude@openim jabber2]$ cvs -d :pserver:anoncvs@jabber.org:/home/cvs -z3 chec
kout msn-transport
cvs server: Updating msn-transport
U msn-transport/AUTHORS
U msn-transport/Makefile
U msn-transport/README
U msn-transport/chat.c
U msn-transport/cmd.c
U msn-transport/conf_room.c
U msn-transport/conf_sb.c
U msn-transport/iq.c
U msn-transport/md5.c
U msn-transport/md5.h
U msn-transport/message.c
U msn-transport/msntrans.c
U msn-transport/msntrans.h
U msn-transport/muser.c
U msn-transport/ns.c
U msn-transport/parser.c
U msn-transport/presence.c
U msn-transport/receive.c
U msn-transport/register.c
U msn-transport/session.c
U msn-transport/stream.c
U msn-transport/subscribe.c
U msn-transport/utils.c
[cavedude@openim jabber2]$ ▮
```

Figure 5-14: Using CVS to retrieve the MSN transport files

```
cavedude@openim.myjabber.org: /usr/local/jabber/jabber2/msn-transport
[cavedude@openim jabber2]$ cd msn-transport
[cavedude@openim msn-transport]$ ls
AUTHORS      conf_sb.c   md5.c       msntrans.h  presence.c  session.c
chat.c       CVS         md5.h       muser.c     README      stream.c
cmd.c        iq.c        message.c   ns.c        receive.c   subscribe.c
conf_room.c  Makefile    msntrans.c  parser.c    register.c  utils.c
[cavedude@openim msn-transport]$ make
gcc -g -Wall -fPIC -I. -I.. -I/usr/local/include  -I../jabberd/ -Wall -g -O2 -Wn
o-unused   -c -o chat.o chat.c
gcc -g -Wall -fPIC -I. -I.. -I/usr/local/include  -I../jabberd/ -Wall -g -O2 -Wn
o-unused   -c -o cmd.o cmd.c
gcc -g -Wall -fPIC -I. -I.. -I/usr/local/include  -I../jabberd/ -Wall -g -O2 -Wn
o-unused   -c -o conf_room.o conf_room.c
gcc -g -Wall -fPIC -I. -I.. -I/usr/local/include  -I../jabberd/ -Wall -g -O2 -Wn
o-unused   -c -o conf_sb.o conf_sb.c
gcc -g -Wall -fPIC -I. -I.. -I/usr/local/include  -I../jabberd/ -Wall -g -O2 -Wn
o-unused   -c -o iq.o iq.c
gcc -g -Wall -fPIC -I. -I.. -I/usr/local/include  -I../jabberd/ -Wall -g -O2 -Wn
o-unused   -c -o md5.o md5.c
gcc -g -Wall -fPIC -I. -I.. -I/usr/local/include  -I../jabberd/ -Wall -g -O2 -Wn
o-unused   -c -o message.o message.c
gcc -g -Wall -fPIC -I. -I.. -I/usr/local/include  -I../jabberd/ -Wall -g -O2 -Wn
o-unused   -c -o msntrans.o msntrans.c
gcc -g -Wall -fPIC -I. -I.. -I/usr/local/include  -I../jabberd/ -Wall -g -O2 -Wn
o-unused   -c -o muser.o muser.c
gcc -g -Wall -fPIC -I. -I.. -I/usr/local/include  -I../jabberd/ -Wall -g -O2 -Wn
o-unused   -c -o ns.o ns.c
gcc -g -Wall -fPIC -I. -I.. -I/usr/local/include  -I../jabberd/ -Wall -g -O2 -Wn
o-unused   -c -o parser.o parser.c
gcc -g -Wall -fPIC -I. -I.. -I/usr/local/include  -I../jabberd/ -Wall -g -O2 -Wn
o-unused   -c -o presence.o presence.c
gcc -g -Wall -fPIC -I. -I.. -I/usr/local/include  -I../jabberd/ -Wall -g -O2 -Wn
o-unused   -c -o receive.o receive.c
gcc -g -Wall -fPIC -I. -I.. -I/usr/local/include  -I../jabberd/ -Wall -g -O2 -Wn
o-unused   -c -o register.o register.c
gcc -g -Wall -fPIC -I. -I.. -I/usr/local/include  -I../jabberd/ -Wall -g -O2 -Wn
o-unused   -c -o session.o session.c
```

Figure 5-15: The MSN transport compiling

Editing the jabber.xml file and building the msntrans.xml file

Here you go — back into the `jabber.xml` file. You can expect to know this document well by the time you finish. Just follow these steps:

1. Open `jabber.xml` in your editor and set up the `browse` entry, as shown in the following code. This process is straightforward and identifies the transport to your client software.

```
<service type="msn" jid="msn.openim.myjabber.org" name="MSN Transport">
        <ns>jabber:iq:gateway</ns>
        <ns>jabber:iq:register</ns>
     </service>
```

    Edit the jid to your server, and this part is done.

2. Next you build the transport linker. Scroll down to the `service` area and right, under the `icq-linker`, place the `msn-linker`, as follows:

```
<service id="msn_linker">
     <host>msn.openim.myjabber.org</host>
     <accept>
       <ip>205.150.219.39</ip>
       <port>9001</port>
       <secret>k7asfon</secret>
   </accept>
   </service>
```

Again, pay close attention to the host name and to the IP address in this entry. The IP address must match the one in your `msntrans.xml` file. See Figure 5-16.

In the /jabber2 directory, open the `msntrans.xml` file in your editor. Copy the following information into it or use the `msntrans.xml` file that's on the CD (modified for your server, of course).

```
cavedude@openim.myjabber.org: /usr/local/jabber/jabber2                    _ □ ✕
   IW   jabber.xml (Modified)       Row 456  Col 1    6:46  Ctrl-K H for help
<service id ="conference.openim.myjabber.org">
       <load><conference>./conference/conference.so</conference></load>
       <conference xmlns="jabber:config:conference">
       <public/>
                   <vCard>
                   <FN>Conference Server</FN>
                   <DESC>This is your Conference Server</DESC>
                   <URL>Http://openim.myjabber.org</URL>
                   </vCard>
       <history>20</history>
       <notice>
       <join> just got here</join>
       <leave> has run away</leave>
       <rename> has changed names to </rename>
       </notice>
</conference>
</service>

<service id="icq_linker">
   <host>icq.openim.myjabber.org</host>
   <accept>
     <ip>205.150.219.39</ip>
     <port>7001</port>
     <secret>k7asfon</secret>
   </accept>
</service>

<service id="msn_linker">
   <host>msn.openim.myjabber.org</host>
   <accept>
     <ip>205.150.219.39</ip>
     <port>9001</port>
     <secret>k7asfon</secret>      </accept>
</service>
```

Figure 5-16: Example of the msntrans_linker entry

```
<jabber>
  <service id="msn_linker">
    <uplink/>
    <connect>
      <ip>205.150.219.39</ip>
      <port>9001</port>
      <secret>k7asfon</secret>
    </connect>
  </service>
  <service id="msn.openim.myjabber.org">
   <msntrans xmlns="jabber:config:msntrans">
    <vCard>
        <FN>MSN Transport</FN>
        <DESC>openim MSN Transport</DESC>
        <URL>http://openim.myjabber.org</URL>
    </vCard>
   </msntrans>
   <load>
      <msntrans>./msn-transport/src/msntrans.so</msntrans>
   </load>
  </service>
</jabber>
```

Save the file, and you're finished with this portion of the server with only the restarting of the server and the agents left to do. Remember this process? We did this earlier in the chapter with the ICQ transport. Okay, once more from the top — follow these steps:

1. Recover the screen session (`screen -r`).

2. Find the process id (`ps aux | grep jabberd`).

3. Kill the main server (`kill xxxxx <pid#>`).

4. Kill the ICQ transport (`kill xxxxx <pid#>`). We recommend using the `pa aux | grep jabberd` command now to make sure that you have all processes stopped.

5. Restart the main server (`./jabberd/jabberd &`).

6. Restart the ICQ transport (`./jabberd/jabberd -c icqtrans.xml`).

7. Start your MSN transport (`./jabberd/jabberd -c msntrans.xml`).

8. Detach the screen again (`screen -d`).

See Figure 5-17 for a look at these commands being used.

```
cavedude@openim.myjabber.org:/usr/local/jabber/jabber2
[cavedude@openim jabber2]$ ps aux | grep jabberd
cavedude 25025  0.2  1.4  2656 1416 pts/0    S    19:11   0:00 ./jabberd/jabberd
cavedude 25026  0.0  1.3  2480 1256 pts/0    S    19:11   0:00 ./jabberd/jabberd
cavedude 25029  0.2  0.9  2752  924 pts/0    S    19:12   0:00 ./jabberd/jabberd
cavedude 25034  0.0  0.6  1592  580 pts/0    S    19:12   0:00 grep jabberd
[cavedude@openim jabber2]$ kill 25025
[cavedude@openim jabber2]$ 20020203T00:12:44: [alert] (-internal): Recieved Kill. Ja
bberd shutting down.

[2]-  Done                    ./jabberd/jabberd
[cavedude@openim jabber2]$ kill 25026
bash: kill: (25026) - No such pid
[cavedude@openim jabber2]$ kill 25029
[cavedude@openim jabber2]$ ./jabberd/jabberd &
[4] 25035
[3]   Done                    ./jabberd/jabberd -c msntrans.xml
[cavedude@openim jabber2]$ ./jabberd/jabberd -c msntrans.xml &
[5] 25037
[cavedude@openim jabber2]$ ./jabberd/jabberd -c icqtrans.xml &
[6] 25038
[cavedude@openim jabber2]$ ▮
```

Figure 5-17: Stop and restart the server with the new transport.

Now you need to test your new transport by using myJabber. Log in to the server with myJabber and expand the Agents list. The MSN transport should appear there with a white bulb, showing that it's offline. Right-click the bulb and choose Properties from the pop-up menu, enter your MSN account information, and click Register. If you're already an MSN Messenger user, your screen should start to fill with subscription requests from *everyone* in your contact list. If it does, you did a good job! If you're not already a user and set up an account for testing purposes, the bulb's turning green is a good sign that it's working. Try sending a message to your online contacts. (Tell them that you're not using the MSN client — it drives them crazy!)

Installing the Yahoo! Agent

Yahoo! Messenger is another popular chat program, widely used throughout the world. The process for setting up its compatibility with the Jabber protocol is, of course, very similar to the other transports' processes, but a couple of commands are different.

Start by getting the source in place in the /jabber2 directory. How you do this, this time — CVS or direct download — is up to you. Remember that, in theory, what's in CVS will be the latest update to any program. Now follow these steps:

cd into your /yahoo-transport directory. You may notice that no `configure` or `makefile` is in the directory. You do see a `configure.in` file, but you won't be able to run it. The author of this transport took a slightly different route. Try the following command:

```
./autogen.sh --with-jabberd=/usr/local/jabber/jabber2/jabberd
```

The command, in reality, looks as follows:

```
./autogen.sh --with-jabber=/full-path/to/the/jabberd/directory
```

`jabberd` is the Jabber daemon and lives in the /jabber2/jabberd directory. This command directs the configuration file to build by using `jabberd`. After it finishes the build, it creates the `makefile`. Type `make`.

Now you're back in familiar territory. After `make` finishes, you need only to edit your new transport into the `jabber.xml` file and test it.

Editing the jabber.xml file and building the yahootrans.xml file

To edit the `jabber.xml` file and build the `yahootrans.xml` file, first add the `browse` entry, as follows:

```
        <service type="yahoo" jid="yahoo.openim.myjabber.org"
name="Yahoo! Transport">

        <ns>jabber:iq:gateway</ns>

        <ns>jabber:iq:register</ns>
    </service>
```

Now build the linker for the transport, as follows:

```
<service id="yahoo_linker">
```

```
    <host>yahoo.openim.myjabber.org</host>
    <accept>
      <ip>205.150.219.39</ip>
      <port>6001</port>
      <secret>k7asfon</secret>
    </accept>
  </service>
```

And now, build the transport's XML file, as follows:

```
<jabber>
  <service id="yahoo_linker">
    <uplink/>
    <connect>
      <ip>205.150.219.39</ip>
      <port>6001</port>
      <secret>k7asfon</secret>
    </connect>
  </service>
  <service id="yahoo.openim.myjabber.net">

    <yahootrans xmlns="jabber:config:yahootrans">
      <instructions> Enter your Yahoo Account and
Password.</instructions>
      <search>Search for Yahoo! users</search>

      <vCard>
        <FN>Yahoo! Transport</FN>
        <DESC>openim Yahoo! Transport</DESC>
        <URL>http://openim.myjabber.org</URL>
      </vCard>
        <disable-tcp/>

    </yahootrans>

    <load>
      <yahoo_transport>./yahoo-
transport/src/yahootrans.so</yahoo_transport>
    </load>

  </service>

</jabber>
```

NOTE In the Yahoo transport, the `yahootrans.so` file is in a different location from the other transports. This one is in the /src directory under the main transport. This location has confused us a couple of times.

All right! The only thing left is to stop the server and restart it with your new Yahoo transport. The command for the Yahoo transport is `./jabberd/jabberd -c yahootrans.xml`. Register with the transport by using your Yahoo logon and send a message.

Installing the AIM Agent

The agent for AOL Instant Messenger is a bit different, requiring some things the others don't need.

The first step, of course, is to get the source files into your /jabber2 directory, in their own subdirectory of /aim-transport. We, being lazy, elect to use CVS again. We also want the very latest source that we can get, and with the aim-transport, this precaution is important. The build that we used at the time of this writing is AIM-Transport 0.9.5.

Change directories to the /aim-transport directory. You notice that no `makefile` is in this source either. You have the `autogen.sh` file, however, so issue the following command:

```
./autogen.sh --with-jabberd=/usr/local/jabber/jabber2/jabberd/
```

Now run the `make` command and let the agent compile. That part is finished; now comes the tricky part.

For the AIM transport to work, you need a valid installation from AIM version 3.5.1670. (It must be that version.) We suggest browsing `ftp://ftp.newaol.com` to find this version or searching on Google (at `www.google.com`). The transport is going to use binaries from this program. So what you're going to do is install the Windows program, AIM, on your Linux server. You can do so in a couple of ways. Some people use WINE, a Windows emulator, to install this program. Our servers are just that, server installs only, so we have no Xwindow installs except on our primary Linux workstations. The easiest way we've found to get this copy of the AIM program in the right place is to install this version on a Windows 98 machine, zip up the entire folder, and FTP it to the server. After you have it there, move it to the /jabber2 directory, unzip it, and rename the directory /aimprogram. The `aimtrans.xml` file refers to this directory for the information it needs to stay online.

Editing the jabber.xml file and building the aimtrans.xml file

To edit the `jabber.xml` file and build the `aimtrans.xml` file, first, of course, add the `browse` entry:

```
<service type="aim" jid="aim.openim.myjabber.org" name="AIM Transport">
        <ns>jabber:iq:gateway</ns>
        <ns>jabber:iq:register</ns>
        <ns>jabber:iq:search</ns>
    </service>
```

Now do the linker to the `aimtrans.xml` file by using the following code:

```
<service id="aim_linker">
    <host>aim.openim.myjabber.org</host>
    <accept>
      <ip>216.94.240.201</ip>
      <port>8001</port>
      <secret>k7asfon</secret>
    </accept>
</service>
```

Figure 5-18 shows the proper location of the linker in the `jabber.xml` file.

```
 cavedude@openim.myjabber.org: /usr/local/jabber/jabber2          _ □ ×
  IW   jabber.xml (Modified)      Row 516  Col 13   3:50  Ctrl-K H for help
    <accept>
      <ip>205.150.219.39</ip>
      <port>7001</port>
      <secret>k7asfon</secret>
    </accept>
 </service>

 <service id="msn_linker">
    <host>msn.openim.myjabber.org</host>
    <accept>
      <ip>205.150.219.39</ip>
      <port>9001</port>
      <secret>k7asfon</secret>
    </accept>
 </service>

 <service id="yahoo_linker">
    <host>yahoo.openim.myjabber.org</host>
    <accept>
      <ip>205.150.219.39</ip>
      <port>6001</port>
      <secret>k7asfon</secret>
    </accept>
 </service>

<service id="aim_linker">
    <host>aim.openim.myjabber.org</host>
    <accept>
      <ip>205.150.219.39</ip>    ▇
      <port>8001</port>
      <secret>k7asfon</secret>
    </accept>
 </service>
```

Figure 5-18: The browse entries for AIM and Yahoo!

Finally, build the `aimtrans.xml` file as follows:

```
<jabber>

  <service id="aim_linker">
    <uplink/>
    <connect>
      <ip>216.94.240.201</ip>
      <port>8001</port>
      <secret>k7asfon</secret>
    </connect>
  </service>

  <service id="aim.openim.myjabber.org">
```

```
    <aimtrans xmlns="jabber:config:aimtrans">
        <instructions> Enter your AIM Account and
Password.</instructions>
      <search>Search for AIM users</search>
      <aimbinarydir>/usr/local/jabber/jabber2/aimprogram</aimbinarydir>
      <vCard>
        <FN>AIM Transport</FN>
        <DESC>myJabber AIM Transport</DESC>
        <URL>http://www.myjabber.org</URL>
      </vCard>
      <disable-tcp/>

    </aimtrans>

    <load>
      <aim_transport>./aim-transport/src/aimtrans.so</aim_transport>
    </load>
</service>

</jabber>
```

Figure 5-19 shows the code for the aim-linker.

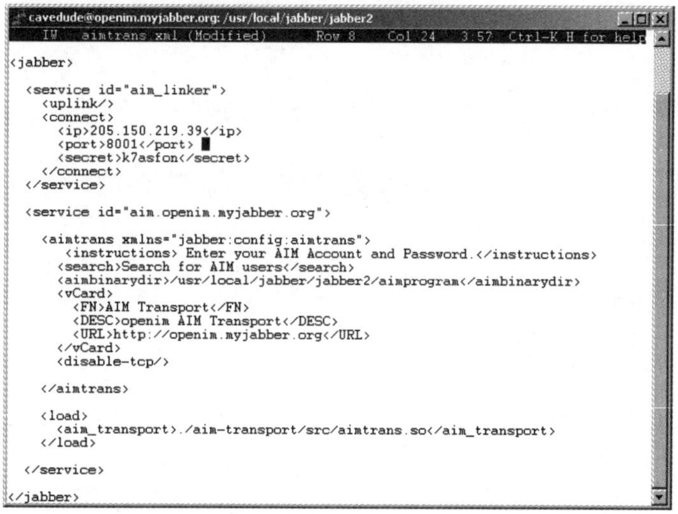

```
cavedude@openim.myjabber.org: /usr/local/jabber/jabber2
   IW   aimtrans.xml (Modified)     Row 8    Col 24   3:57  Ctrl-K H for help
<jabber>

  <service id="aim_linker">
    <uplink/>
    <connect>
      <ip>205.150.219.39</ip>
      <port>8001</port>
      <secret>k7asfon</secret>
    </connect>
  </service>

  <service id="aim.openim.myjabber.org">

    <aimtrans xmlns="jabber:config:aimtrans">
       <instructions> Enter your AIM Account and Password.</instructions>
      <search>Search for AIM users</search>
      <aimbinarydir>/usr/local/jabber/jabber2/aimprogram</aimbinarydir>
      <vCard>
        <FN>AIM Transport</FN>
        <DESC>openim AIM Transport</DESC>
        <URL>http://openim.myjabber.org</URL>
      </vCard>
      <disable-tcp/>

    </aimtrans>

    <load>
      <aim_transport>./aim-transport/src/aimtrans.so</aim_transport>
    </load>

  </service>

</jabber>
```

Figure 5-19: The aimtrans.xml file

Here is the big test! Stop your server and all the transports you have running. Remember to recover and detach your screen sessions. We are going to write a shell script in the next section to start the entire server, including all transports, with one simple command. If the server starts, your code to this point is correct and you have passed the XML test.

Jabber Quick Start Shell Script

Earlier in the chapter, we promised you a shell script to start this whole thing, so here it is. Create a new file in your editor called `start` (or you can call it `bill` if you want; `start` just makes sense to us), add the following code to it (placing the file in the /jabber2 directory), and save it:

```
#!/bin/bash
./jabberd/jabberd &
./jabberd/jabberd -c aimtrans.xml &
./jabberd/jabberd -c yahootrans.xml &
./jabberd/jabberd -c msntrans.xml &
./jabberd/jabberd -c icqtrans.xml &
```

You now need to make this file executable, by using the following command:

```
chmod  -c +x start
```

Just to make sure the file will run, look at the permissions on the file with the following command:

```
ls −l
-rwxrwxr-x    1 cavedude   cavedude         214 Jun 25 14:56 start
```

See Figure 5-20 for a better look a the output from the `ls −l` command and the use of the `start` command.

The `−x` is the flag for executable, so you're ready to go. Start your new server with the following command:

```
./start &
```

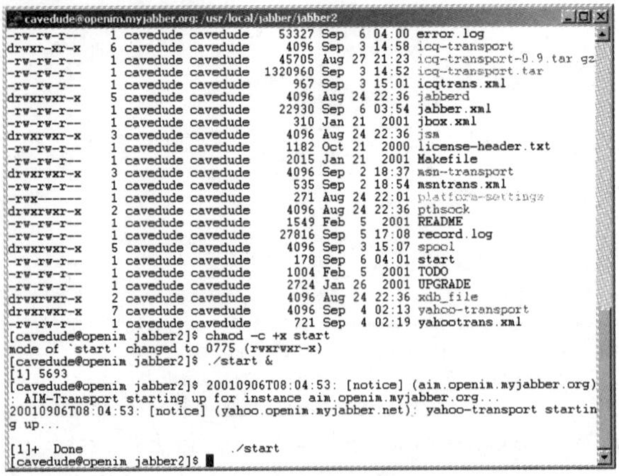

Figure 5-20: The use of chmod and the start script

A Word about Routers and Firewalls

If you're using a router or you installed a good commercial-grade firewall on your gateway system, you have some things to look at: You need to make sure that the ports you've specified are open to two-way traffic. These are ports 6001, 7001, 8001, and 9001. If you have a transport or "agent" acting funny or giving you strange messages as it tries to log on, badly configured ports may be the issue. If the transports refuse to start, and you're positive the XML is correct, this is most likely the problem. Refer to your router or firewall documentation for information on setting up the hardware for the port assignments.

Summary

In this chapter, we've covered downloading the conference server by using CVS, compiling the code, and editing the `jabber.xml` file to run the Conference module internal to the main server. You now have a running Jabber server that enables the use of group chat, person-to-person chat, and server-to-server for either one of them. If you have any questions so far, we highly recommend that you reread what we've done to this point. The next chapter covers the inclusion of the advanced transports and can be a bit confusing.

You now have an operational Jabber server that needs only some testing. We've discussed the basics of XML programming for Jabber, and we've shown you the pitfalls that you can get into if you get into a hurry. Your server is running in what is called the "out-of-process" mode. Each of the separate transports or processes is started separately and can be restarted separately if necessary.

Chapter 6

Testing Your Setup

In This Chapter

♦ Getting connected

♦ Logging in

♦ Checking the Conference agent

♦ Checking the various agents

This brief chapter is about testing everything that you've done so far and getting your server ready to use in Part III. Everything that we've shown you up to this point should have given you all the basic information about the server that you need to keep it running and useable for testing purposes. You're now simply going to test the different functions and make sure that everything is working.

Getting Connected

Bring the Linux box with the server online and log in with your Jabber user ID. We suggest doing so via Telnet from the machine that you intend to program with. If you've set up your directories and permissions correctly, you should be in the /jabber 2 directory. (Remember that /jabber2 is only the name that we use; yours can be anything that you want.) If you're unsure whether you're in the correct directory, make a quick list of the directory (`ls`) or request the present working directory (`pwd`).

We normally start a new server in debug mode so that we can watch the test as it progresses. The command to start in debug is `./jabberd/jabberd -D` (the D, of course, standing for *debug*). The server should fill your Telnet session with line after line of text and, finally, reach a point where it tells you that no users are online. This process takes only a matter of seconds even on a slow machine. If you get an error concerning XML parsing and the server doesn't start, the cause is most likely badly formed XML in the `jabber.xml` file. One of our most common mistakes is to place a comment inside another comment. If you've done this, too, you need to go through the `jabber.xml` file line by line until you find the offending section.

Logging In

You're going to use the myJabber client to test with, so open it and build a new profile. The server name is the full DNS name of your server. If you're not using DNS, you can log on to the server by using its local IP address.

> **NOTE** For you to log on by using the local IP address, the server itself must be configured to do so. At the very top of the `jabber.xml` file are the lines where you add the host name. Even if you enter a host name there and just aren't ready to use the DNS name, you can add the local IP by copying the host line and replacing the DSN name with your local IP. In our local network, for example, our server is at 10.0.0.5.

Click the connect icon in myJabber. The Telnet session should fill the screen with text and then stabilize. Look at the following example:

```
Sun Dec  2 19:37:01 2001  util.c:64 dropping 503 packet <presence
type='probe' from='terry@openim.myjabber.org'
to='terry@openim.myjabber.org'/>
Sun Dec  2 19:37:01 2001  mtq 81B6448 leaving to pth
Sun Dec  2 19:37:01 2001  mio.c:268 write_dump writing data: <message
from='openim.myjabber.org' to='terry@openim.myjabber.org'>
       <subject>Welcome!</subject>
       <body>Welcome to the Jabber server at openim.myjabber.org -- we
hope you enjoy this
          experiance! For information about how to use Jabber,Refer to
your Jabber programing Book from Hungry Minds INC or the CD
       provided with the book/</body>
    <x xmlns='jabber:x:delay' from='terry@openim.myjabber.org'
stamp='20011203T00:36:59'>Offline Storage</x></message>
Sun Dec  2 19:37:49 2001  users.c:82 checking users for host
openim.myjabber.org
Sun Dec  2 19:37:49 2001  users.c:63 freeing tsmelser
Sun Dec  2 19:37:49 2001  users.c:63 freeing cavedude
Sun Dec  2 19:37:49 2001  users.c:63 freeing srlee
Sun Dec  2 19:37:49 2001  usercount 1   total users
```

Notice in the last line `usercount 1 total users`. Success! You also see the "Welcome" message in the server output. This message is sent to new users. (We're assuming, of course, that you've not jumped ahead of us and already logged on once or twice.)

That's pretty much it. The server works! We don't, at the moment, need to start each of the transports. If something was wrong with the XML for them, the server itself wouldn't have started.

You now need to stop the server and restart the whole package permanently. Press Ctrl+C and look for the following output:

```
20011203T00:45:03: [alert] (-internal): Recieved Kill.  Jabberd shutting
down.
Sun Dec  2 19:45:03 2001   dnsrv.c:386 dnsrv: Read error on coprocess: 4
Interrupted system call
Sun Dec  2 19:45:03 2001   dnsrv.c:408 pid 18427, exit status: 0
Sun Dec  2 19:45:03 2001   dnsrv.c:416 child returned 0
Sun Dec  2 19:45:03 2001   dnsrv.c:429 child dying...
Sun Dec  2 19:45:04 2001   mio.c:809 MIO is shutting down
Sun Dec  2 19:45:04 2001   dialback.c:137 miod cleaning out socket 18
with key
5736962612ec363087b83fc6edfe346bbe875095@openim.myjabber.org/myjabber.ne
t to hash 811E1E8
Sun Dec  2 19:45:04 2001   log.c:175 <log type='record'
from='openim.myjabber.org'>in dialback 1 216.xx.240.xxx
myjabber.net</log>
Sun Dec  2 19:45:04 2001   mio.c:354 freed MIO socket
Sun Dec  2 19:45:04 2001   dialback.c:137 miod cleaning out socket 17
with key myjabber.net/openim.myjabber.org to hash 810C938
Sun Dec  2 19:45:04 2001   deliver.c:303 Unregistering myjabber.net with
instance s2s
Sun Dec  2 19:45:04 2001   log.c:175 <log type='record'
from='myjabber.net'>out dialback 4 216.94.240.236
openim.myjabber.org</log>
Sun Dec  2 19:45:04 2001   mio.c:354 freed MIO socket
Sun Dec  2 19:45:04 2001   client.c:243 pthsock_client_read called with:
m:81E6DB8 flag:4 arg:81E6E98
Sun Dec  2 19:45:04 2001   client.c:248 io_select Socket 15 close
notification
Sun Dec  2 19:45:04 2001   mio.c:354 freed MIO socket
Sun Dec  2 19:45:04 2001   base_accept.c:100 process XML: m:8130878
state:4, arg:81307E0, x:804EF0C
Sun Dec  2 19:45:04 2001   mio.c:354 freed MIO socket
Sun Dec  2 19:45:04 2001   base_accept.c:100 process XML: m:81304E0
state:4, arg:8130448, x:804EF0C
Sun Dec  2 19:45:04 2001   mio.c:354 freed MIO socket
Sun Dec  2 19:45:04 2001   base_accept.c:100 process XML: m:812FD00
state:4, arg:812FC68, x:804EF0C
Sun Dec  2 19:45:04 2001   mio.c:354 freed MIO socket
Sun Dec  2 19:45:04 2001   base_accept.c:100 process XML: m:812F538
state:4, arg:812F4A0, x:804EF0C
Sun Dec  2 19:45:04 2001   mio.c:354 freed MIO socket
Sun Dec  2 19:45:04 2001   dialback_in.c:170 dbin read: fd 8 flag 4
Sun Dec  2 19:45:04 2001   mio.c:354 freed MIO socket
Sun Dec  2 19:45:04 2001   mio.c:354 freed MIO socket
```

That's the shutdown sequence from jabberd. Kind of gruesome, huh? Now to start the server permanently. This includes the transports and conferencing, plus the local JUD (Jabber Users Directory).

Open a screen session by typing `screen`; then give the following command to use the startup script that you wrote in Chapter 5.

```
./start
```

The output at this point varies. Most of the time, it looks something like the following example:

```
[cavedude@openim jabber2]$ ./start
[cavedude@openim jabber2]$ 20011203T00:46:26: [notice]
(aim.openim.myjabber.org): AIM-Transport starting up for instance
aim.openim.myjabber.org...
20011203T00:46:26: [notice] (yahoo.openim.myjabber.org): yahoo-transport
starting up...
```

We've never seen all the transports give a `start` line after the use of the start script, but we've seen every one of them output a `start` line.

The server is running, and you now need to close the screen session to keep it running. Use the following command: `screen -d`. (The `-d` tells the screen program to detach.) You should get a line similar to the following:

```
[cavedude@openim jabber2]$ screen -d

[remote detached]
[cavedude@openim jabber2]$
```

The server is now running and is going to stay running. The `screen` command is a rather neat little tool. Yes, you can start something and keep it running in other ways, but this way was the fastest for our purposes and is very dependable.

Now check the server with the following quick command:

```
ps aux | grep jabberd
```

You should get something that looks like the following example:

```
[cavedude@openim jabber2]$ ps aux | grep jabberd
cavedude 18431  0.4  1.8  3552 1728 pts/0      S   19:46   0:07
./jabberd/jabberd
cavedude 18432  0.0  1.4  3152 1336 pts/0      S   19:46   0:00
./jabberd/jabberd
cavedude 18433  0.0  0.9  2768  912 pts/0      S   19:46   0:00
./jabberd/jabberd
cavedude 18435  0.0  1.0  2796 1024 pts/0      S   19:46   0:00
./jabberd/jabberd
cavedude 18436  0.0  1.4  2644 1408 pts/0      S   19:46   0:00
./jabberd/jabberd
```

```
cavedude 18443  0.0  0.9  2752  924 pts/0    S   19:57   0:00
./jabberd/jabberd
cavedude 18459  0.0  0.6  1592  580 pts/2    S   20:14   0:00 grep
jabberd
[cavedude@openim jabber2]$
```

That's the openIM server with all transports running; yours should look much the same.

Checking the Conferencing Agent

The next step is to test the conference transport. This procedure is really simple. In myJabber, press F4. In the server block, type the name of your conference server as you set it up in the `jabber.xml` file in Chapter 4.

For openIM the server is `conference.openim.myjabber.org`.

In the chat-room block, type anything that you want for a room name (e.g., `test`). Put your name in the nickname block and click Connect.

A group-conference window should open, and in it, your name should appear on the right-hand side. A notice saying that you've joined should appear in the main text area.

That's it! The conference transport works. If the process doesn't happen just exactly as we describe it in this section, something is wrong with the XML code in the `jabber.xml` file, most likely in the `services` area.

Checking the Various Agents

Your last task is to check to see that the agents (or transports) are running and connecting to the services they're designed to work with. This task, too, is a very simple one that involves only registering with the services. You did so in Chapter 3 with the myJabber client, so it should be old stuff to you. Right-click a transport in the Agents list and choose Properties from the pop-up menu. Enter your user information and click Register. You should get a subscription request from each service as it connects and the bulb that we use in myJabber should turn green. Add a contact or two in each service and try talking to them. Does it work? Success!

Summary

We've come a long way together in these six chapters, and we hope the information we've provided has helped you get to this point in comfort, with a bit of fun along the way. You now have a functioning Jabber server, have a basic understanding of Jabber and its beginnings, and are familiar with the myJabber client produced by sltsCommunications and the myJabber team.

Part III

Creating Your Own Instant Messaging Client

In This Part

Chapter 7

Working with Jabber COM Libraries

In This Chapter

♦ What Jabber COM libraries do

♦ Advantages of using a COM library

♦ COM library choices

♦ Example: using Matrix

♦ Installing Matrix

In this chapter, we look at a couple of available COM libraries that can make creating your instant messaging client much easier. We show you an example of the difference in code requirements between handling the socket and XML layer yourself and using a COM library. Finally, we show you a couple of examples on how to use the Matrix COM Library and how to install it.

What Jabber COM Libraries Do

The components of a Jabber COM library work as a layer between your client and the Jabber server (see Figure 7-1), taking care of socket connections and producing and parsing the XML necessary for the server. Normally these libraries also handle SSL as well as any other low-level socket and XML parsing. The libraries provide access to the raw XML stream so that, if necessary, the client can manipulate the stream.

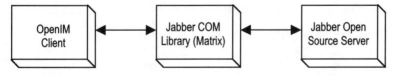

Figure 7-1: COM library layer

To give you some idea what the COM libraries do, the following example shows the steps necessary to create a connection and to log in to our OpenIM Jabber server:

1. Create a Winsock connection on port 5222. This task requires either dropping the `Winsock` object on your form or creating a reference to the library in your Visual Basic project. After you make the reference, you need to handle the events from the `Winsock` control. The following code fragment shows the connection code to open a socket to the Jabber server:

```
winsock1.RemotePort = 5222
winsock1.RemoteHost = openim.myJabber.org
winsock1.Connect
```

2. After you establish the connection to the port on the Open Source Jabber Server, you start your XML stream. The following code shows the XML that the Open Source Jabber Server requires. You send this XML stream from the `winsock1_connect` subprocedure, as follows:

```
<?xml version="1.0" encoding="UTF-8" ?>

<stream:stream
to="openim.myJabber.org"
xmlns="jabber:client" xmlns:stream=http://etherx.jabber.org/streams>
```

If the XML syntax is correct, the server should respond with the following XML list. The `winsock_dataArrival` event will fire, and you will need to parse out the data that the socket layer receives. At this point, the parsing of the XML code is not too bad, as you can pretty well guarantee that you receive only the one string of XML. But as the client starts its connection and begins to get `RosterItems`, agent items, messages, and other notifications, you get several pieces of XML all at once, and you may not receive it all in one chunk but rather end up with the `winsock1_dataArrival` event getting called a couple of times before all the data arrives. This situation causes a problem for parsing, as you have no guarantee of getting a complete XML message in one chunk. You must, therefore, keep track of the incoming data and parse the XML only after you know that you've received a complete stream of XML information.

This code block is what the server's XML response looks like:

```
<?xml version="1.0" encoding="UTF-8" ?>

<stream:stream
from="openim.myJabber.org"
xmlns="jabber:client" xmlns:stream=http://etherx.jabber.org/streams>
```

At this point, the XML stream is established with the Jabber server, and you can send your login information. The following XML shows the required information:

```
<iq type="set" id="MX_1">
 <query xmlns="jabber:iq:auth">
        <username>cavedude</username>
        <password>arrgh</password>
        <resource>openIM</resource>
 </query>
</iq>
```

If your logon attempt is successful and the XML is correctly formatted, the server returns the following XML:

```
<iq type="result" id="MX_1"/>
```

Remember that we've shown you only the basic steps and necessary XML. We didn't actually write the code to establish this connection or the code to parse the XML input and output. Now try the same thing using an example call to Matrix to establish a connection to the server, as follows:

```
Set cSession = New MatrixServer.cSession
cSession.ServerAddress = "openim.myJabber.org"
cSession.UserName = "cavedude"
cSession.Password = "arrgh"
cSession.Resource = "openIM"
cSession.Port = "5222"
cSession.Connect
```

That's it — you should have a connection. Figure 7-2 shows an example of the XML that passes back and forth during a connection process using the myJabber client. As you're creating your client, you will include a form similar to this one so that you can watch the debug output.

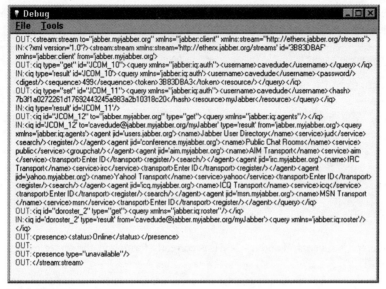

Figure 7-2: Debug output

The following example shows the XML necessary to send a message to a roster user. (In the section "COM Library Choices" later in this chapter, you see an example of sending the same message by using both the JabberCOM COM library and the Matrix COM Library.)

```
<message  id="MX_4" to="cavegal@openim.myjabber.org"          type="normal"
from="cavedude@openim.myjabber.org">
    <subject>Hey!</subject>
    <body>
        just me saying hi
    </body>
</message>
```

Next is a subscription request. (In the section "COM Library Choices" later in the chapter, we show you the same example sent from the JabberCOM library and the Matrix COM Library.)

```
<presence to="cavegal@openim.myjabber.org" type="subscribe"/>
```

After you send a subscription request, the roster user needs to reply. The following example shows the reply returned by the roster user:

```
<presence to=cavedude@openim.myjabber.org type="subscribed"/>
```

Now whenever the user logs in, you receive the complete presence information for that roster user, as shown in the following code:

```
<presence from="cavegal@openIM.myjabber.org/myJabber"
to="cavedude@openim.myjabber.org">
    <show>away</show>
```

```
    <status>Gone for lunch</status>

</presence>
```

Keep in mind that you receive the presence information for each person on your roster list as well as that for all transports running on the server you're logging in to.

NOTE The Jabber Programmer's Guide, available at `http://docs.jabber.org/jpg/`, gives a comprehensive overview of the details involved in sending XML information to the Jabber server. We have also included this guide on the CD that accompanies this book.

As you can see from the raw XML examples, you have a very good reason to use one of the COM libraries. The code is clean, and the Matrix COM Library handles all the XML parsing. If for some reason you encounter an error logging in to the Jabber server, the Matrix COM Library fires an event and returns the error information to the client.

COM Library Choices

The following sections discuss some of your COM library choices.

JabberCOM

The first COM library to be available was *JabberCOM*. Developed alongside winjab, it's been widely used for Windows clients. The library was written in Delphi, which, although it is a very good object-oriented programming language, isn't as widely used in Windows development as Visual Basic or C++.

myJabber uses the JabberCOM library but is moving away to its own after experiencing several compatibility problems with JabberCOM. (We couldn't fix the problems as we didn't have a Delphi compiler.) The JabberCOM library provides pretty good documentation, but we found the support from the author very slow or nonexistent. The code is open source and is available for download from `http://jabbercom.sourceforge.net`.

As you soon see, connecting to a Jabber server is very easy with JabberCOM. The following code shows an example of doing so:

```
Private WithEvents cSession as MatrixServer.Session

jSession.Server = "openIM.myJabber.org"
jsession.Port = 5222
jSession.UserName = "cavedude"
jSession.Password = "arrgh"
jSession.Resource = "OpenIM"
jSession.UseSSL = true
jSession.DoConnect False, jatAuto
```

`WithEvents` enables the client to have the JabberCOM COM library raise events to the client.

Everything else is pretty self-explanatory, with the exception of the `DoConnect` event. The first argument of `DoConnect` involves whether we're registering a new user and the constant `jatAuto` is telling JabberCOM to connect by using the best authentication type. JabberCOM starts with ZeroK authentication; if that's not available on the Jabber server, it uses digest, and if that isn't available, it falls back to plain text.

Now take a quick look at the following code, which sends a message by using the JabberCOM library:

```
Dim JMsg As JabberMsg

    Set JMsg = JSession.CreateMsg

    JMsg.ToJID = "cavegal.openIM.myJabber.org"
    JMsg.Subject = "Hey!"
    JMsg.Body = "just me saying hi"
    JMsg.MsgType = jmtNotmal
    JSession.SendMessage JMsg
```

As you can see, this code initializes a new instance of `JabberMsg`, sets the `ToJID` to the roster user to whom you're sending the message, adds the body of the message, and uses the `SendMessage` function of the JabberCOM library to send the message to the Jabber server for delivery to the roster user.

The following code shows the call that's necessary to send a subscription request to a roster user:

```
jSession.SendPresence "cavegal@openim.myjabber.org", jptSubscribe,
"Please let me add you to my list", Nothing
```

The first argument is the roster user to whom you're sending the request; the next is a constant that tells the JabberCOM library that you want to subscribe to the user; the next is the text that gives the reason for the request; and the last argument is set to nothing.

If `cavegal.openIM.myjabber.org` accepts your subscription request, the following code sends the response to the JabberCOM library:

```
jSession.SendPresence "cavedude@openim.myjabber.org", jptSubscribed, "",
Nothing
```

If she chooses to deny the request, the following code sends that response instead:

```
jSession.SendPresence "cavedude@openim.myjabber.org', jptUnsubscribed,
"", Nothing
```

Notice that the only difference is the `jptUnSubscribed` constant that's passing back.

> **NOTE** A subscription request is a request that you send to a roster user asking that person to allow you to add him or her to your roster list. After you are subscribed to a user, you can see the user's presence (online, away, etc.).

Jabcpp

As the name implies, Jabcpp is written in C++, and it's written as a cross-platform library for both client and server applications to use. The library comes with a wrapper that makes it a COM component for easy client development. Although fairly new as of the writing of this book, this library shows huge potential, and the developer's been a large contributor to the Jabber Open Source Server. The code is open source, and you can download it from `http://sourceforge.net/projects/jabcpp`.

Matrix

Matrix is our own COM library. We decided to create our own library because Jabcpp wasn't ready at the time and we were having too many problems with JabberCOM.

Matrix is written in Visual Basic by sltsCommunications, and at the time of this writing, it isn't open source. This situation may change in the very near future. The Matrix COM Library's focus is to enable a client to communicate with a Jabber server as easily as possible. As you saw in the preceding examples, the methods and events of Matrix make communicating with a Jabber server very easy. Matrix is written as a set of classes, starting with a base socket class. The design of Matrix enables you to add or change functionality very quickly.

The following, written by one of the developers of the Matrix COM Library, introduces the general ideas and the future direction of Matrix:

> What is Matrix? Matrix is a framework made by developers for developers. It allows you to quickly implement a protocol that is supported in Matrix and to extend it yourself if you need to. All this is possible by packaging all the protocol-specific functions inside Matrix so that it handles all this for you and allows you to receive actions and data through events and easy-to-use objects and functions.

> Matrix was designed so that developers could implement the protocol they choose in a very short amount of time. A simple client can be created in a matter of hours. How does Matrix make this possible? Through XML. Matrix is top-to-bottom based on XML. "But I don't know XML," you say. You don't need to know XML; our easy-to-use objects and functions don't *require* you to know XML, but we do expose in our very efficient XML Node, in case you want to modify, send, or retrieve specific data yourself.

> The future of Matrix is limitless. At the moment, Matrix supports the Jabber protocol, which in turn (depending on the server configuration) can communicate with other instant messaging networks such as MSN, AOL, Yahoo!, and ICQ. Matrix can also support, for example, ICQ directly rather than going through the Jabber protocol that

supports those other networks. Matrix can connect to Napster or Gnutella; it's not dependent on any one protocol. Matrix can be extended in any direction for network purposes in the future. Matrix may someday support your network!

As you can see, Matrix is very flexible, user-friendly, and quick to implement. Its being based on XML and being represented as a COM object makes all this possible. You could quite possibly spend more time designing GUIs and screens than adding functionality to connect to a network!

Basic concepts of Matrix

To show you the basic concepts of Matrix, in this section we run through a lot of the same examples that we show you for JabberCOM, but we try to explain in a little more detail what's happening in each one.

The Matrix server requires you to create it by using events, as in the following example:

```
Private WithEvents cSession as MatrixServer.Session
```

The WithEvents event enables the client to have the Matrix server raise events to the client. This becomes clear as we begin to write our OpenIM client. Figure 7-3 shows an example of the flow of events and methods between the objects.

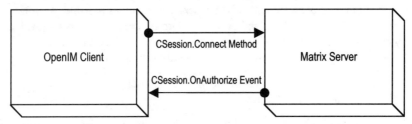

Figure 7-3: Example flow of events and methods

As we go through the creation of the OpenIM client, you should start to get a fairly good feel as to how the Matrix server communicates with the client. We recommend at this point that you review the documentation we provide for the Matrix COM Library (see Appendix C) in order to become familiar with some of the available properties, methods, and events.

Creating a message and sending one is just as easy as creating a connection to the server. The following code shows the cavedude user sending a message to cavegal:

```
Dim myMessage As New MatrixServer.cMessage

cSession.CreateMessage myMessage

myMessage.MSG_Type = MSG_Normal
myMessage.Subject = "Hi ya!"
myMessage.ToJID = "cavegal@openim.myjabber.org
```

```
myMessage.Body = "just me saying hi"
myMessage.SendMessage
```

This code sends a standard *message*. If you changed MSG_TYPE to MSG_Chat, the code would send a *chat* message to cavegal.

In cavegal's client, the OnMessage event fires and the client then does whatever's necessary to display the message. The onMessage event receives the message, as shown in the preceding code, but also has myMessage.FromJID.

Now say that you want to add cavegal to your roster list. A simple one-line call sends a subscription request to cavegal, as follows:

```
cSession.Sendpresence "cavegal@openimmyjabber.org", MX_Subscribe
```

The subscription request asks cavegal whether you can add her to your roster. cavegal's client receives an OnSubscriptionRequest event. The client will then have code to ask cavegal whether she wants to accept the subscription. If she does, she returns the following:

```
cSession.Sendpresence "cavedude@openim.myjabber.org",
MX_Subscribe_Accept
```

If she decides that she doesn't want cavedude to see her presence, she returns the following instead:

```
cSession.Sendpresence "cavedude@openim.myjabber.org", MX_Subscribe_Deny
```

cavedude's client receives either an OnSubscriptionAccept event or an OnSubscriptionDenied event.

> **NOTE** The examples we've provided for Matrix aren't all that different from those of the other COM libraries. The syntax may be slightly different, but the concepts are essentially the same. We've provided only a couple of examples here. In the following chapters, we put these events and procedures to work as you create your client.

The XML Node

The XML Node object is an important part of the COM object, as it gives you a way to handle XML parsing inside the client app. You may never need to do this task, but it's a handy way to implement to a client new functionality that may not be available through a COM library. If you create custom namespaces to add additional functionality to your client that's not available as a standard namespace in the Jabber server, you must use the XML Node to manipulate the XML stream for that namespace. We recommend that you not create a client that's incompatible with other Jabber clients, as the idea of Jabber is compatibility with as many systems as possible. That said, making your clients compatible while still maintaining functionality that other clients lack is possible.

You should notice that, by using Matrix, you really don't need to handle any kind of XML whatsoever, unlike with the JabberCOM library, which under most circumstances still passes XML to your client for parsing.

Registering the Matrix COM Library

To use the Matrix COM Library, you of course need to install it on your computer. After you obtain the Zip file, either from our CD or from the Web site, you need to unzip the file into your \system folder. This folder is typically c:\windows\system on Windows 95, 98, and ME and c:\winnt\system32 on Windows NT, 2000, and XP. After the file is in your system folder, you need to register it. On the Windows taskbar, select Start ⇨ Run and enter the command shown in Figure 7-4.

> **NOTE** The documentation for the Matrix COM Library appears in Appendix C of this book. This material gives you an overview of the properties, methods, and events that the Matrix COM Library includes. The latest version of the Matrix COM Library available at the time of writing is on the CD, but we suggest you download the latest version of the library from `www.openim.myjabber.org`.

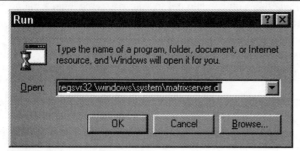

Figure 7-4: Sample Run command

If you enter the command correctly, regsvr32 should produce the dialog box shown in Figure 7-5.

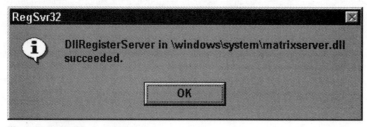

Figure 7-5: Sample regsvr32 reply

We performed this installation on a Windows 98 machine, so remember to change the \windows\system directory to your appropriate system folder.

Summary

By now, you should have a basic understanding of how COM libraries are of benefit in the development of a Jabber client. At this point, you should be able to find and obtain a copy of one of the libraries; you should know the basic properties, methods, and events of the Matrix

COM Library; and you should be ready to start writing your own Jabber instant messaging client.

Chapter 8

Getting Connected

In This Chapter

- ◆ Creating the MainForm
- ◆ Adding a Debug form
- ◆ Creating a Login form
- ◆ Sending a connection request
- ◆ Logging on to the development server
- ◆ Preparing the TreeView for data
- ◆ Adding transports/agents
- ◆ Getting a roster list
- ◆ Sending and receiving subscription requests
- ◆ Registering with a transport/agent

We now begin the process of creating your own instant messaging client. By the end of this chapter, you create a client that can connect to the development server, and you'll be able to view the XML debug information going back and forth between the client and the server. You can also at that point add transports to your roster and accept or decline subscription requests.

ON THE CD-ROM You can find the code for this chapter on the CD-ROM in the \openIM\chapter08 folder.

Creating the MainForm

The first step in creating the `MainForm` is to create a folder on your computer in which to store the OpenIM source code. (We call ours OpenIM.) Just follow these steps:

1. Start Visual Basic. In the New tab of the New Project window, click on the Standard EXE icon and then click Open (see Figure 8-1).

Figure 8-1: The New Project window

2. You should see a new project and a blank form onscreen. On the Visual Basic menu bar, select MenuItem ⇨ Project1 Properties. Change the `Project Name` to `OpenIM` and change the `Project Description` to `OpenIM an Open Source Jabber Client`. Enter any version information that you want to set on the Make tab of the Project Properties window. After you finish, click OK to store the changes and close the Project1 — Project Properties window.

> **TIP** On the Make tab of the Project Properties window, we set the Auto Increment flag so that every compile changes the version number.

3. In the Properties window for the form, change `Form1` in the `(Name)` field to `MainForm`. We've always set the name of our `MainForm` in the project to `MainForm`.

> **NOTE** You may or may not agree with the coding practices we use, so feel free to use your own coding styles. These are just the methods we prefer.

4. Set the `caption` of the form in the Properties window to `OpenIM`. At this point, you also set the `BorderStyle` property to `Fixed Single`. As we're trying to help you get an

instant messaging client working in a short time, we'll leave the resize code up to you. At this point, you may want to change the icon for the form. We chose one of the standard graphics that installs with Visual Studio. Set any colors that you want to change.

5. You need to add a reference to the `matrixserver.dll` file. From the Project window, click References. Search down your list for references until you find Matrix Server For Jabber and click the check box next to it. Then click OK. Figure 8-2 shows an example of my References — Project1 window.

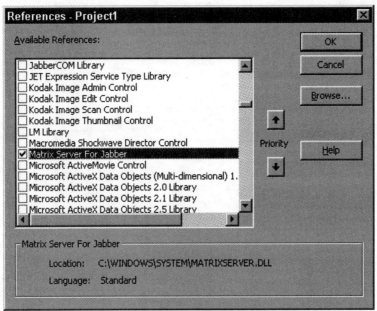

Figure 8-2: Setting a reference to the matrixserver.dll file

You should have a reference set to the library that does the communicating with the development server. If you don't see the component in the list, you quite possibly haven't registered it yet. At the end of Chapter 7, you find the instructions for registering the Matrix COM Library.

NOTE For the rest of the book, whenever we refer to the development server, we're talking about either the server at `openim.myjabber.org` or the server that you installed on your Linux computer.

6. Double-click anywhere on the `MainForm` to open the code window and go to the `(General)` section of the code window and enter the following code:

```
Public WithEvents cSession As MatrixServer.cSession
```

If you set the reference correctly on the Matrix server, the IntelliSense feature of Visual Basic shows you the Matrix server name. To see that all went as planned, check the left drop-down list of the code window for a new reference for `cSession` and the right drop-down list for several new events (see Figure 8-3). The events in the right drop-down list are all the events that the Matrix server fires in response to outgoing and incoming requests from the development server.

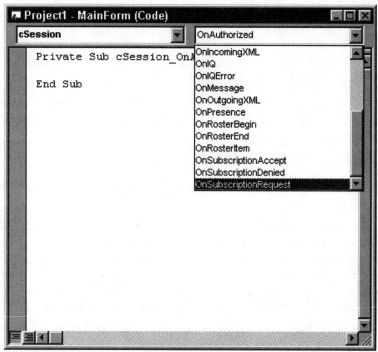

Figure 8-3: New events after adding cSession

7. You need to add a couple of extra components to your OpenIM project. Right-click the Visual Basic Toolbox and select Components from the pop-up menu. In the list of controls in the Components dialog box that appears, look for Microsoft Windows Common Controls 6. Click the check box next to it and then click OK. This step should add nine new controls to your toolbox.

NOTE The version of Visual Basic we are using to write this client is Version 6, with the latest Service Pack installed. However, Visual Basic 5 should work as well. We suggest loading the latest service packs for Visual Studio.

8. To add a `StatusBar` control to the `MainForm`, click the `StatusBar` control in the Toolbox and draw it onto your `MainForm`. You use the `StatusBar` to tell you your connection status. Open the Properties window for the `StatusBar` and set the `style` property to `sbrSimple`. Open the code window for the `MainForm` and, in the `cSession_OnAuthorized` event, set the `simpletext` of the `StatusBar` to `Connected` by using the following code:

```
StatusBar1.SimpleText = "Connected"
```

This will set the text of the `StatusBar` to `Connected` once we have been authorized by the Jabber server.

After the Matrix COM Library fires this event, it means that the client successfully connected and authenticated to the Jabber server.

9. In `cSession_OnDisConnected`, you need to add code to set the `simpletext` of the `StatusBar` to `Disconnected`. This way, users have a visual cue as to their status on the Jabber server.

```
StatusBar1.SimpleText = "Disconnected"
```

10. Click TreeView on the Visual Basic Toolbox dialog and draw the TreeView to fill the rest of the `MainForm`.

11. You need to add some code to close the program and shut everything down nice and clean. We've found that the best way to close down an application is to make sure that all the forms the program is using are unloaded. You can create a module so that you have a place to put a few utilities, as you need them. On the Visual Basic menu bar, select Project ⇨ Add Module. On the Add Module screen, click Open to create a new module. In the Properties window for the module, change the (`name`) property to `mUtils`.

The `mUtils` module should be open. If it isn't, open the code window for it and enter the following code to create a subprocedure that closes all windows associated with your project:

```
Public Sub CloseForms()
' This will make sure that all of the forms
' get closed when exiting the application
Dim iFormCount As Integer
Dim i As Integer
    ' The form is not open we might get an error.
    ' So we just resume next to carry on with the rest of the forms
    On Error Resume Next

    ' store the number of forms
    iFormCount = Forms.Count - 1
    For i = iFormCount To 0 Step -1
```

```
        Unload Forms(i)
        Set Forms(i) = Nothing
    Next

End Sub
```

12. Now you can add the code to the Exit menu item to shut down the application. Open the code window for the `MainForm` and, in the `mnuOpenIM_Exit_Click` sub, enter the following code:

```
Private Sub mnuOpenIM_Exit_Click()

    ' make sure we close down the matrix connection cleanly
    If cSession.Active Then cSession.Disconnect

    ' make sure all associated forms are closed
    CloseForms
    ' unload the MainForm to completely shut down the application
    Unload me
End Sub
```

13. As you can see from the comments in the code, you're just making sure that the connection to the Matrix server is closed after checking to see whether it's active. Next, call your new subprocedure, which ensures that all forms associated with the program are unloaded. Finally, unload your `MainForm`, which should terminate the application.

Creating the Debug Form

Your next step is to create a Debug form; we've always found this window handy in writing a client so that we can see the information going to and from the server. This window is really going to show only the XML that you're sending and receiving, but it really helps in looking for problems in your code. It helps to pick out spelling errors in user logins and passwords as well as debug any custom XML that you may be passing. If you're having any trouble with the server's not returning your requests, this window is the first place to look, as you're more than likely experiencing a problem with the XML that you're sending. To create your Debug window, follow these steps:

1. From the Visual Basic menu bar, select Projects ⇨ Add Form. Click the Form icon and then click the Open button. For the new form, go to the Properties window and change the (name) to `frmDebug` and the `caption` to `Debug`; then set the `BorderStyle` to `1 - Fixed Single` and, again, set the icon and colors the way that you want them. Now, from the Toolbox window, drag and drop a text box onto the Debug form and resize it to fit almost the entire form. In the Properties window for the text box, set the `MultiLine` property to `True`, set the `Enabled` property to `False`, and set the `ScrollBars`

property to 2 – vertical. Clear the Text property so that it no longer contains text1. Now drop two command buttons on the form and center them at the bottom. In the properties of the first command button, set the Caption to Clear. In the properties for the second command button, set the Caption to &Close and the Default property to True. After you finish, you should have something that looks similar to the window shown in Figure 8-4.

Figure 8-4: Sample Debug window

2. Double-click the Clear command button and enter the following code:

```
Text1.text = ""
```

This button gives you a quick way to clear the Debug window — you find that, as you add more and more code to the client, the volume of data that goes to the Debug window can become excessive, and you need to clear the window occasionally.

3. Double-click the Open command button and, under the command2_click event in the code window, enter the following code:

```
Unload Me
```

```
The code window should look something like this

Private Sub Command2_Click()
    Unload Me
End Sub
```

The preceding code, as you're no doubt aware, unloads the Debug window after you click the Close button.

4. Now you need to set some code to actually deliver the XML output to the Debug window. Go to the `MainForm` and open the code window; in the `cSession_OnIncomingXML` event, enter the following code so that the Matrix server fires the `cSession_OnIncomingXML` event every time that it receives XML from the development server:

```
If frmDebug.Visible = True Then
        frmDebug.Text1 = "IN: " & XML_Node.XML & vbcrlf
End If
```

The first thing you do next is check to see whether the Debug window is onscreen and then set the output to the text box on the Debug window. Checking to make sure that the Debug window is visible is your way of turning debug printing on and off. (The Debug window's being visible is your way of knowing that debug information should be written to the window.) You add the `IN:` to it so that you know that `XML_Node1.XML` is incoming XML data, and you add a carriage return linefeed to start a new line after it displays in the Debug window.

5. In the `cSession_OnOutgoingXML` event, enter the following code:

```
If frmDebug.Visible = True Then
        frmDebug.Text1 = "OUT: " & XML_Node.XML & vbcrlf
End If
```

The only difference in the code in the `cSession_OnOutgoingXML` event and the `xSession_InComingXML` event is that now you use `OUT:` instead of `IN:` to show that the XML is outgoing from the client.

6. Because you need a way to load and unload the Debug window, you need to add a menu item to your `MainForm`. Close the code window and highlight the `MainForm`. From the menu bar, select Tools ⇨ Menu Editor. Add a top-level menu called openIM and another called Tools.

NOTE In naming top-level menu items, we try to stick to the following naming conventions: We start with mnu and add the caption to it, so as an example for the Tools menu, the name would be `mnuTools`. For second-level menu items, we use the top-level name, an underscore, and the caption from the menu item. Again, as an example, a Debug second-level menu item under the Tools menu would be `mnuTools_Debug`.

You've added a couple of extra menu items as well so that, after you finish, the Menu Editor should look something like what you see in Figure 8-5.

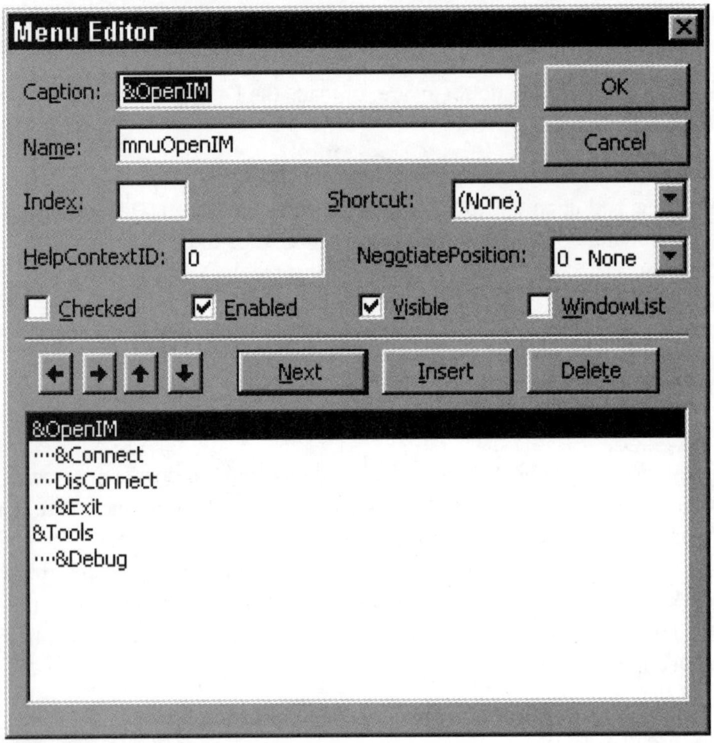

Figure 8-5: Menu Editor

7. On your MainForm, select Tools ⇨ Debug. In the code window, enter the following:

```
FrmDebug.show
```

The preceding code loads the Debug window and displays it onscreen after you choose it from the menu of your client.

8. Save your project by selecting File ⇨ Save from the menu bar.

Creating a Login Form

Now you need to add a Login form — a place to enter the information that the server requires to enable you to log in. Just follow these steps:

1. Create a new form by following the procedures for adding a new form in the preceding section. Change the name in the Properties window to `frmLogin` and set the `BorderStyle` to `1 - Fixed Single`, and the `Caption` to `OpenIM Login`.

2. You now need to add five labels to the form; from the Toolbox, drag and size a label control. Change the `Alignment` property of the label to `Right Justify`. Then copy and paste it onto the form four times. On the first attempt, Visual Basic prompts you as to whether you want to create a control array. You can answer "Yes" to this query. After you have added all five labels, arrange them in a row down the left side of the window. Change the `Caption` properties so that the first label is `Server:`, the second is `Port:`, the third is `User Name:`, the fourth is `Password:`, and the last is `Resource:`.

3. From the Toolbox, drop a text box onto the form and place it next to the Server caption. Do this four more times so that you have a text box next to each of the labels from Step 2. Set the `(Name)` property of each of the text boxes as shown in the following table.

Caption Name	Textbox (Name) Property
Server	`TxtServer`
Port	`TxtPort`
User Name	`txtUserName`
Password	`txtPassword`
Resource	`txtResource`

4. For the Password text box, set the `PasswordChar` to `*`. You also need to clear the `text` property so that it's empty for each of the text boxes.

5. Drag and size a check box onto the form, placing it below the last text box. Set the `(Name)` property to `chkNewAccount` and the caption to `Create a new account`. This check box enables a user who doesn't already have an account on the server to create a new one.

6. Drag and size two command buttons onto the form and place them at the bottom of the form. In the properties for the first button, change the `Caption` to `&Login` and set the `Default` property to `True` and the `(Name)` property to `cmdLogin`.

> **NOTE** Setting the Default property to `True` on a command button makes it the default button. In other words, if the user presses the Enter key while that form is active, the code for that button is activated.

7. Set the `Caption` of the second button to `&Close` and the `(Name)` to `cmdClose`. Figure 8-6 shows the completed Login form.

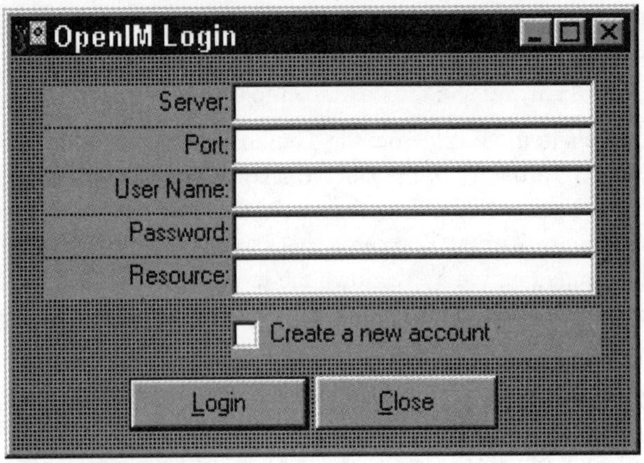

Figure 8-6: Login form

8. Now you need a way to display this window from the `MainForm`, so click the `MainForm` window, then choose OpenIM ⇨ Connect. This action places you back into the code window. Now enter the following:

```
FrmLogin.show
```

9. Go back to your Login form. Double-click the Close button to open the code window and then add the following code to close the form when the button is clicked:

```
Unload me
```

Now you're ready to write some code to connect you to the development server. Double-click the `MainForm` and make sure that you're in the `Form Load` subprocedure. You're going to create a new instance of the Matrix COM Library. In Step 6 of Creating the `MainForm` in the general area of the form, you created a reference to it. Now you're going to create a new object that you can use to access the properties and methods of the Matrix COM Library. We do this by setting the `csession` object to a new `matrixserver.csession` object.

```
Set csession = new matrixserver.csession
```

Sending a Connection Request

Double-click the Login command button on the Login form. You're now going to add the code that we showed you in Chapter 7 for connecting to the server. You set each of the properties of one of the text boxes and use the check box to determine whether you're going to register a new user.

Your code should look like the following example:

```
With MainForm.cSession

    .ServerAddress = txtServer.Text
    .Port = txtPort.Text
    .UserName = txtUserName.Text
    .Password = txtPassword.Text
    .Resource = txtResource.Text
    If chkNewAccount.Value = vbChecked Then
        .Connect True
    Else
        .Connect False
    End If
End With
Unload me
```

Notice the `Unload me` at the bottom of the code; you may want to comment this out for the first couple of attempts at connecting with the server. Normally, after you're connected, you don't need the Login Form any more, so you can close it.

In the `Form_Load` of the Login form, you may want to set the `.ServerAddress`, `Port`, and so on. We normally do so for testing purposes, but *remember* later in the development cycle to remove this code. You can easily set these properties by using the following code:

```
txtServer.Text = "openim.myjabber.org"
txtPort.Text = "5222"
txtUserName.Text = "cavedude"
txtResource.Text = "OpenIM"
```

Notice that you don't set the password here, just in case you forget to remove this code later on.

The following list shows the properties to which you're sending data, tells you what you use them for, and provides a description of the `Connect` method for each one:

1. `ServerAddress`: The FQDN (fully qualified domain name) or an IP address to the Jabber server that you want to connect to.

2. `Port`: The port number on which the Jabber server is listening for incoming requests; this number is normally port 5222.

3. `UserName`: The username that you're using to log in to the Jabber server; in the example, it's `cavedude`.

4. `Password`: The password that you use for authentication to the Jabber server. In the example, it's set to `argh`.

5. `Resource`: The Jabber `Resource` is the current resource that you use for the current session. This resource is normally either the client you're using — such as OpenIM — or a location such as Home, Office, Laptop, and so on.

6. `Connect`: The `Connect` method takes a value that's either true or false. If you set the value to true, the Matrix server assumes that you want to create a new account; if false, it logs you in to the Jabber server.

Before you actually connect to the server, you need to add some code to the Disconnect menu item so that you can shut down your connection to the server cleanly. Open the code window for your `MainForm` and enter the following code in the `mnuOpenIM_DisConnect_Click()` event:

```
If cSession.Active Then cSession.Disconnect
```

> **NOTE** The `Active` property of the Matrix COM Library is set to true if you're connected to the Jabber server or false if you're not. This property is read-only. This iproperty should be checked for a `True` value before executing code, which requires an active connection to the development server, such as one resulting from sending a message.

You should now have enough code in place to test a connection to the development server.

Make sure that you save your project and then press F5 to start your project; if all goes well and your code contains no syntax errors, you should see your `MainForm` window. On the menu bar, select Tools ⇨ Debug to open your Debug window. After you open the Debug window, choose OpenIM ⇨ Connect from the window's menu bar. Your Login form should appear. Follow these steps:

1. In the `Server Name` field, enter the FQDN of your development server; if you're using our development server, the name is `openim.myjabber.org`.

2. Set the port to `5222` (unless you set it for something different in your development Jabber server). Port 5222 is the default value for almost all Jabber servers.

3. Enter a user name. (We're using `cavedude` for our user name; make sure that you don't use this name, however, as only one person can log on to a server using the same name.)

4. Enter a password for your user.

5. Enter a resource. (We use `OpenIM`; you can use the same thing or change it to whatever you want.)

6. If you have not created an account on the development server before, make sure that you check the Create a New Account check box.

7. Click Connect.

If everything is set up correctly and you entered all the code that we've discussed, you should now be connected to the development server and your windows should look similar to those in Figure 8-7. Notice the debug information in the Debug window; the XML code that we talked about in Chapter 7 should be visible. The First Line should be the XML to open the stream to the Jabber server. Notice that the stream isn't closed at the bottom of the Debug window; that's because the stream remains open for the duration of the client session with the server. Calling the `DisConnect` method of the Matrix server closes the stream.

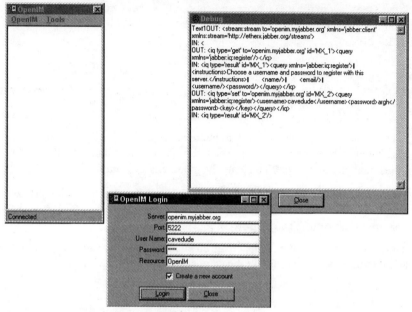

Figure 8-7: Screen view of connected client

It isn't fancy and it doesn't do any more than connect you to the server, but as you can see from the status bar of the main OpenIM window, you're connected! Before long, you can send messages to all your Jabber friends with your own client.

Getting the TreeView Ready for Data

The first thing that you need to do is add an ImageList from the Toolbox to your project. Click the ImageList in the Toolbox and draw it on your form somewhere. Remember that this control doesn't appear onscreen at runtime, so you can place it anywhere on the form. Then just follow these steps:

1. Right-click the ImageList that you put on your form and choose Properties from the pop-up menu. On the General tab of the dialog box that appears, set the size to 16 _ 16. Click the Images tab and pick three icons to represent the states of online, away, and offline. (We use the traffic lights that come with Visual Studio.) Set the `Key` and `Tag` for each one to match the icon, so if it's an Away icon, for example, set the `Key` and `Tag` properties to `Away`.

ON THE CD-ROM We include the graphics that we use for this project in the \openIM\graphics folder on the CD.

2. Pick a graphic to represent the transport/agent icon, and set the `Tag` and `Key` properties to `Transport`.

3. Right-click the TreeView in the `MainForm` and choose Properties from the pop-up menu; on the General tab of the Properties window that appears, set the `Imagelist` property to `imagelist1`.

NOTE A transport/agent is the connection point for other services that may be available on the Jabber server. Examples of transports are AIM, ICQ, Yahoo!, and MSN. You use these transports to connect to the other instant messaging systems.

Now you need to create another module in which to put the code that's specific to the OpenIM project. We prefer a module that includes all the little setup-type routines and any other code specific to the project that you may reuse. To create the module, follow these steps:

1. From the Visual Basic menu bar, select Projects ⇨ Add Module and then click Open after the Add Module screen appears. In the Properties window for the new module, change the `(Name)` property from `Module1` to `mOpenIM`.

2. In the General section of the new module, create an enum to track the value of your new images. The following code listing shows the enums as you should add them:

```
Public Enum eIcons
    ICON_Blank
    ICON_Online
    ICON_Away
    ICON_Offline
    ICON_Transport
End Enum
```

3. After you've added this code, create a new subprocedure to set up the beginning of your TreeView, as follows:

```
Public Sub SetupTreeview()
Dim nodx As Node


    With MainForm.TreeView1
        'Create the top level nodes for our TreeView
        Set nodx = .Nodes.Add(, , "OnLine", "OnLine")
        nodx.Image = eIcons.ICON_Online
        nodx.Bold = True

        Set nodx = .Nodes.Add(, , "OffLine", "OffLine")
        nodx.Image = eIcons.ICON_Offline
        nodx.Bold = True
```

```
        Set nodx = .Nodes.Add(, , "Transport", "Transport")
        nodx.Image = eIcons.ICON_Transport
        nodx.Bold = True

        'set the properties for the TreeView to have it display
        'the way we want it
        .Style = tvwTreelinesPlusMinusPictureText
        .LineStyle = tvwRootLines
        .BorderStyle = ccFixedSingle
        ' reduce the indentation of the trees so it
        ' doesn't take up as much room on the screen
        .Indentation = 250

    End With

End Sub
```

> **NOTE** We don't go into much detail regarding the controls that ship with Visual Basic. We're assuming that you
> know Visual Basic well enough to know how these controls work. If you're unfamiliar with one of the controls that
> we use in this project, we highly recommend that you scan the Help in Visual Basic to get an idea of how they
> work.

As you can see from the preceding code, you're setting the top-level nodes for your TreeView. The first top-level node (online) you use to list any roster users that you've added who are currently online. The second lists any roster users that you've added who aren't currently logged in to the server, and the third lists the transports that are running on the server and whether you're logged in to them.

4. After this code is in place, open the MainForm code window and, in the Form_load sub, add the following line to call the sub as the OpenIM MainForm is loading:

```
SetupTreeview
```

If you run your project, you should see the new top-level nodes in your main window (see Figure 8-8).

Figure 8-8: Window displaying top-level nodes

Now that you have the TreeView set up, you can send some data to it. The first thing that you do is add code to the TreeView for any transports the server has running and also to make it show whether you're logged into it. Follow these steps:

1. Open the code window for the MainForm and, in the
    `cSession_OnAuthorized()` event, type the following code:

```
cSession.FetchAgents
```

This line prompts the Matrix server to browse the development server for any transports it's running. The Matrix server then fires the `cSession_OnAgentBegin` event. You can use this event to initialize any items that are required before you start receiving transport/agent items.

After the Matrix server receives information about an agent, it fires `cSession_OnAgentItem`. `cSession_OnAgentItem` receives a `cAgentItem`. With the information that the `cAgent` item contains, you have enough information to use the agent.

2. In `cSession_OnAgentItem`, add the following code to add to the root node transport in your TreeView any agents that are running on the server:

```
Dim nodx As Node

    Set nodx = TreeView1.Nodes.Add("Transport", tvwChild, Agent.JID,
Agent.Name, eIcons.ICON_Offline)
```

In the code listing above, you can see that you set the key of the node to the JID (Jabber User ID) of the transport for two reasons: to make sure that you don't duplicate any keys (as we note earlier, only one person can log in as a JID at a time) and because you need the JID for later use.

With this code in place, run your project and log in to the development server. Click the little plus sign next to the Transport caption, and six transports should appear in a list under it (see Figure 8-9), assuming that you set up all the transports that we list earlier in the book or are using our development server.

Now you need to add some code to clean up the list on a disconnect. In the General section of the mOpenIM module, insert the following code:

```
Public Sub ResetTreeview()
    'Empty the TreeView
    MainForm.TreeView1.Nodes.Clear
    'now reset our primary nodes
    SetupTreeview

End Sub
```

The preceding code clears all nodes out of the TreeView and then calls the `SetupTreeview` sub to reset the three top-level nodes. After this subprocedure is in place, create a new subprocedure in the General section of the `mUtils` module by using the following code:

```
Public Sub DoDisconnect()
  If MainForm.cSession.Active Then MainForm.cSession.Disconnect
  ResetTreeview
End Sub
```

The `DoDisconnect` subprocedure replaces the code in `mnuOpenIM_DisConnect_Click()`; in this function, delete the code that you put there earlier and replace it with `DoDisconnect`. You need a disconnect in a couple of different places in the code, so for the sake of code reuse, we created the `DoDisconnect` subprocedure.

If you run your project, log in to the development server, and then disconnect from the development server by using the Disconnect menu item on your `MainForm`. The TreeView should return to its original state (refer to Figure 8-8).

After the Matrix server pushes all the transports/agents to your client, the Matrix server fires `cSession_OnAgentEnd`.

Now that the agents are loading into your TreeView, you need to register some of the transports. Transports such as MSN, ICQ, Yahoo!, and AIM require you to enter an account on that server to use the transport. But before you can do so, you need to load your roster list, because you're going to start receiving subscription requests from some of the transports. As an example, if you're using MSN or Yahoo! with one of their clients and you register with the transport on the development server, the server pushes a list of your contacts to you.

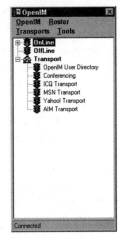

Figure 8-9: Client with agents list

Getting a Roster List

Retrieving your roster list from the server isn't much different from getting your transports/agents. In the `cSession_OnAgentEnd` sub in your `MainForm`, make the following call to the Matrix server:

```
cSession.FetchRoster
```

This line prompts the Matrix server to browse the development server for a list of your personal roster items. The Matrix server then fires the `cSession_OnRosterBegin` event. In OpenIM we do not use this event.

After the Matrix server receives information about a roster item, it fires `cSession_OnRosterItem`. `cSession_OnRosteritem` receives a `cRosterItem` object. The information that you receive from `cRosterItem` contains enough information for you to add a `rosterItem` to your TreeView.

In `cSession_OnRosterItem`, you need to add any roster items to the TreeView, so at this point, you add the roster item to the root node Offline until the Matrix server sends you a `cSession_OnPresence` event for that roster user. The following code shows you how to add the roster items to the TreeView:

```
Dim nodx As Node

If PresItem = MX_RosterItem Then
   'look up the JID in our current TreeView nodes
   item = FindTreeviewNode(TreeView1, RosterItem.JID)
   If item = 0 Then
```

```
    Set nodx = TreeView1.Nodes.Add("OffLine", tvwChild, RosterItem.JID,
RosterItem.nickName, eIcons.ICON_Offline)
  End if
End if
```

Notice the use of `PresItem`. You use this to ensure that you load only the `RosterItems` and not transports/agents into your TreeView in the Offline parent node.

After you receive all the `RosterItems`, the Matrix COM Library fires `cSession_OnRosterEnd`. This is a good place to let everyone know that you're available. You do so by sending your presence to the server. In the `cSession_OnRosterEnd` sub in the `MainForm`, add the following code:

```
cSession.SendPresence "", MX_Available
```

This code sends your presence to the development server so that your status appears as online to the server and to anyone who subscribed to your presence.

Next you need to add some code to the `cSession_OnSubscriptionRequest` sub. The Matrix server fires this event whenever someone wants to subscribe to your presence. `cSession_OnSubscriptionRequest` receives the JID of the person sending the request and the type of request received. At this point, you're interested only in the `MX_Subscribe` subtype.

```
If SubType = MX_Subscribe Then
      If MsgBox(" you have recieved a subscription request from" & _
        vbCrLf & JID & vbCrLf & " accept?", vbYesNo, _
        "Subscription Request") = vbYes Then

          cSession.SendPresence JID, MX_Subscribe_Accept
      Else
          cSession.SendPresence JID, MX_UnSubscribe_Deny
      End If
End If
```

In the preceding code, you're checking to determine whether the subtype is a subscription request and opening a message box to determine whether you want to accept the subscription request from the other user. If you answer Yes in the message box, you send an accept to the request; otherwise, you send a deny.

You also need to subscribe to any `RosterItems` that subscribe to you to see them online. You must create another menu on your `MainForm`, next to the OpenIM menu item, and label it `Roster`. To the second-level Roster menu, add a Presence menu item and then, under it, add Subscribe and Unsubscribe menu items. The following table shows the entries that you need to make. Figure 8-10 shows our current Menu Editor.

Caption	Name	SubMenu
&Roster	mnuRoster	No
Log On	mnuRoster_Presence	Yes
Log Off	mnuRoster_Presence_Subscribe	From Presence, Yes
Properties...	mnuRoster_Presence_UnSubscribe	From Presence, Yes

NOTE The SubMenu column in the table denotes that you should move the SubMenu in one level by pressing the right arrow button on the Menu Editor. The Subscribe and Unsubscribe should be in one more level so that they appear on a submenu of the Presence menu item.

Figure 8-10: Menu Editor displaying Presence menu items

From your `MainForm`, choose Roster ⇨ Presence ⇨ Subscribe. In the code window, enter the following code to send a subscription request to the currently highlighted user in your TreeView. (We've added some debugging code to make sure that you've highlighted a user, but you may want to add more to inform the user of any errors he or she makes.)

```
Private Sub mnuRoster_Presence_Subscribe_Click()
```

```
        If Not TreeView1.SelectedItem.Parent Is Nothing Then
            If TreeView1.SelectedItem.Parent = "OnLine" Or _
                TreeView1.SelectedItem.Parent = "OffLine" Then
                cSession.SendPresence TreeView1.SelectedItem.Key,
MX_Subscribe
            Else
                MsgBox " you must pick a Roster Item from your list first"
            End If
        End If
End Sub
```

You need to check to make sure that the parent node of the child node you've highlighted isn't nothing. This check confirms that you've selected a child node in the TreeView that's either a RosterItem or a transport. Because you want to subscribe only to a RosterItem, you check to determine whether the ParentNode is online or Offline, which confirms that it's a RosterItem. You use the SendPresence method of the Matrix COM Library to send the subscription request to the RosterItem.

The Matrix server fires an event if the person accepts your request and a different one if the person denies your request. In your MainForm code window, add the following code to cSession_OnSubscriptionAccept to open a message box telling you that your subscription is accepted:

```
MsgBox "The Roster User " & JID & "has accepted our subscription
request", vbInformation
```

To open a message box telling you that the subscription is denied, use the following code:

```
MsgBox "The Roster User " & JID & "has denied our subscription request",
vbInformation
```

Now you'll receive visual notification of an accept or deny on a subscription request.

CROSS-REFERENCE Please consult the Matrix documentation in Appendix C for constants that the Matrix COM Library uses.

Next you need to write some code for the cSession_OnPresence event. The Matrix COM Library raises this event any time a change occurs in a RosterItem's presence or a change in presence in one of the agents/transports. The sub receives the following parameters: the JID of the item; a PresItem that holds the type of item from which you're receiving the presence, such as a RosterItem, Agent, Groupchat Item, and so on; an available flag as to whether the item is available or going offline; and a status string that tells you the current status of the item (which, in the case of a RosterItem, may be something such as At Lunch or Gone Home). The cSession_OnPresence event's last parameter receives the raw XML in cases where you want to manipulate the XML yourself.

You now need to create another utility to add to your mUtils module; you use this utility to find a node in a TreeView item.

To help check for items in your TreeView, you add another function to your mUtils module. This function takes two arguments and returns a `long`, which is the index of the node in the TreeView if it's found or 0 if it's not found. Enter the following code to add this function:

```
Public Function FindTreeviewNode(myTreeview As TreeView, sKey As String)
as long
Dim x As Long

    With myTreeview
        For x = 1 To .Nodes.Count
            If UCase(.Nodes.Item(x).Key) = UCase(sKey) Then
                FindTreeviewNode = x
                Exit Function
            End If
        Next x
    End With


End Function
```

Your new function takes two parameters; the first is the TreeView control that you want to search and the second is the key of the TreeView node that you want to find. The function returns a `long`, which is 0 if the node isn't found or the index of the node in the TreeView if it is.

The reason you need this function right now is that, as you may recall, you added all `RosterItems` to the list in the Offline root node and added all the transports/agents to the root node Transports. You must find them in the list to change the presence of the item from online to offline or vice versa. In this case, that means setting the stoplight icon to green for online and red for offline.

Add the following code to `cSession_OnPresence` in the code window of your `MainForm`:

```
Dim nodx As Node
Dim sJID As String
Dim Item As Long
Dim sOldKey As String
Dim sNickName As String

    'look up the JID in our current TreeView nodes
    Item = FindTreeviewNode(TreeView1, JID)
    ' also if the node can't be found then we shouldn't be changing
    ' it anyway
    If Item > 0 Then
        'let's hold onto the Old JID and NickName before removing the
        ' node
```

```
            sOldKey = TreeView1.Nodes.Item(Item).Key
            sNickName = TreeView1.Nodes.Item(Item).Text
            TreeView1.Nodes.Remove (Item)
            If Available = True Then
                'we are interested only in transports/agents and RosterItems
at the moment
                Select Case PresItem
                    Case MX_RosterItem
                        Set nodx = TreeView1.Nodes.Add("OnLine", tvwChild,
sOldKey, sNickName, eIcons.ICON_Online)

                    Case MX_AgentItem
                        Set nodx = TreeView1.Nodes.Add("Transport",
tvwChild, sOldKey, sNickName, eIcons.ICON_Online)
                End Select
            Else
                'we are interested only in transports/agents and RosterItems
at the moment
                Select Case PresItem
                    Case MX_RosterItem
                        Set nodx = TreeView1.Nodes.Add("OffLine", tvwChild,
sOldKey, sNickName, eIcons.ICON_Offline)

                    Case MX_AgentItem
                        Set nodx = TreeView1.Nodes.Add("Transport",
tvwChild, sOldKey, sNickName, eIcons.ICON_Offline)
                End Select

            End If
    End If
```

You can see from the code that the first thing that you need to do is try to find the item in your TreeView that sent its presence. If you find it, you store the JID and the nickname of the TreeView item and delete the node. If not, you ignore it, as you shouldn't be getting presence requests from anything other than what's in your TreeView. You then check to determine whether the item sending presence is available or not; either way, you check to determine whether it's a transport/agent or a `RosterItem`. This way, you can add the node back in under the correct parent node. You then add a new node with the correct parent and the icon for offline or online.

Registering with a Transport/Agent

Agents can be a little tricky to work with at first. To register with an agent, you need to retrieve the registration information from the transport. The Matrix COM Library keeps information on each of the transports, including the necessary registration fields. As you're querying a transport for its registration data, you don't know how many fields it's going to return, so you need to create a form that you can add fields to dynamically, based on the information you receive from the Matrix COM Library.

Add a new form to your project and, in the Properties for the form, change the (Name) property to frmAgentProperties; set the icon property to the same one that you used for the Transport Parent Node in the Treeview; set the BorderStyle property to 1 – Fixed Single and the Caption property to Transport Properties.

Now draw three new command buttons onto the form and place them at the bottom. Change the (Name) property on the first button to cmdRegister and the Caption to Register. Change the (Name) property on the second button to cmdDelete and the Caption to Delete. And finally, on the last button, change the (Name) property to cmdClose and the Caption to Close; also set the Default property on this button to True.

Add a label to the top of the form and make it almost as wide as the form; change the (Name) property to lblName and set the Alignment to 2 – Center and the Caption to Transport. (You dynamically set the caption later, but knowing what it's for helps in designing the form.) Change the font to about a 12-point bold. You use this font to display the name of the transport.

Next, add another label just below the first one and set the (Name) property to lblInstructions. You use this field to display the instructions on how to register with the transports.

Add another label, changing the (Name) property on this one to lblFieldName and setting the Alignment to 1 – Right Justify. Also set the Index property to 0, which enables you to create an array of this label. Each of these labels displays the field name of information that the transport requires.

The last thing that you need is a text box; change the (Name) property to txtFieldValue, and set the Index to 0. You use the text box array to enter the data for the different fields that the transports require.

After you finish, you should have something similar to what appears in Figure 8-11.

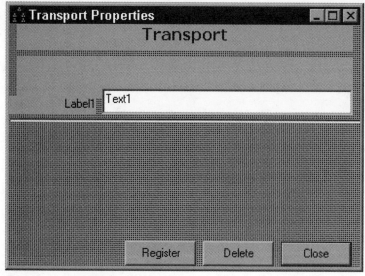

Figure 8-11: Agent form in design mode

Double-click the Close button you put on your `frmAgentProperties` form and, in the code window that appears, add the following code to the `cmdClose_Click` sub:

```
Unload Me
```

You need to add a sub to your form to add the fields that you set up as arrays. You also use this to suppress unwanted transport fields and to adjust the layout of the form to accommodate the fields that you add. Make sure that you set the function to `public` so that it can be called from outside of the form.

```
Public Sub AddField(FieldName As String, FieldValue As String)

    'Here we check if the field name being added is the name field; if
so we don't want it in a text box but rather in the label at the top of
the form

    If FieldName = "name" Then
        lblName.Caption = FieldValue
        Exit Sub
    End If

    'Here we check if the field name being added is the instructions
field; if so we also don't
    'want this to appear in a text box but rather in the label
underneath the name label
    If FieldName = "instructions" Then
        lblInstructions.Caption = FieldValue
```

```
        Exit Sub
    End If

    'These fields we don't need to worry about, so we don't include them
in our form
    If FieldName = "service" Or FieldName = "search" Or FieldName =
"register" Or FieldName = "registered" Or FieldName = "transport" Or
FieldName = "key" Then
        Exit Sub
    End If

    'Load a new instance of txtFieldValue and lblFieldName
    Load txtFieldValue(txtFieldValue.UBound + 1)
    Load lblFieldName(lblFieldName.UBound + 1)

  'if this is a password field, let's set the passwordchar for the
textbox
  ' we don't want to be able to see the passwords in clear text on the
form
    If FieldName = "password" Then
        txtFieldValue(txtFieldValue.UBound).PasswordChar = "*"
    End If

    'Move the newest textbox below the previous one and make it visible
    txtFieldValue(txtFieldValue.UBound).Top =
txtFieldValue(txtFieldValue.UBound - 1).Top +
txtFieldValue(txtFieldValue.UBound).Height + 30
    txtFieldValue(txtFieldValue.UBound).Visible = True
    'Set the value of the text box to the value of the field
    txtFieldValue(txtFieldValue.UBound).Text = FieldValue

    'Move the new instance of lblFieldName below the previous one and
make it visible
    lblFieldName(lblFieldName.UBound).Top =
txtFieldValue(txtFieldValue.UBound).Top +
txtFieldValue(txtFieldValue.UBound).Height / 3
    lblFieldName(lblFieldName.UBound).Visible = True
    'Set the value of the new label to the field value
    lblFieldName(lblFieldName.UBound).Caption = FieldName


    'Move the command buttons below the last field
    cmdClose.Top = txtFieldValue(txtFieldValue.UBound).Top +
txtFieldValue(txtFieldValue.UBound).Height + cmdClose.Height - 100
    cmdDelete.Top = txtFieldValue(txtFieldValue.UBound).Top +
txtFieldValue(txtFieldValue.UBound).Height + cmdDelete.Height - 100
    cmdRegister.Top = txtFieldValue(txtFieldValue.UBound).Top +
txtFieldValue(txtFieldValue.UBound).Height + cmdRegister.Height - 100
```

```
    'Resize the form to accommodate all the new controls on the form to
make sure that they're visible.
    Me.Height = cmdClose.Top + cmdClose.Height + 500
End Sub
```

As you can see, most of the code in this sub deals with resizing and moving the fields around on the form. The code at the beginning of the sub decides what to do with certain fields and suppresses fields that you don't need to display to the end user.

Before you continue any further with the code for this form, you need to add some code to the `MainForm` to display the `frmAgentProperties` form and fill in the labels on the form.

Open the `MainForm`, start the Menu Editor again and add a menu item right after the entries for Roster. Title the new menu item `&Transports`, remembering as you set the name to use `mnuTransports`. Then add three submenu items; the following table shows the caption and name for each of these menu items.

Caption	Name	SubMenu
&Transport	MnuTransport	No
Log On	MnuTransport_LogOn	Yes
Log Off	MnuTransport_LogOff	Yes
-	MnuTransport_Separator	Yes
Properties...	MnuTransport_Properties	Yes

NOTE You use the – entry as a separator; it draws a line across your menu to separate a menu item from others.

You should be able to right-click the transports as well, so in the `TreeView1_MouseUp` event of your `MainForm`, add the following code:

```
    'If mouse button clicked was the right button
    If Button = vbRightButton Then
        'show the Transport menu
        PopupMenu mnuTransport
    End If
```

This code checks to determine whether you clicked the right mouse button, and if so, it displays the menu for the transports that you created in the table above by using the Menu Editor.

Now you need to add the code to open the new Transport Property form that you created and view the registration information for that transport. You put the code in the `mnuTransports_Properties_Click` sub, which is called any time the user clicks the Properties submenu for the Transports menu.

```
Dim fnd As Integer
Dim itm As Variant

    'Make sure the item clicked is a child of the transport node
    If TreeView1.SelectedItem.Parent.Text = "Transport" Then
        Load frmAgentProperties
        frmAgentProperties.Tag = TreeView1.SelectedItem.Key
        'Search for the agent with the JID of the selected item and give
us
        'the reference # in the agents collection of that agent
        fnd = cSession.FindAgent(TreeView1.SelectedItem.Key)

        'Loop through the fields collection that makes up this agent
that
        'we want to include on the form
        For Each itm In cSession.Agents(fnd).Fields
            'Call the function AddField to add a new field with the
values
            'from the current field
            frmAgentProperties.AddField itm.Name, itm.Value
        Next
        frmAgentProperties.Show
    End If
```

Before you actually work with the form, you want to check to make sure that the parent node of the TreeView is Transport. Doing so ensures that you're working with a transport/agent and not a rosteritem. If it's a transport, you load your new `frmAgentProperties` form and set the `tag` of the form to the JID (Jabber ID) of the transport. You set this tag so that you can use it from the form later to delete or register with the transport. Next, you call the `cSession.FindAgent` method to query the Matrix COM Library for information about the transport. Then you cycle through each of the fields that the transport requires for registration; for each field, you call the `AddField` sub that you created in the `frmAgentsProperties` form. After you add all the fields, you display the `frmAgentProperties` form. Figure 8-12 shows an example of the transport form after it loads with the information for the ICQ transport.

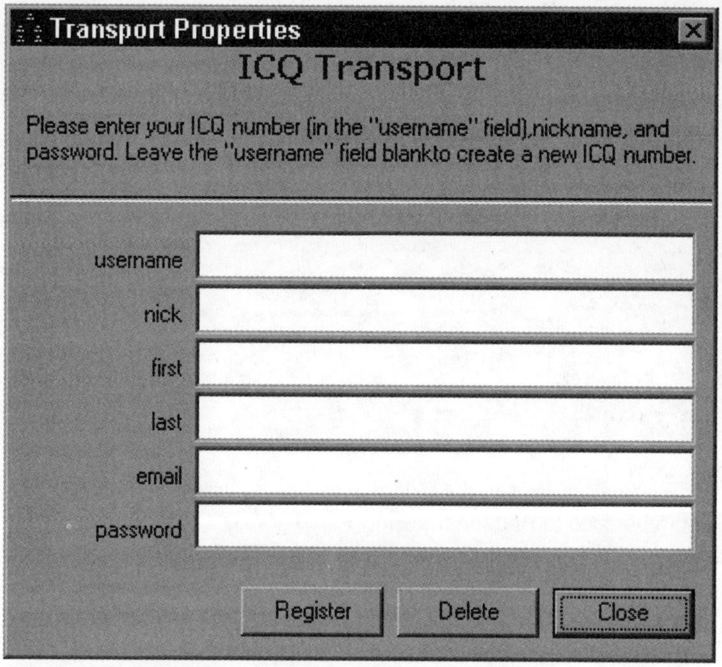

Figure 8-12: Transport Properties with ICQ Transport information

In the design view of Visual Basic, open `frmAgentsProperties` and double-click the Register button. You must add the code to register with the transport. In the `cmdRegister_Click` sub, enter the following code:

```
Dim fnd As Integer
    Dim fnd2 As Integer
    Dim Counter As Integer

    'Basically this loops through all the labels (which represent
required
    'fields from the agent for registration) and submits the values
entered
    'to the agent itself, then calls the update function of the agent to
send off
    'the registration

    'Find the agent we are currently modifying and wish to register
    fnd = MainForm.cSession.FindAgent(Me.Tag)

    'If found we continue with the registration
    If fnd > 0 Then
```

```
            'Loop through all the labels and find the associated field
inside the agent
        For Counter = 0 To lblFieldName.Count - 1
            fnd2 =
MainForm.cSession.Agents(fnd).FindField(lblFieldName(Counter).Caption)
            'If found we set the value found in the agent to the value
in the text box
            If fnd2 > 0 Then
                MainForm.cSession.Agents(fnd).Fields(fnd2).Value =
txtFieldValue(Counter).Text
            End If
        Next
    End If

    'Call update function of agent to send off the registration request
    MainForm.cSession.Agents(fnd).Update
```

When you set the labels earlier, you set them to the field names that the transport needs return to it for a registration. Again, you need to find the transport in the Matrix COM Library so that you're sure that you're dealing with the right transport. You use the JID that you stored earlier to find it in the Matrix Transport List. After you find the transport in the list, you can cycle through each of your fields and find the corresponding field in the properties of the agent in the Matrix COM Library. As you find them, you set the value of the properties to the values that you entered on the `frmAgentsProperties` form. After you set all the values that you need, you call the `update` method of `cSession.Agents` to get the Matrix COM Library to push the information back to the transport running on the development server.

> **NOTE** Although some of the transports enable you to register a new user, we recommend that you register by using the client that was designed for the transport, such as the ICQ client, MSN Messenger, and so on. (Assuming that you don't already have an account set up with them.)

To see how this code all works, run your project from Visual Basic and log in to the development server. Remember to open your Debug window so that you can see any XML that's passing between the Matrix COM Library and your development Jabber server. Open the Transport Treeview list by pressing the + sign next to it in the window. You should see a list of agents. Right-click the ICQ Transport and click Properties on the pop-up menu that appears. A form similar to the one shown in Figure 8-12 should appear. You can see from the directions at the top of your Transport Properties form that you need to enter the UIN (ICQ number) in the username field and enter a password for our account. You also see in the instructions that, if you leave the username field blank, doing so creates a new account. (We've had only partial success with this, and as mentioned previously, we recommend that you create an account before using the transport.)

Fill in your ICQ number in the `username` field and enter in the `password` field the password that you used as you created your account; notice that the `password` field is acting like a true `password` field in that it's masking the input. As you may recall, we requested the masking of the password in creating the `AddField` earlier in the chapter.

Now click the Register button, and if all goes well, you should receive a subscription request from the transport. After you receive the request and answer Yes, the stoplight icon should change from red to green to indicate that the transport is now online.

Go ahead and register with the rest of the transports; you should notice that each transport uses different fields than the others. One of the benefits of the Jabber server is that each transport can explain its properties to the client through standard XML code. Although it requires a little more work on the client side, the overall goal is very well defined. If you add a new transport to the server, the client shouldn't require any additional coding for you to use it.

Remember that, as we mention earlier, MSN and Yahoo! both store your list of contacts on the server, so if you register with these transports, you receive subscription requests from anyone that's on your contact list.

Summary

In this chapter, we showed you how to create your basic instant messaging client, enabling you to register with transports/agents, receive subscription requests from other instant messaging users and view whether the users are online or offline. In the next chapter, you begin communicating with other IM users and finish up some extra goodies with the `RosterItem`.

In upcoming chapters, you add more functionality to the `RosterItem`, adding messages and chats. This is really just the base of the client, and as we said earlier, we recommend that you add much more error checking to the code. (For the sake of keeping the code listings focused on the Jabber connection and messages, we've left most of the error handling out in this chapter.)

Chapter 9

More on RosterItems

In This Chapter

♦ Resource usage

♦ Viewing properties for a RosterItem

♦ Updating a RosterItem

♦ Adding a RosterItem

♦ Deleting a RosterItem

♦ Searching for a user

In this chapter, we show you how to write the code to view a RosterItem's properties and add, update items, and delete RosterItems from your roster. We then describe how you can create a form and use the transport search facilities (if available) to search for a user on the transport that you request.

ON THE CD-ROM You can find the code for this chapter on the CD-ROM in the \openIM\chapter09 folder. This code also includes the code from Chapter 8.

Resource Usage

As you may know, a resource is added to the end of the JID whenever the Matrix COM Library sends an OnPresence event to it. When you receive your list of roster users from OnRosterItem, you receive it without a resource, but after that, you receive it with a resource. As we mention earlier in the book, a resource can be a place or perhaps the name of the client you're currently using. We normally use the name of the client; whether people know we are at work or at home doesn't matter to us, although it may be important to you.

We're now going to show you how to create a new function that removes the resource from the JID so that you can find the roster user in your Offline parent node. Follow these steps:

1. Open the mOpenIM module and add the following code to the module:

```
Public Function RemoveResource(JID As String) As String
Dim lBegPos
```

```
    lBegPos = InStr(1, JID, "/", vbTextCompare)
    If lBegPos > 0 Then
        RemoveResource = Left(JID, lBegPos - 1)
    Else
        RemoveResource = JID
    End If

End Function
```

You use the Visual Basic `Instr` function to check the full JID for the presence of a `/`; if it exists, anything past that is a resource, and you remove both the resource and the `/`.

2. In your code for the `MainForm`, go to the `cSession_OnPresence` event and make the changes shown in the following code. (We've indicated which lines have been added, removed, or changed.)

```
Private Sub cSession_OnPresence(ByVal JID As String, PresItem As
MatrixServer.eItemType, ByVal Available As Boolean, ByVal Status As
String, ByVal XML_Node As MatrixServer.cXML_Node)
Dim nodx As Node
Dim sJID As String
Dim item As Long
Dim sOldKey As String
Dim sNickName As String
*ADDED Dim JIDNoResource As String

    *ADDED ' remove the resource to see if they are in our list
    *ADDED JIDNoResource = RemoveResource(JID)
    'look up the JID in our current treeview nodes
    *CHANGED item = FindTreeviewNode(TreeView1, JIDNoResource)
    *ADDED If item = 0 Then
    *ADDED     item = FindTreeviewNode(TreeView1, JID)
    *ADDED End If
    ' if the node can't be found, we shouldn't be changing
    ' it anyway
    If item > 0 Then
        'let's hold onto the old JID and NickName before removing the
        ' Node
        *REMOVED 'sOldKey = TreeView1.Nodes.item(item).Key
        sNickName = TreeView1.Nodes.item(item).Text
        TreeView1.Nodes.Remove (item)
        If Available = True Then
```

```
                    'we are interested only in transports/agents and
rosteritems at the moment
            Select Case PresItem
                Case MX_RosterItem
                    *CHANGED  Set nodx = TreeView1.Nodes.Add("OnLine",
tvwChild, JID, sNickName, eIcons.ICON_Online)

                Case MX_AgentItem
                    *CHANGED  Set nodx = TreeView1.Nodes.Add("Transport",
tvwChild, JID, sNickName, eIcons.ICON_Online)
            End Select
        Else
            'we are interested only in transports/agents and roster
items at the moment
            ' take the resource off the JID when storing in the offline
parent node
            ' in case the user logs back in under a different resource
            *ADDED  JIDNoResource = RemoveResource(JID)
            Select Case PresItem
                Case MX_RosterItem
            *CHANGED        Set nodx = TreeView1.Nodes.Add("OffLine",
tvwChild, JIDNoResource, sNickName, eIcons.ICON_Offline)

                Case MX_AgentItem
            *CHANGED        Set nodx = TreeView1.Nodes.Add("Transport",
tvwChild, JIDNoResource, sNickName, eIcons.ICON_Offline)
                End Select

        End If
    End If
End Sub
```

We've added a call to our new `RemoveResource` function and used the JID that returned to
determine whether the `RosterItem` was already in the TreeView. If not, we check the
TreeView nodes with the resource still attached to the JID. Now, instead of using the `OldKey`
value that may or may not have contained the resource, we use the JID that passed in to the
`OnPresence` function. If the `RosterItem` is going Offline, we remove the JID so that it's
the same as it was when the `OnRosterItem` event added it. That way, if the roster user logs
back in under another resource, we can still find the JID in the Offline list.

NOTE In testing changes that we've made to a client app, we normally use another client (in our case,
myJabber), create a second account, and subscribe to ourselves in the new client. This procedure enables us to
test without needing a roster user online to test with.

You can test the preceding code by logging in with your client and account and then logging in with OpenIM and going on and offline with your test account and your other client. You see the RosterItem moving from the offline to the online parent node in the TreeView.

Viewing Properties for a RosterItem

One of the things that we like to do whenever we receive a request for subscription or add a RosterItem is to give it a NickName that makes more sense than the JID. To do so, we need the capability to view the properties for the RosterItem and to edit the NickName. We also want the capability to view the information that the presence status stores.

To create these capabilities, you need to start by creating a new form; follow these steps:

1. Change the (name) property from Form1 to frmRosterProperties and the Caption to Roster Properties. Make sure you set the BorderStyle property to 1 - Fixed Single unless you want to deal with having to resize the form.

2. Add two buttons to your form; set the (Name) property of the first one to cmdUpdate and set the Caption to &Update; set the Default property of this button to True. For the second button, set the (Name) property to cmdClose and the Caption to &Close.

3. Add four labels. The following table shows the properties for these labels. (We use an array for labels, so we put one label on the form, set the Alignment property, and then copy and paste the label, as we do in Chapter 8. This action saves us from having to set the Alignment property for each label.)

Label Index	Alignment	Caption
0	1 - Right Justify	JID
1	1 - Right Justify	NickName
2	1 - Right Justify	Status
3	1 - Right Justify	ShowType

4. After you add these labels, add another label next to the JID label, set the (Name) property to lblJID and the BorderStyle property to 1 - Fixed Single, and clear the Caption property. Create another label next to the Status label and set the (Name) property to lblStatus and the BorderStyle property to 1 - Fixed Single, and clear the Caption property. And finally, add one more label next to the ShowType label. Set the (Name) property to lblShowType and the BorderStyle property to 1 - Fixed Single, and clear the Caption property.

5. Create a text box next to the NickName label, set the (Name) property to txtNickName, and clear the text property.

After you finish, you should have a form similar to that shown in Figure 9-1.

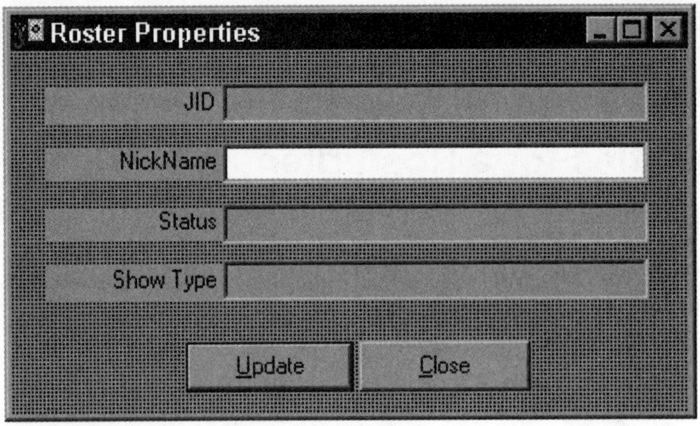

Figure 9-1: Design view of Roster Properties form

6. Double-click the Close button and add the following code to the `cmdClose_Click()` sub:

```
Unload Me
```

7. You need to add a new menu item to the Roster menu on the `MainForm` to display your Roster Properties form. Follow the same procedures that we use in Chapter 8 to add the new menu item, making sure that you set the `Caption` to `&Properties` and the `Name` to `mnuRoster_Properties`. We also add a separator between the Presence and Properties menu items to break up the menu a bit for easier reading.

8. In the `MnuRoster_Properties_Click` sub of the `MainForm`, add the following code:

```
Dim lRosterItmIndex As Long
Dim lPresItm As Long
Dim JIDNoResource As String

    'Make sure the item clicked is a child of the Transport node
    If TreeView1.SelectedItem.Parent.Text = "OnLine" Or _
    TreeView1.SelectedItem.Parent.Text = "OffLine" Then

        ' remove the resource to see if they are in our list
        JIDNoResource = RemoveResource(TreeView1.SelectedItem.Key)

        ' find the Roster Item in the csession RosterItem collection
        lRosterItmIndex = cSession.FindRosterItem(JIDNoResource)
        If lRosterItmIndex > 0 Then
            With frmRosterProperties
```

```
                .lblJID = cSession.Roster(lRosterItmIndex).JID
                .txtNickName =
cSession.Roster(lRosterItmIndex).nickname
                'find the presence item for this Roster Item
                lPresItm =
cSession.FindPresence(TreeView1.SelectedItem.Key)
                If lPresItm > 0 Then
                    .lblStatus = cSession.Presence(lPresItm).Status
                    ' convert the Showtype enum into a readable form
                    Select Case cSession.Presence(lPresItm).Showtype
                        Case eShowType.MX_None
                            .lblShowType = ""
                        Case eShowType.MX_Away
                            .lblShowType = "Away"
                        Case eShowType.MX_chat
                            .lblShowType = "Available for Chat"
                        Case eShowType.MX_ExtendedAway
                            .lblShowType = "Extended Away"
                        Case eShowType.MX_DND
                            .lblShowType = "Do Not Disturb"
                    End Select
                End If
                ' show the Roster Properties form
                .Show
            End With
        End If
End If
```

The first thing you do is make sure that the item highlighted in the TreeView is a child of either the OnLine or OffLine parent node. If it is, remove the resource from the JID and find the RosterItem in the cSession.Roster collection. After you find it, set the lblJID on the Roster Properties form to the JID of the RosterItem and the lblNickName to the NickName of the RosterItem.

9. Find the PresenceItem for the currently selected RosterItem in the csession.Presence collection; if you find one, set lblStatus to the status of the RosterItem and lblShowType to the ShowType property of the RosterItem. Notice that on the ShowType we convert the enum to a human-readable string.

10. After you set up all the variables in the previous step, you display the Roster Properties form. Figure 9-2 shows an example of the information for cavegal.

Roster Properties

JID	cavegal@openim.myjabber.org
NickName	cavegal@openim.myjabber.org
Status	I Stepped away for a minute, Be Right Back!
Show Type	Away

Update   Close

Figure 9-2: Example Roster Properties form

Updating a RosterItem

Now that you can display the information, you need to add code to cmdUpdate_Click on the frmRosterProperties form to enable users to update the NickName.

The basic idea is to enable the user to enter a new NickName, find the RosterItem in the csession.Roster collection, and send an update request back to the Matrix COM Library for that item; the Matrix COM Library then sends a request to the Jabber server to update your personal XML file with the new information. Then you update the TreeView to show the new NickName. The following code shows how to update the TreeView:

```
Dim lRosterItmIndex As Long
Dim lIndex As Long
Dim tvNode As Node

    With MainForm
        lRosterItmIndex = .cSession.FindRosterItem(lblJID.Caption)
        If lRosterItmIndex > 0 Then
            .cSession.Roster(lRosterItmIndex).nickname =
txtNickName.Text
            .cSession.Roster(lRosterItmIndex).Update
        End If
        ' find this node in the treeview
        ' don't assume the same node is highlighted as when we loaded
this form
        lIndex = FindTreeviewNode(.TreeView1, lblJID.Caption)
        If lIndex > 0 Then
            Set tvNode = .TreeView1.Nodes(lIndex)
            tvNode.Text = txtNickName.Text
```

```
        End If
    End With
    Unload Me
```

At this point, you should probably revise the `TreeView1_MouseUp` sub in the `MainForm` so that a user can right-click a `RosterItem` and open the Roster menu. Rather than show you the changes you need to make, we recommend that you just enter the following code. (Notice that we check the parent node to see which pop-up to display. Checking the parent node also stops the pop-ups from appearing on the parent nodes.)

```
'If mouse button pressed was the right button
    If Button = vbRightButton Then
        If Not TreeView1.SelectedItem.Parent Is Nothing Then
            If TreeView1.SelectedItem.Parent.Text = "Transport" Then
                'show the Transport menu
                PopupMenu mnuTransports
            ElseIf TreeView1.SelectedItem.Parent.Text = "OnLine" Or _
                TreeView1.SelectedItem.Parent.Text = "OffLine" Then
                'show the Transport menu
                PopupMenu mnuRoster
            End If
        End If
    End If
```

Adding a RosterItem

Now you can view properties for a `RosterItem`. How do you add someone to your roster? If you're adding someone who is a Jabber user, this procedure is pretty easy. You can also add users from the different transports (MSN Messenger, AIM, and so on).

This task requires you to ask the user which transport to use to add the `RosterItem`. As before, because you may need a drop-down list to display the agents/transports, you will want to create a reusable function to do the job. In the mOpenIM module, add the following sub:

```
Public Sub FillTransportCombo(myCombo As ComboBox)
Dim iAgentCount As Integer
Dim x As Integer

    iAgentCount = MainForm.cSession.Agents.Count
    For x = 1 To iAgentCount
        myCombo.AddItem MainForm.cSession.Agents.item(x).Name
    Next x

    If MainForm.cSession.Agents.Count > 0 Then myCombo.ListIndex = 0

End Sub
```

All you're doing is retrieving the list of agents from the Matrix COM Library and adding the agents to the combo box. Later, you can use the `ListIndex` property of the combo box to retrieve information about the agent.

To create a form to add a `RosterItem`, follow these steps:

1. Change the `(name)` property from `Form1` to `frmAddRosterItem` and the `Caption` to `Add Roster Item`. Again, make sure you set the `BorderStyle` property to `1 - Fixed Single` so that you don't need to deal with form resizing. (We set the `Icon` to the same one that we used for the `MainForm`. It's `OpenIM.ico`, which you find in the \OpenIM\Chapter09\graphics directory on the CD-ROM.)

2. Add the labels as per the following table.

Label Index	Alignment	Caption
0	1 - Right Justify	Transport
1	1 - Right Justify	JID
2	1 - Right Justify	NickName

3. Next to the label with the caption `Transport`, add a combo box. Set the `(Name)` property to `cboTransport` and the `Style` property to `2 - Dropdown List`. Next, add a text box beside the JID label and change the `(Name)` property to `txtJID`; you may also want to clear the `text` property. Add another text box next to the NickName label, change the `(Name)` property to `txtNickName`, and clear the `text` property of this text box as well.

4. Add two command buttons to the bottom of the form. For the first command button, set the `(Name)` property to `cmdADD` and the `Caption` to `&ADD`; for the second command button, change the `(Name)` property to `cmdClose` and the `Caption` to `&Close`. You may also want to set the `Default` property to `True` on the `cmdAdd` command button.

   After you complete the preceding steps, you should have a form similar to the one shown in Figure 9-3.

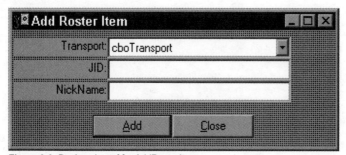

Figure 9-3: Design view of frmAddRosterItem

5. In the `cmdClose_Click` sub in the code window for `frmAddRosterItem`, enter the following code to close the form if the Close button is clicked:

```
unload me
```

6. In the `Form_Load` sub, add a call to your new function to fill the combo box; notice that we supply the combo box as a parameter when we call `FillTransportCombo` so that you can reuse this function in other places in your client.

```
FillTransportCombo cboTransport
```

7. Now you need a way to display your new form. Use the Visual Basic Menu Editor to add a new entry under the Roster menu, changing the `caption` to `Add` and the `Name` to `mnuRoster_Add`. View the code for the `MainForm` and in the `mnuRoster_Add_Click`.

8. Add the following code to display the new `frmAddRosterItem` form:

```
'make sure we have logged in first
If cSession.Active Then
    frmAddRosterItem.Show
End If
```

Notice that we check to make sure we have an active connection with the Jabber server — without an active connection, the Add Roster User form doesn't work, so we don't open the form unless we do have an active connection.

You need to create another public sub to parse the JID from the server. The idea is that `JID@myserver.com` breaks up into `JID` and `myserver.com`, removing the `@`. You'll find this sub quite handy as you develop the client further. Follow these steps:

1. Open the mOpenIM module and create the following sub:

```
Public Sub ParseJID(sJID As String, sUserName As String, sServer As
String)
Dim lMyPos As Long

    If sJID > "" Then
        lMyPos = InStr(1, sJID, "@", vbTextCompare)
        If lMyPos > 0 Then
            sUserName = Left(sJID, lMyPos - 1)
            sServer = Mid(sJID, lMyPos + 1, Len(sJID) - lMyPos)
        Else
            sUserName = sJID
        End If
    End If
```

```
End Sub
```

The sub takes three arguments: The first is the complete JID; the second is the variable that returns the username part of the JID; and the third is the variable that returns the server name part of the JID.

2. Open the code window for `frmAddRosterItem` and, in `cmdAdd_Click`, add the following code:

```
Dim tmpRosterItem As cRosterItem
Dim lRosterItmIndex As Long
Dim sUserName As String
Dim sServer As String

    Set tmpRosterItem = New cRosterItem
    ' make sure we have a JID to ADD
    If txtJID.Text > "" Then
        ParseJID txtJID.Text, sUserName, sServer
        With MainForm
            ' create a new Roster Item
            .cSession.CreateRosterItem tmpRosterItem
            ' if it's a Jabber ID, just add as is
            If cboTransport.ListIndex = 0 Then
                ' make sure they added a server in the JID
                If sServer = "" Then
                    'if not, assume they are on our server
                    sServer = .cSession.ServerAddress
                End If
                tmpRosterItem.JID = sUserName & "@" & sServer
            Else
                'if it's another transport change the @ to %
                'and add the transport onto the ID
                tmpRosterItem.JID = Replace(txtJID.Text, "@", "%") &
"@" & .cSession.Agents(cboTransport.ListIndex + 1).JID
            End If
            ' if nickname is blank set it to JID
            If txtNickName.Text = "" Then
                tmpRosterItem.NickName = txtJID.Text
            Else
                tmpRosterItem.NickName = txtNickName.Text
            End If
            ' Add the Roster Item to the List
            .cSession.Roster.Add tmpRosterItem, tmpRosterItem.JID
            'Find the index for the new roster Item
```

```
            lRosterItmIndex =
.cSession.FindRosterItem(tmpRosterItem.JID)
            If lRosterItmIndex > 0 Then
                ' found it, so update it in our roster list
                .cSession.Roster(lRosterItmIndex).Update
                ' now send a presence request so we subscribe to them
                .cSession.SendPresence tmpRosterItem.JID, MX_Subscribe
            End If

        End With

    End If
```

Now to discuss the code and what it's doing: The first thing you do is create a new cRosterItem object to hold the information for your new RosterItem. You then check to make sure that the user has put a JID into the txtJID field. (Without a JID, you can't add a new RosterItem.) The next step is to call your new ParseJID sub so that you can determine whether the user has entered both a username and a server name. You then use your cSession object to create a new RosterItem. You need to determine whether the transport you're going to register the user with is the Jabber User Database or one of the other transports. (We deal with the JUD first.)

You check to determine whether sServerName is empty, and, if it is, you decide for the user that he's trying to add a user on the same server that he's connected to. If the sServer variable is empty, you assign cSession.ServerAddress, which is the client's server. After you make sure that you've set up a server, you concatenate the sUsername variable and the sServerName variable, making sure that you add the @ between the two.

What if it's one of the other transports, such as ICQ's or MSN Messenger's? The JID is a little different for these transports. In the case of MSN Messenger, a completed JID looks something like the following example: *username*%hotmail.com@msn.openim.myjabber.org.

Notice that the Hotmail address has the @ changed to a percent sign, and the transport address is added on the end with an @. The Jabber server parses the JID at the @ so that it knows what transport to send the request to; after it's done that, in the case of this MSN Messenger example, the MSN-t or MSN Transport takes the percent sign and changes it back to an @ to deliver the message to the Hotmail account.

As users normally add a new RosterItem as *username*@hotmail.com, you must take the precaution of changing any @ in the JID to %. Then you add the transport to the end, making sure that you add a @ between the two again. As we mentioned earlier in this section, you use the combo box ListIndex property to get the right transport JID from the Agents Collection on the Matrix COM server.

You should now have a correct JID, either for a JUD or for one of the other transports.

The next thing you do is to determine whether the client user entered a NickName; if not, you set the NickName to the JID. At this point, you could parse off the username and set the NickName to the username, but we leave that as an exercise for you.

After you set those pieces of data, you send an update to the `RosterItem` to update your roster on the server. Then you send a subscription request to that user.

Figure 9-4 shows an example of the Add Roster Item window in action.

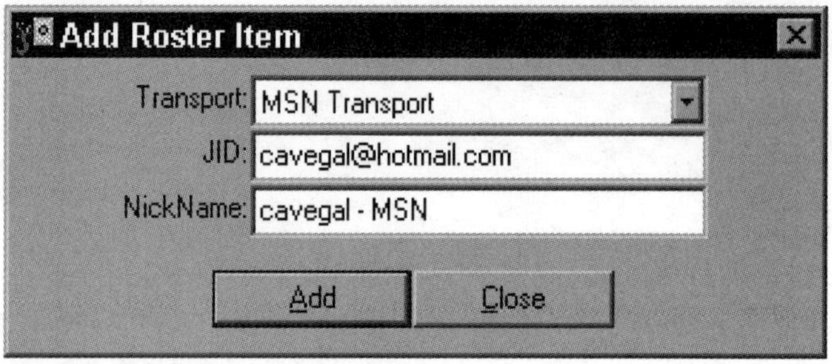

Figure 9-4: Add Roster Item window

Deleting a RosterItem

Say you've added someone to your roster and now you want that person off your list. Deleting `RosterItems` is a pretty simple process. Basically, you want them removed from your TreeView and from your `RosterList` on the server.

1. Use the Visual Basic Menu Editor on the `MainForm` to add a new entry to your Roster menu; change the `Caption` to `Remove` and the `Name` to `mnuRoster_Remove`.

2. In the `MainForm` Code window, move to the `mnuRoster_Remove_Click` sub and enter the following code:

```
Dim lRosterItmIndex As Long

    If Not TreeView1.SelectedItem.Parent Is Nothing Then
        If TreeView1.SelectedItem.Parent = "OnLine" Or _
            TreeView1.SelectedItem.Parent = "OffLine" Then
            If MsgBox("Do you really want to delete " &
TreeView1.SelectedItem.Text & " ?", vbYesNo) = vbYes Then
                lRosterItmIndex =
cSession.FindRosterItem(RemoveResource(TreeView1.SelectedItem.Key))
                If lRosterItmIndex > 0 Then
                    cSession.Roster(lRosterItmIndex).subscription =
MX_Remove
                    cSession.Roster(lRosterItmIndex).Update
                End If
```

```
            TreeView1.Nodes.Remove TreeView1.SelectedItem.Index
        End If
    Else
        MsgBox " You must pick a Roster Item from your list first"
    End If
End If
```

As always, check to make sure that the node you highlighted is actually a roster node.

3. Open a message box to make sure that the user really wants to delete that `RosterItem` (better safe than sorry). If the user clicks the Yes button on the message box, you find the `RosterItem` in the roster collection of the Matrix server, set the subscription to `MX_Remove`, and update the `RosterItem` by using the `Update` event. Setting the `RosterItem`'s `Subscription` property to `MX_Remove` prompts the Matrix COM server to send the `Remove` to the Jabber server, removing it from your roster. After you do so, you remove the item from the TreeView, and — voilà! — the delete is complete.

Searching for Users

With most transports, you can search for users. In the case of Jabber, the search looks at the JUD (Jabber User Database). This database may be a local one or it may be the main JUD running at Jabber.org. In the case of the transports that enable us to search, the database of that transport is searched. In the case of ICQ, a request is sent to the user database on the ICQ server that AOL runs.

> **NOTE** Some transports have the capability to search for users and others don't. As of the writing of this book, you can search the JUD and ICQ. This situation may change as more functionality is added to any of the transports.

Begin by adding a new form to your project; follow these steps:

1. Change the (name) property of the form to `frmSearch`, the caption to `Search` and, again, the `BorderStyle` property to `1 - Fixed Single` so the form doesn't resize. Change the `icon` property to the search icon that we include in the \graphics directory on the CD-ROM.

   The following table lists the buttons to add to your form and the property values that you need to set.

(name)	Caption	Default
cmdSearch	Search	True
cmdClear	Clear	False
cmdClose	Close	False

You use the Search Form labels and text boxes in the same fashion as you do the `frmAgentProperties` form. The information that returns from the agent dynamically creates and fills the labels.

2. As you do with the `frmAddRosterItem` form, you need to add a combo box to this form to list the available transports. Add a label to your form and change the `Caption` property to `Transport`, and set the `Alignment` property to `1 - Align Right`. Next to the label with the caption `Transport`, add a combo box. Set the `(Name)` property to `cboTransport` and the `Style` property to `2 - Dropdown List`.

3. Add a label and set the `(name)` property to `lblInstructions`. You use this field to show the instructions on how to search by using the transport.

4. Add another label, changing the `(name)` property to `lblFieldName` and setting the `Alignment` property to `1 - Right Justify`. Also set the `Index` property to `0`, which enables you to create an array of this label. Each of these labels displays the field name of information the transport requires.

5. Add a text box, changing the `(Name)` property to `txtFieldValue` and setting the `Index` to `0`. You use the text box array to enter the data that's searchable on the transport.

6. Add a ListView to the form as a place to display your search results. Change the `(Name)` property to `lvSearchResults` and the `View` property to `3 - lvwReport`. Set the `FullRowSelect` property to `True` and the `labeledit` property to `1 - lvwManual`.

After you complete these steps, you should see a form similar to that shown in Figure 9-5.

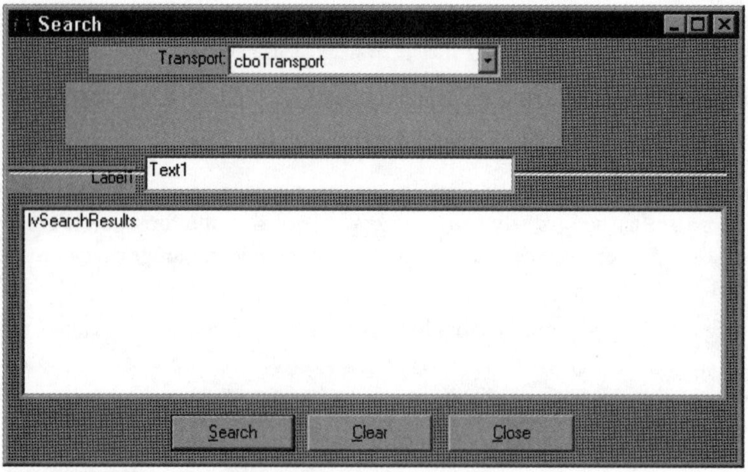

Figure 9-5: Design view of Search Form

7. In the `Form_Load` sub of the code window in your `frmSearch` form, add the following code:

```
'fill the combo box with a list of transports
    FillTransportCombo cboTransport
```

Notice that we use the subprocedure that you wrote in the previous section to fill the combo box with a list of the transports/agents.

8. You need to add the following code in cboTransport_Click to get the search fields you want. Call the GetSearchFields method of the agent in the Matrix server to have it return a list of the search fields available for the server/transport. After the Matrix server receives a list of the fields from the Jabber server, it fires the cSession.OnSearchFields event.

```
' send a request to the matrix server to return the search fields
MainForm.cSession.Agents(cboTransport.ListIndex + 1).GetSearchFields
```

In cmdClose_Click, add the following code:

```
Unload me
```

In the code window, add the following subprocedure:

```
Public Sub AddField(FieldName As String, FieldValue As String)

    'Here we check if the field name being added is the instructions
field; if so, we don't
    'want this to appear in a text box but rather in the label
underneath the Name label
    If FieldName = "instructions" Then
        lblInstructions.Caption = FieldValue
        Exit Sub
    End If


    'These fields we don't need to worry about so we don't include them
in our form
    If FieldName = "service" Or FieldName = "search" Or FieldName =
"register" Or FieldName = "registered" Or FieldName = "transport" Or
FieldName = "key" Then
        Exit Sub
    End If

    'Load a new instance of txtFieldValue and lblFieldName
    Load txtFieldValue(txtFieldValue.UBound + 1)
    Load lblFieldName(lblFieldName.UBound + 1)
```

```
    'Move the newest text box below the previous one and make it
visible
    txtFieldValue(txtFieldValue.UBound).Top =
txtFieldValue(txtFieldValue.UBound - 1).Top +
txtFieldValue(txtFieldValue.UBound).Height + 30
    txtFieldValue(txtFieldValue.UBound).Visible = True
    'Set the value of the text box to the value of the field
    txtFieldValue(txtFieldValue.UBound).Text = FieldValue

    'Move the new instance of lblFieldName below the previous one and
make it visible
    lblFieldName(lblFieldName.UBound).Top =
txtFieldValue(txtFieldValue.UBound).Top +
txtFieldValue(txtFieldValue.UBound).Height / 3
    lblFieldName(lblFieldName.UBound).Visible = True
    'Set the value of the new label to the field value
    lblFieldName(lblFieldName.UBound).Caption = FieldName

    'Move the listview below the fields
    lvSearchResults.Top = txtFieldValue(txtFieldValue.UBound).Top +
txtFieldValue(txtFieldValue.UBound).Height + cmdClose.Height - 100
    'Move the command buttons below the Listview
    cmdClose.Top = lvSearchResults.Top + lvSearchResults.Height +
cmdClose.Height - 100
    cmdSearch.Top = lvSearchResults.Top + lvSearchResults.Height +
cmdSearch.Height - 100
    cmdClear.Top = lvSearchResults.Top + lvSearchResults.Height +
cmdClear.Height - 100

    'Resize the form to accommodate all the new controls on the form to
make sure they're visible.
    Me.Height = cmdClose.Top + cmdClose.Height + 500
End Sub
```

You need this function to populate the `frmSearch` form with the fields that you can use to search for a user. This code is much the same as the code you use in the `frmAgentProperties` form.

9.   In the `cmdClear_Click()` sub, add the following code:

```
    ' clear any values that were entered in the search form so we can
start over.
    For x = 1 To frmSearch.txtFieldValue.UBound
        frmSearch.txtFieldValue(x).Text = ""
```

```
Next x
' clear the search list view
lvSearchResults.ListItems.Clear
' clear the column heads of the list view
lvSearchResults.ColumnHeaders.Clear
```

This code just resets all the text boxes to empty again and clears the search results of the ListView; it also clears the column headers of the ListView so that they're refilled on the next search. You set up this button so that the user can start a new search without needing to exit the form.

10. In the cmdSearch_Click sub, you need to add the following code to tell Matrix to have the transport perform the search on the server by using the user information. In the case of the JUD, you're connected to the Jabber server if it's running a local JUD or to the public JUD on the Jabber.org server.

```
Dim x As Long

    ' clear the search fields collection in the Matrix server
    MainForm.cSession.SearchFields.Clear

    ' refill the search fields collection with the information from the
search form
    For x = 1 To txtFieldValue.UBound
        If txtFieldValue(x).Text > "" Then
            MainForm.cSession.SearchFields.Add lblFieldName(x).Caption,
txtFieldValue(x).Text
        End If
    Next x

    'call the agent search method
    MainForm.cSession.Agents(cboTransport.ListIndex + 1).search
```

11. Make sure that the SearchFields collection on the Matrix server is cleared. Next populate the SearchFields collection with the information that you gather from the Search Form. The names of the fields you want to search are the captions on the labels as you assigned them after you received the OnSearchFields event. The text fields hold the information the user enters, which is what the user wants to search for. You send Matrix only the fields for which the user enters information. (No point in sending back blank information.)

12. You now need to add a new menu item to the Roster menu to access the Search Form. First, use the Visual Basic Menu Editor on the MainForm to add a new entry to your Roster menu, changing the Caption to Search and the Name to mnuRoster_Search.

13. In the `mnuRoster_Search_Click` sub, add the following code to open the Search
    Form. (Again, check to see whether you have an active connection before trying to display
    the form.)

```
'make sure we have logged in first
If cSession.Active Then
    frmSearch.Show
End If
```

14. In `cSession_OnSearchFields`, add the following code:

```
Dim x As Long

    For x = frmSearch.txtFieldValue.UBound To 1 Step -1
        Unload frmSearch.txtFieldValue(x)
        Unload frmSearch.lblFieldName(x)
    Next x

    For x = 1 To SearchFields.Count
        frmSearch.AddField SearchFields(x).FieldName,
SearchFields(x).FieldData
    Next x
```

As you can see in the code, you first clear the search fields from the Search Form so that you
start with a clean form. Next you step through the `SearchFields` collection that the Matrix
COM Library sent and populate your Search Form with the values of the `SearchFields`
collection.

Before you can continue the search, you need to add another utility function to your mUtils
module, so follow these steps:

1. Open the code window for the module and add the following code:

```
Private Function FindlvColumnHeader(mListView As ListView, sHeader As
String) As Long
Dim x As Long
    With mListView
        For x = 1 To .ColumnHeaders.Count
            If .ColumnHeaders.Item(x).Text = sHeader Then
                FindlvColumnHeader = x
                Exit Function
            End If
        Next x
        FindlvColumnHeader = 0
    End With
```

```
End Function
```

This handy little function returns the item number of the ListView Header if it finds it on the ListView or 0 if it doesn't find the item number. You use this function in filling your lvSearchResults ListView, but as you can see, you could use it anytime you need to check for a column header in a ListView. You see it in action in the code for your cSession_OnSearchResults event.

2. Open the code window for the MainForm. You're now going to add the code to fill your lvSearchResults ListView. Find the cSession_OnSearchResults event and enter the following code:

```
Dim x As Long
Dim lField As Long
Dim lvItem As ListItem


        With frmSearch.lvSearchResults

            If Searchresults.Count = 0 Then
                Set lvItem = .ListItems.Add
                .ColumnHeaders.Add , , "Results"
                lvItem.Text = "No Results Found"
                lvItem.Key = "NoResults"
            Else
                .ListItems.Clear
                .ColumnHeaders.Clear
                For x = 1 To Searchresults.Count
                    'add a new listview Item
                    Set lvItem = .ListItems.Add
                    ' add the SearchItem as the key and first field
                    ' this will normally be the JID
                    lvItem.Text = Searchresults.item(x).SearchItem
                    lvItem.Key = Searchresults.item(x).SearchItem
                    .ColumnHeaders.Add , , "Item"
                    ' cycle through the fields if there are any

                    If Not Searchresults.item(x).Fields Is Nothing Then
                        For lField = 1 To
Searchresults.item(x).Fields.Count
                            ' add new columns as required
                            If
FindlvColumnHeader(frmSearch.lvSearchResults,
Searchresults.item(x).Fields(lField).FieldName) = 0 Then
```

```
                            .ColumnHeaders.Add , ,
Searchresults.item(x).Fields(lField).FieldName
                        End If
                        ' add sub items
                        lvItem.SubItems(lField) =
Searchresults.item(x).Fields(lField).FieldData
                    Next lField
                End If
            Next x
        End If
    End With
```

Looking at the preceding code, you notice that the first thing you check for is to determine whether any search results returned. You do so by checking the count property of the search results collection; if it's 0, no results returned. You display that fact in the lvSearchResults ListView. If results returned, you clear the ListView in case the user has already made a search but not clicked the Clear button on the Search form. Next you create a loop to loop through all the results that the Matrix COM Library returns. You add a new ListView item for each search result and loop through the Fields' collection of the Search result object to fill in the ListView with any of the fields that return. The fields are the same ones that return to your Search Form after you query the Matrix COM Library for the search fields. Figure 9-6 shows an example of a Search window after a search.

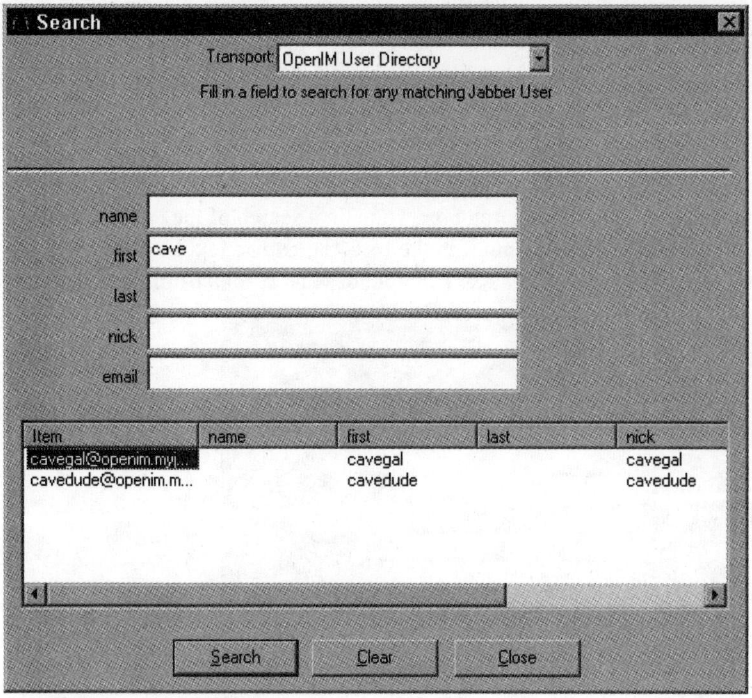

Figure 9-6: Example of a user search

You need to add code to the ListView so that, if the user double-clicks an item, that action opens the `Add Roster Item` form, which displays the information for that roster user.

In `lvSearchResults_DblClick` of the `frmSearch` form, add the following code:

```
Dim iSubitm As Integer

    frmAddRosterItem.Show
    frmAddRosterItem.cboTransport.ListIndex = cboTransport.ListIndex
    frmAddRosterItem.txtJID = lvSearchResults.SelectedItem.Text

    ' try a couple of different ways to see if there is a nickname we
can use in the listview
    iSubitm = FindlvColumnHeader(lvSearchResults, "nickname")
    If iSubitm = 0 Then
        iSubitm = FindlvColumnHeader(lvSearchResults, "nick")
    End If

    If iSubitm = 0 Then
        iSubitm = FindlvColumnHeader(lvSearchResults, "nick name")
    End If
```

```
    If iSubitm > 0 Then
        frmAddRosterItem.txtNickName =
lvSearchResults.SelectedItem.SubItems(iSubitm-1)
    End If
```

The code above is pretty simple stuff: You just show the `frmAddRosterItem` form, pass the transport Index number from the Search Form to the `frmAddRosterItem` form, and then fill the `txtJID` text box with the name in the search box. Then do a search of the column headers for something that may be a NickName and put it in the `txtNickName` text box of the `frmAddRosterItem` form. Figure 9-7 shows an example of what results from this procedure.

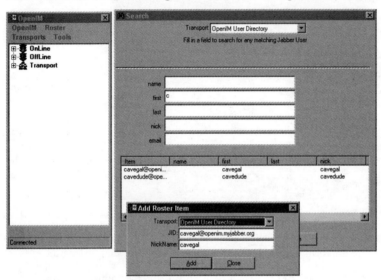

Figure 9-7: Add Roster Item form Search window

Summary

Your OpenIM client should now have enough functionality in place to manipulate the roster. You've added the code that enables you to add, update, and delete `RosterItems` as well as to view the properties of a `RosterItem`. You can now also search for a user in the JUD and some of the other transports.

Chapter 10

Sending Your First Message

In This Chapter

- ◆ Creating the message form
- ◆ Sending a message
- ◆ Creating the receive form
- ◆ Receiving messages
- ◆ Replying to a message
- ◆ Working with multiple recipients

In this chapter, we write the code that enables you to send a message to another user, send messages to multiple recipients (cc: them), and receive messages from other users.

ON THE CD-ROM You can find the code for this chapter on the CD-ROM in the \openIM\chapter10 folder. This code also includes the code from previous chapters.

Creating the Message Form

This is the moment you've been waiting for — it's time to start communicating with our roster users! Using instant messages is the easiest and simplest way of communicating with others.

Jabber instant messaging works somewhat like a conventional e-mail message. You create your message with the address of the person to whom you want to send it, maybe carbon copying (cc:) someone else or blind copying (bcc:) another user, and then you add a subject line, type your message, and send it off.

If your intended recipient is online, the program instantly delivers the message. In other words, the recipient is notified right away, either by the message's appearing in its own window on-screen or by some other visual cue, that you sent a message. So unlike with e-mail, the receiving client doesn't need to poll the server periodically to get the messages, but rather the server "pushes" the message to the client right away. If the user isn't online, the message goes into that user's spool file for holding until the recipient does log in, at which time the user receives notification of the message or messages that await.

Now, we're ready to add some simple messaging to your OpenIM client, so just follow these steps:

1. Create a new form in your OpenIM project. Set the (name) property of the form to frmMessage, the borderstyle property to 1 - fixed single, the caption to OpenIM Message, and, finally, set the icon to message.ico. (You can find this file in the \graphics directory for this chapter on the CD-ROM.)

2. Add four labels. The following table shows the properties for the labels. Again, we used an array for labels, so we put one label on the form, set the alignment property to 1 - Right Justify, and copy and paste the label as we do in Chapter 9. Set the caption for each of the labels as shown in the table.

Label Index	Alignment	Caption
0	1 - Right Justify	To:
1	1 - Right Justify	CC:
2	1 - Right Justify	Bcc:
3	1 - Right Justify	Subject:

> **NOTE** In the message code we are creating here, we use only one name each in the to:, cc:, and bcc: lines. If you want, you can use multiple recipients, and doing so is a good exercise for later. We'll show you the basic concept later in this chapter, but leave it to you to create an address book–style addition system.

3. Next to the To: label, add a combo box to your frmMessage form. (We later add your roster list to this drop-down.) Set the (name) property of the combo box to cboTo and clear the text property. Now create two more combo boxes; place the first one next to the CC: label and change the (name) property to cboCC; place the next beside the Bcc: label and set the (name) property to cboBCC. Make sure that you clear the text properties on both of these as well.

4. Add a standard text box next to the Subject: label. Set the (name) property to txtSubject and clear the text property. We'll use this text box to add a subject line to our message.

5. Add another text box on the frmMessage form and expand it so that it's several lines deep; this is where you type your message to send out, so you need room for multiple lines of text. Set the (name) property to txtMessage and clear the text property. Then set the Multiline property to true and the Scrollbars property to 2 - Vertical.

6. Add two buttons to the bottom of the form. For the first button, set the (name) property to cmdSend and set the caption to &Send. For the second button, set the (name) property to cmdClose and the caption to &Close.

Notice that you don't set the `default` property to `true` on either of these buttons because you need the capability to press the Return key and have it start a new line in the multiline `txtMessage` text box (as opposed to its sending the message).

You should now have a form that looks similar to that shown in Figure 10-1. It's starting to look a whole lot like an e-mail form, isn't it?

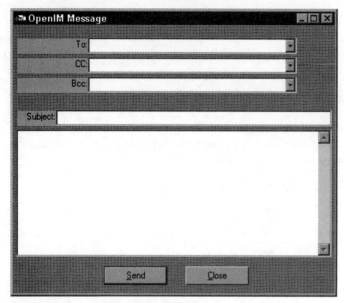

Figure 10-1: Design view of a message form

Sending a Message

Now it's time to add your typical code to the `cmdClose_Click` event of the `frmMessage` window:

```
Unload me
```

To create another utility function that populates a combo box with your roster list, follow these steps:

1. Open the mOpenIM module and enter the following code:

```
Public Sub FillRosterCombo(myCombo As ComboBox)
Dim x As Long

    'clear the combobox
    myCombo.Clear
    ' now populate it with the roster items
    With MainForm
```

```
        For x = 1 To .cSession.Roster.Count
            If .cSession.FindItemType(.cSession.Roster.item(x).JID) =
MX_RosterItem Then
                myCombo.AddItem .cSession.Roster.item(x).JID
            End If
        Next x

    End With


End Sub
```

This code is fairly simple: You loop through the collection of roster items that the Matrix COM Library holds, checking each one to make sure that the `ItemType` is a roster item. The `ItemType` can be any in the following table.

Constant	Description
`MX_RosterItem`	A roster Item
`MX_AgentItem`	An agent or a transport
`MX_GroupChatItem`	A groupchat room Item
`MX_Unknown`	We don't know what it is

If the ItemType is an `MX_RosterItem`, add it to the combo box's drop-down list.

2. Now you're ready to start setting up your Message window. Add a new menu item to your `MainForm` menu. Set the `caption` to `Send Message` and the `name` to `mnuRoster_SendMessage`.

3. Open the code window for `MainForm` and, in the `mnuRoster_SendMessage_Click` event, add the following code:

```
If cSession.Active = True Then
        frmMessage.Show
End If
```

As before, check to make sure that you have an active session with the Matrix COM Library before displaying the form. If you don't have an active session, even filling the combo boxes with your roster items will fail, and, obviously, sending a message to a server without an active connection is a little tough!

4. Close up the form and add the code to the `frmMessage` form. The first thing that you need to do is to add the calls to populate the combo boxes by using the

FillRosterCombo sub procedure that you created earlier in this chapter. In the
Form_Load() sub of the frmMessage form, enter the following code:

```
'fill the comboboxes with the Users Roster Items
    FillRosterCombo cboTo
    FillRosterCombo cboCC
    FillRosterCombo cboBCC
```

As you can see, you just call your new sub three times, each time passing it the next
combo box.

5. In the cmdSend_Click event, enter the following code:

```
Dim MSG As cMessage

    'check to make sure we have someone to send this message to
    If cboTo.Text > "" Then
        ' create the message
        Set MSG = MainForm.cSession.CreateMessage

        ' set the message type to a normal message
        MSG.MSG_Type = MSG_Normal

        MSG.ToJID = cboTo.Text

        MSG.Subject = txtSubject.Text

        MSG.Body = txtMessage.Text

        ' if we have a cc to send to add it to the envelope
        If cboCC.Text > "" Then MSG.AddCC cboCC.Text

        ' if we have a bcc to send to add it to the envelope
        If cboBCC.Text > "" Then MSG.AddBCC cboBCC.Text

        MSG.SendMessage

        Unload Me
    Else
        MsgBox " you must enter an address in the To Box to send this
message", vbInformation
    End If
```

6.   The first thing that happens is that you create a new instance of the `cMessage` object from the Matrix COM Library. Check to make sure you have someone to send the message to by checking the value of the `txtTo` text box. Then call the `CreateMessage` function to initiate the `MSG` object in the Matrix COM Library. Set the `Msg_Type` property to `MSG_Normal`. The following table shows the different values that you can set this property to.

Constant	Description
MSG_Normal	A normal instant message
MSG_Chat	A chat message
MSG_Headline	A news headline such as a newsfeed (normally accompanied by a URL)

Set the `ToJID` property to the address that was entered by the user in the `cboTo` combo box of your form and then set the `Subject` and the `Body` of the message to `txtSubject.Text` and `txtBody.Text`, respectively. Check to see whether any JIDs are in the `txtCC` and `txtBCC` text boxes and whether you need to add them to the message as well. Call `SendMessage` and — voilà! — your message is sent. After that, just call the `form unload` sub procedure so that the user doesn't need to dismiss the form from the screen.

In these steps, we left the style of the combo boxes as `0 - Dropdown Combo`, so that you can send a message to someone who's not on your roster list. This does leave open the possibility of someone's entering a bad address. We recommend calling the `parseJID` function to make sure that at least the formation of the JID is correct, although the user still can enter a bad username or server. We leave to you the task of adding the error-handling code to check the JIDs.

Figure 10-2 shows the message just before you send it from the OpenIM client that you're currently writing.

Figure 10-3 shows the message arriving in our myJabber client.

NOTE This example represents the simplest form of messaging. A protocol draft for Jabber discusses the use of XHTML-Basic for creating formatted messages.

Although this enables you to send formatted messages, the standard plain-text message also still goes out so that a client that doesn't support formatted text can still view the message. This situation may occur if the client you're sending to is using SMS, or short messages, such as those typically used on a cell phone.

Keep in mind that another Jabber client may not receive your message but that the recipient may be a different instant messaging system, a wireless device, a cell phone, or even an e-mail client. Several transports in development for the Jabber server enable the server to send messages to these different types of systems.

You can read more about XHTML at `http://www.w3.org/TR/xhtml1/`. The draft protocol for Jabber XHTML message formatting can be found at `http://docs.jabber.org/draft-proto/html/xhtml.html`.

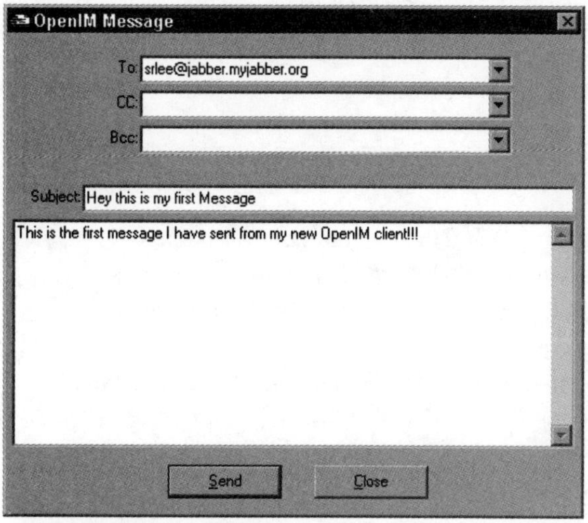

OpenIM Message
To: srlee@jabber.myjabber.org
CC:
Bcc:
Subject: Hey this is my first Message
This is the first message I have sent from my new OpenIM client!!!
Send
Close

Figure 10-2: Message ready to be sent

View Message
To:
From: cavedude (cavedude@openim.myjabber.org/OpenIM)
Subject: Hey this is my first Message
Recieved: 06-Oct-2001 10:51:13 AM
This is the first message I have sent from my new OpenIM client!!!

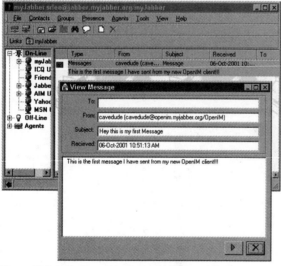

Figure 10-3: Message arriving in the myJabber client

Creating the Receive Message Form

Clearly there's little point in sending a message if you can't receive one, so now we'll write the code in your OpenIM client to receive a message.

> **NOTE** As we mentioned earlier in this chapter, you don't need to poll the server to see whether you have any new messages; the server "pushes" the messages to you. The Matrix COM Library then fires the `OnMessage` event in your client, at which point you must display it for the user. Keep in mind that you could receive more than one message at a time, so you need the capability to display more than one message window. We will show how to do that in the next section of code.

The first thing you must do is to design the form to display the message, so follow these steps:

1. Create a new form in your OpenIM project and then set the `(name)` property of the form to `frmReceiveMsg`, set the `caption` to `Message From`, set the `icon` to the `message.ico` that you used on your `frmMessage` form, and set the `BorderStyle` property to `1 - Fixed Single`.

2. Create a label on your form and position it in the top-left corner. Change the `Caption` property to `Subject:`. Create another label next to it and change the `(name)` property to `lblSubject` and clear the `Caption` property.

3. Create a text box, making sure that you size it so that it's large enough for a multiline message to appear on the form. Set the `(name)` property to `txtMessage`, change the `MultiLine` property to `true` and the `ScrollBars` property to `2 - Vertical`.

4. Add two buttons to the bottom of the form. Change the `(name)` property of the first button to `cmdReply`, change the `default` property to `true`, and set the `caption` to `&Reply`. On the second button, set the `(name)` property to `cmdClose` and the `caption` to `&Close`.

Figure 10-4 shows the design view of the `frmRecieveMsg` form we've just created.

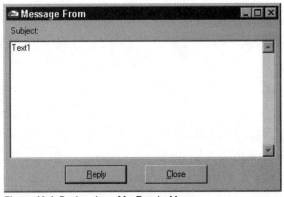

Figure 10-4: Design view of frmReceiveMsg

5. In `cmdClose_Click` of your `frmReceiveMsg` form, type the following code. You will notice a slight difference in the code from the usual `cmdClose_Click` code.

```
colReceiveMsg.Remove Str(Me.hWnd)
Unload me
```

    You're going to be dealing with a collection of `frmReceiveMsg` forms, so you need to remove the form from the collection as well as unload it. (We go into more detail shortly.)

6. In the `txtMessage_KeyPress` sub procedure, add the following code so that the user can't type in the window in which the original message appears. (You could set the `enabled` property to `false`, but then the text in the box would appear grayed and the scrollbars wouldn't work.)

```
KeyAscii = 0
```

    This code just sets to 0 any key that the user tries to type, so the user can type nothing at all in the `txtMessage` box. But it still allows the scrollbars to work.

Receiving Messages

Now we'll work on the code for receiving messages. Just follow these steps:

1. Open the code window for the mOpenIM module and add the following code to the General Declarations section of the module:

```
Public colReceiveMsg As New Collection
```

    The code above creates a collection that will be used to hold the instances of your `frmReceiveMsg` forms.

> **TIP** If you've never used collections before, we recommend that you review the Visual Basic Help files to gain a better understanding of how collections work.

2. Open the code window for your `MainForm`, go to the `cSession_OnMessage` event, and enter the following code:

```
    Select Case MSG.MSG_Type

        Case MSG_Normal
            Dim myReceiveFrm As New frmReceiveMsg
            ' we are receiving a simple message
            'load a new instance of the Receive Message form
            'Load frmReceiveMsg
            With myReceiveFrm
                ' set the tag so we can use it later to reply to the
message
```

```
                .Tag = MSG.FromJID
                ' fill the form with the message
                .Caption = "Message From " & MSG.FromJID
                .txtMessage = MSG.Body
                .lblSubject = MSG.Subject
                .Show
          End With
          ' add the form to our collection of Receive forms
          colReceiveMsg.Add myReceiveFrm, Str(myReceiveFrm.hWnd)

     End Select
```

Notice that the `cSession_OnMessage` sub passes in one argument, which is the `MSG` structure of type `MatrixServer.cMessage`. After the Matrix COM Library receives a message, it parses out the XML and fills the structure with the information for the message.

You first determine what type of message that you're receiving; at this point, the only message you're interested in is of type `MSG_Normal`. You next dimension a new instance of the `frmReceiveMsg` form. After you dimension the new form, you need to fill the fields of the form with the information that the Matrix COM Library passes in the `MSG` structure. (Notice that we set the `Tag` property of the form to `FromJID`; doing so enables you to later use `Tag` to reply to the message from the user.) After you populate your form with the data, you call the `show` method to display the form to the user. Then you add your newly dimensioned form to the `colReceiveMsg` collection.

You may notice that we use the `hwnd` property of the form as the key in the collection; the `hwnd` property is the handle to the window and is guaranteed to be unique. The key must be a string, so we wrap the `hwnd` in the `str()` function of Visual Basic to change the value of `hwnd` from a `long` to a string.

You're now ready to receive a message.

Open up another client and send a message to the user that you're running in the OpenIM client. Try to send a couple of messages before you close the Message window so that you can see your Message window collection at work. Figure 10-5 shows an example of the OpenIM client receiving two messages from my myJabber client.

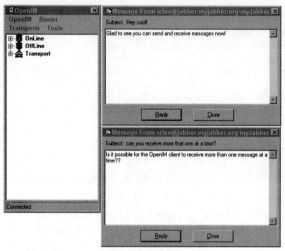

Figure 10-5: OpenIM receiving messages

Replying to a Message

Obviously, just as is the case with e-mail, you want the capability to reply to a message that someone sends you. So you need to put your Reply button on `frmReceiveMsg` to work, as the following steps describe:

1. Open the code window for the `frmReceiveMsg` form and, in the `cmdReply_Click` sub procedure, enter the following code:

```
With frmMessage
        'set the To ComboBox of the Message Form to the tag of this
form
        ' remember the tag of this form holds the JID that sent us the
message
        .cboTo.Text = Me.Tag
        ' fill the subject line and add a RE: to is so it shows as a
reply
        .txtSubject = "Re: " & Me.lblSubject.Caption
        ' attach the original message to the message textbox
        .txtMessage = vbCrLf & "** original Message ** " & vbCrLf &
Me.txtMessage

        ' show the form
        .Show
        .txtMessage.SetFocus
end With
```

The code shows that you're just going to reuse your `frmMessage` window to reply to the message. But instead of showing a blank form, you set some of the fields on the form to the values that you already know from the message that you received.

2. Now you need to set the `To` combo box to the `FromJID` that you stored in the `tag` property of the receive form.

3. Set the `Subject` text box to the subject from the `frmReceiveMsg` form and add a `Re:` in front of the Subject so that the user receving the message knows that it's a reply to his or her message.

4. Set the body of the `frmMessage` form to the original message that you received, adding a carriage-return linefeed, the text **** original Message **** and a carriage-return linefeed.

5. Then show the form by calling the `.Show` procedure and set the focus to the `txtMessage` text box so that your correspondent can add his or her text. (We set the original carriage-return linefeed so that, after we set focus to the `txtMessage` text box, the cursor is on a blank line.)

That's it! Now just send a message to your OpenIM client from another client, and after you receive the message, click the Reply button. Your `frmMessage` window appears with the fields of the form already filled in. Figure 10-6 shows an example of how it looks.

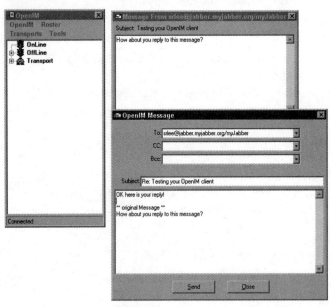

Figure 10-6: Replying to a message

Working with Multiple Recipients

We've left the multiple recipients to the end because, as is the formatted XHTML, the Message Envelope Information Extension is also a protocol draft. But we felt that we should at least touch on it here.

> **NOTE** You can read more about this protocol draft at `http://docs.jabber.org/draft-proto/html/envelope.html`.

For our purposes here, we just show you how to add additional recipients to your CC: and Bcc: text boxes. Most e-mail clients and Jabber clients separate each recipient in these lists with a semicolon. So the CC: data may appear as `cavegal@openim.myjabber.org`; `srlee@jabber.myjabber.net`. You need to create a function to separate each of the JIDs that you enter. Just follow these steps:

1. Open your mOpenIM module code window and enter the following code:

```
Public Function splitJIDS(sJIDList As String) As String()
Dim JIDArray() As String

 ' split up the list given to us at every semi-colon
 If sJIDList > "" Then
    myArray = Split(sJIDList, ";", , vbTextCompare)
    splitJIDS = JIDArray
 End If

End Function
```

   The `split` function is a Visual Basic function that takes a string and breaks it into an array of strings at every occurrence of a delimiter, which in this case is the semicolon. So you need to call the `split` function and return an array of the JIDS.

2. You next need to make a couple of changes to `cmdSend_Click` in your `frmMessage` form. Following is the complete function with the changes made to allow multiple JIDs in both the CC: and the Bcc: text boxes:

```
Dim MSG As cMessage
Dim JIDArray() As String
Dim x As Long

    'check to make sure we have someone to send this message to
    If cboTo.Text > "" Then
        ' create the message
        Set MSG = MainForm.cSession.CreateMessage
```

```
            ' set the message type to a normal message
            MSG.MSG_Type = MSG_Normal

            MSG.ToJID = cboTo.Text

            MSG.Subject = txtSubject.Text

            MSG.Body = txtMessage.Text

            ' if we have a cc to send to add it to the envelope
            If cboCC.Text > "" Then
                JIDArray = splitJIDS(cboCC.Text)
                For x = 1 To UBound(JIDArray)
                    MSG.AddCC JIDArray(x)
                Next x
            End If

            ' if we have a bcc to send to add it to the envelope
            If cboBCC.Text > "" Then
                JIDArray = splitJIDS(cboBCC.Text)
                For x = 1 To UBound(JIDArray)
                    MSG.AddBCC JIDArray(x)
                Next x
            End If

            MSG.SendMessage

            Unload Me
        Else
            MsgBox " you must enter an address in the To Box to send this
message", vbInformation
        End If
```

Notice that we call the splitJIDS function and then run a loop to cycle through the array of JIDs. Other than the change for the loop around the MSG.AddCC and MSG.AddBCC, the rest of the function remains the same.

In fact, the Matrix COM library actually sends the message multiple times to the different JIDs that you add. If you watch the debug window, you see your message going out over and over until it's sent the message to all the JIDs.

Summary

Now you've created the code to send a message, receive a message, and reply to a message. As you can see, these tasks aren't all that difficult. We suggest that you may want to add an address book so that you can select multiple recipients for your message. Maybe add some checking to the To:, CC:, and Bcc: fields to make sure that the JIDs that you enter are valid, and of course, you may want to add the proposed XHTML-Basic–formatted message. In the next chapter, you code OpenIM to do a one-on-one chat.

Chapter 11

Working with vCards

In This Chapter

♦ Creating a vCard form

♦ Coding for the vCard window

In this chapter, we show you how to write the source code to add to the OpenIM project the functionality to retrieve and view the vCard of a `RosterItem` and to update and view your own vCard.

ON THE CD-ROM You can find the code for this chapter on the CD-ROM, in the \openIM\chapter11 folder. This code also includes the code from previous chapters.

vCards are the electronic equivalent of business cards. Most of the current instant messaging and e-mail clients can provide some form of information about the user that you can add to your contact/roster list. ICQ provides several pages of information about a user, as you can see in Figure 11-1.

Figure 11-1: ICQ vCard

One's ability to view an incoming vCard depends on the type of information that the recipient's program supports. Unfortunately, there is no "industry standard" defining the structure of a vCard. If the sender's program includes several pieces of information that the receiving program doesn't support, you will not be able to view that information. Figure 11-2 shows an example of a vCard that was attached to an e-mail we received in Microsoft Outlook. In this case the vCard was displayed "properly" because the original vCard was sent from Outlook. Outlook uses its own address book to display the vCard and allows you to save the information to your own list of contacts.

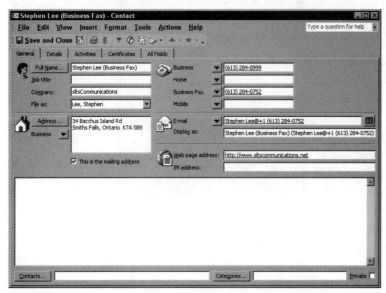

Figure 11-2: vCard received in an e-mail and displayed by Microsoft Outlook

The program you're using probably collected your vCard information from you when you installed it. Once you've entered the information, you can update it at any time to include new e-mail addresses or change existing information.

The Jabber protocol defines a spec for the vCards, and you can review information about vCards in the Jabber programmer's guide. The link to this information is at the following URL: `http://docs.jabber.org/jpg/html/main.html#REFVCARD-TEMP`. You can also view a brief description of the protocol at `http://docs.jabber.org/proto/html/vcard-temp.html`.

The use of `temp` in the namespace of the vCard stems from the fact that the vCard spec for Jabber was never finished. At the time the core Jabber developers added the vCard namespace to Jabber, they used the spec that the Internet Engineering Task Force (IETF) defines at `http://www.ietf.org/rfc/rfc2426.txt?number=2426`.

The RFC was never finalized by the IETF, and, consequently, the Jabber vCard namespace has kept the `temp` until it is finalized or a new spec is created. Some talk about a new vCard format for Jabber is circulating. You can find the information for the new vCard spec at www.vcard-xml.org. For now, we suggest sticking to the `vcard-temp` namespace.

Figure 11-3 shows the vCard window in myJabber, using the namespace that the Jabber documentation defines.

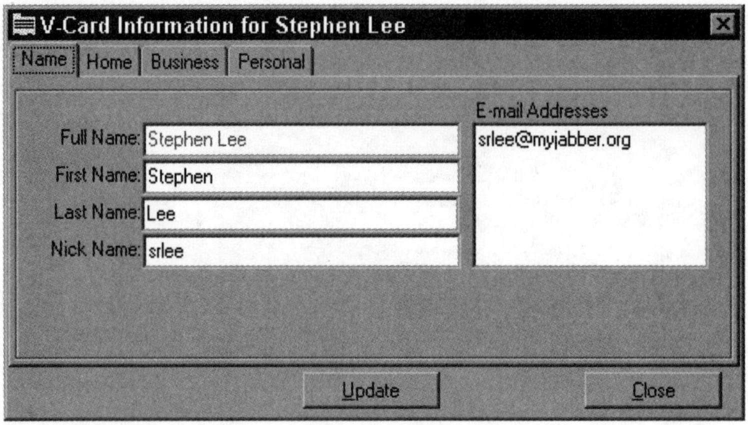

Figure 11-3: myJabber vCard

By now, you should have a basic understanding of the vCard concept, so in the following section, we show you how to add vCards to your OpenIM project.

Creating the vCard Form

You need to create a new form in your OpenIM project, which we started in Chapter 8. (In that chapter, we discuss how to add a new form to your project.) To do so, follow these steps:

1. In the `properties` window of the new form, set the `(name)` property of the form to `frmVcard`, making sure that you set the `borderstyle` to `1 - fixed single`. Set the `caption` of the form to `vCard Information`. (We set the `icon` property to the OpenIM icon in the \OpenIM\Chapter11\graphics directory on the CD-ROM.)

2. Next, add a frame to your form by clicking on the `Frame` component in the Visual Basic Toolbox and drawing it on the form. Set the `caption` to `Personal Information` in the `properties` window of the `Frame` component. Add another frame below the first one and set the `caption` to `Home`; then add one frame more below the one you just added and set the `caption` to `Business`.

3. In the `Personal Information` frame, add the labels from the following table. (Remember that you can create the labels as control arrays as we did in Chapter 8.)

Label Index	Alignment	Caption
0	1 - Right Justify	Full Name:
1	1 - Right Justify	First Name:
2	1 - Right Justify	Last Name:
3	1 - Right Justify	Nick Name:
4	1 - Right Justify	Birthday:
5	1 - Right Justify	Web:

4. In the Home frame, add the following labels:

Label Index	Alignment	Caption
6	1 — Right Justify	Street:
7	1 — Right Justify	City:
8	1 — Right Justify	Region:
9	1 — Right Justify	Postal Code:
10	1 — Right Justify	Country:

5. Next add a frame inside the Home frame and set its caption to Phone Numbers. In the Phone Numbers frame, add the following labels:

Label Index	Alignment	Caption
11	1 — Right Justify	Voice:
12	1 — Right Justify	Fax:
13	1 — Right Justify	Message:

6. In the Business frame, add the following labels:

Label Index	Alignment	Caption
14	1 — Right Justify	Street:
15	1 — Right Justify	City:
16	1 — Right Justify	Region:
17	1 — Right Justify	Postal Code:
18	1 — Right Justify	Country:

7. Next, add a frame inside the Business frame and set its caption to Phone Numbers. In the Phone Numbers frame, add the following labels:

Label Index	Alignment	Caption
19	1 — Right Justify	Voice:
20	1 — Right Justify	Fax:
21	1 — Right Justify	Message:

8. You now need to add text boxes for each of your labels. The following list shows the (name) property that each text box requires. For each text box, click on the `TextBox` component in the Visual Basic Toolbox and draw the text box next to one of the labels you added earlier.

`txtFullName`	`txtHomePhone`
`txtFirstName`	`txtHomeFax`
`txtLastName`	`txtHomeMessage`
`txtNickName`	`txtBusinessStreet`
`txtBirthDay`	`txtBusinessCity`
`txtWeb`	`txtBusinessRegion`
`txtHomeStreet`	`txtBusinessPostalCode`
`txtHomeCity`	`txtBusinessCountry`
`txtHomeRegion`	`txtBusinessPhone`
`txtHomePostalCode`	`txtBusinessFax`
`txtHomeCountry`	`txtBusinessMessage`

The (name) properties should tell you which text box goes next to each label. Make sure, too, that you clear the `text` property of each text box by deleting the text in the properties window for each text box.

9. Add two buttons to your form as we did in Chapter 8; set the (name) property of the first one to `cmdUpdate` and set the `caption` to `&Update`; set the `Default` property of this button to `true`. For the second button, set the (name) property to `cmdClose` and the caption to `&Close`.

After you're done, you should have a form that looks like the one in Figure 11-4.

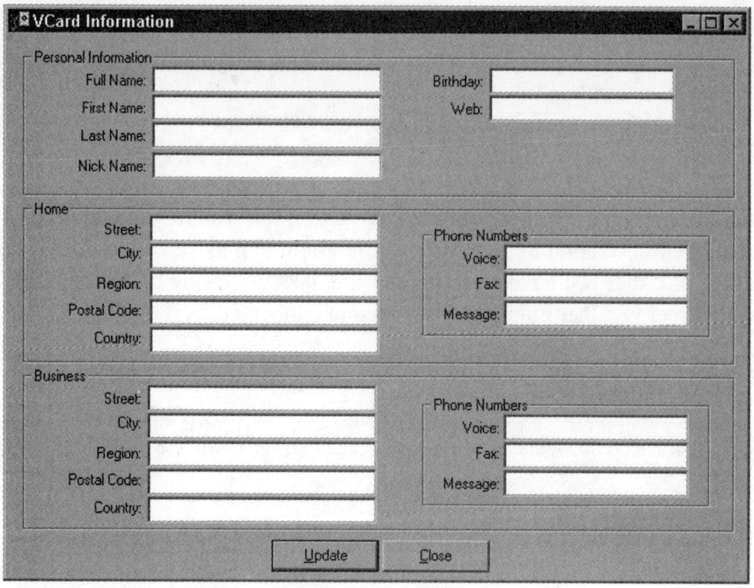

Figure 11-4: Design view of a vCard form

Coding for the vCard Form

Follow these steps to code for the vCard form:

1. Double-click the Close button on the `frmVcard` form to open the code window and place you in the `cmdClose_Click()` event and add the following code in the `cmdClose_Click()` event:

```
Unload Me
```

2. You want to add two menu items to your `MainForm`, starting with the Roster Menu. Add a new menu item, setting the `caption` to `&Vcard...` and the `name` property to `MnuRoster_Vcard`. Add this menu item right below the `Properties` menu item of the Roster Menu. Next add a new menu item to the Tools Menu item; set the `caption` to `My Vcard...` and the `name` property to `mnuTools_MyVcard`. Add this menu item right below the `Debug` menu item in the Tools menu.

3. Open the `Mainform` code window and in the `MnuRoster_Vcard_Click` event, enter the following code:

```
' check for active Jabber Session
    If cSession.Active Then
        With TreeView1
            ' make sure the selected Item has a parent then we know
            ' that it is a roster item or transport
```

```
            If Not .SelectedItem.Parent Is Nothing Then
                cSession.SendVCardRequest .SelectedItem.Key
            End If
        End With
    End If
```

In the code above the first thing we check for is to make sure that you have an active session as we mentioned in Chapter 8. Any time you're going to make a call to the Matrix COM Library, make sure that you have an active session, because trying to retrieve vCard information from a server is rather pointless if you're not connected.

4. Make sure that the `selecteditem` in the `treeview` has a parent, which ensures that the selected item is either a `rosteritem` or a `transport`.

NOTE You can retrieve vCard information about the `transports` as well. See Chapter 8 for a definition of transports.

5. After you make your checks, call the `cSession.SendVCardRequest` method. This method takes one argument, which is the JID (Jabber User ID) for the item for which you want to retrieve the vCard.

6. In the `mnuTools_MyVcard_Click` event, add the following code so that you can modify and view your own vCard:

```
If cSession.Active Then
    cSession.SendVCardRequest cSession.UserName & "@" &
cSession.ServerAddress
    End If
```

7. Again, make sure that you have an active session and then call the `cSession.SendVCardRequest` method. This time, you pass the `UserName` and `ServerAddress` of the person using your OpenIM client.

In both cases, the Matrix COM Library then passes the request to the Jabber server in XML format and waits for a reply. After the Jabber server returns the reply to Matrix, the Matrix COM Library parses out the returned XML and fills the `vcard` class with the information. After the Matrix COM Library fills the `vcard` class, it raises the `cSession_OnVCardResult` event.

8. In the `cSession_OnVCardResult` event of the `MainForm`, enter the following code:

```
With frmVcard

    'set the caption for the vcard window so full name shows
    .Caption = "Vcard Information for " & vcard.FullName
```

```
        If RemoveResource(FromJID) = cSession.UserName & "@" &
cSession.ServerAddress Then
            ' this is our vcard allow us to update it
            .cmdUpdate.Visible = True
            .Frame1.Enabled = True
            .Frame2.Enabled = True
            .Frame3.Enabled = True
        Else
            ' view vcard only
            .cmdUpdate.Visible = False
            .Frame1.Enabled = False
            .Frame2.Enabled = False
            .Frame3.Enabled = False

        End If
            ' personal information
            .txtFullName.Text = vcard.FullName
            .txtFirstName.Text = vcard.Firstname
            .txtLastName.Text = vcard.LastName
            .txtNickName.Text = vcard.NickName
            .txtBirthDay.Text = vcard.BirthDate
            .txtWeb.Text = vcard.WebPage

            ' Home info
            .txtHomeStreet.Text = vcard.HomeStreet
            .txtHomeCity.Text = vcard.HomeCity
            .txtHomeRegion.Text = vcard.HomeRegion
            .txtHomePostalCode.Text = vcard.HomePostalCode
            .txtHomeCountry.Text = vcard.HomeCountry
            .txtHomePhone.Text = vcard.HomePhone
            .txtHomeFax.Text = vcard.HomeFax
            .txtHomeMessage.Text = vcard.HomeMessage

            'business Info
            .txtBusinessStreet.Text = vcard.BusinessStreet
            .txtBusinessCity.Text = vcard.BusinessCity
            .txtBusinessRegion.Text = vcard.BusinessRegion
            .txtBusinessPostalCode.Text = vcard.BusinessPostalCode
            .txtBusinessCountry.Text = vcard.BusinessCountry
            .txtBusinessPhone.Text = vcard.BusinessPhone
            .txtBusinessFax.Text = vcard.BusinessFax
            .txtBusinessMessage.Text = vcard.BusinessMessage
```

```
                        ' show the vcard form now
                        .Show
            End With
```

The `cSession_OnVCardResult` event passes in three arguments; the first is the JID of the item that sends the vCard information. The next is the `vcard` class that holds the information for this vCard; and the final is the raw XML code.

In `cSession_OnVCardResult`, the first thing to do is to check to see whether the vCard that's returning is your own. You do this by checking the `fromJID` against your own JID to see if it matches. If it does, then the vCard is yours; that way, you can set controls on the `frmvcard` form so that you can modify the vCard. Remember that you don't want the capability to modify someone else's vCard.

> **TIP** Rather than setting each control on the form to `enable`, we use the frames to enable and disable all controls within the frame. (Anything that is within a frame is disabled if the frame is disabled.) This approach makes adding new fields much easier later on, and you don't need to worry about enabling and disabling them then.

9. After determining whether to enable the user to modify the fields and whether to display the Update button, set the `txtfields` on the form to the prevalent fields in the `vcard` class. After filling the form, call the `show` method of the form to display the form to the user.

You now need to add the code to update the vCard of the person using the OpenIM client. Open the `frmvcard` code window and, in the `cmdUpdate_Click` event, add the following code:

```
Dim myVcard As New cVcard

    With myVcard
      ' personal information
      .FullName = txtFullName.Text
      If .FullName = "" Then
          .FullName = txtFirstName.Text & " " & txtLastName.Text
      End If
      .Firstname = txtFirstName.Text
      .LastName = txtLastName.Text
      .NickName = txtNickName.Text
      .BirthDate = txtBirthDay.Text
      .WebPage = txtWeb.Text

      ' Home info
      .HomeStreet = txtHomeStreet.Text
```

```
        .HomeCity = txtHomeCity.Text
        .HomeRegion = txtHomeRegion.Text
        .HomePostalCode = txtHomePostalCode.Text
        .HomeCountry = txtHomeCountry.Text
        .HomePhone = txtHomePhone.Text
        .HomeFax = txtHomeFax.Text
        .HomeMessage = txtHomeMessage.Text

        'business Info
        .BusinessStreet = txtBusinessStreet.Text
        .BusinessCity = txtBusinessCity.Text
        .BusinessRegion = txtBusinessRegion.Text
        .BusinessPostalCode = txtBusinessPostalCode.Text
        .BusinessCountry = txtBusinessCountry.Text
        .BusinessPhone = txtBusinessPhone.Text
        .BusinessFax = txtBusinessFax.Text
        .BusinessMessage = txtBusinessMessage.Text
    End With

    ' send the updated vcard info to Matrix
    MainForm.cSession.UpdateVcard myVcard

    ' unload the form
    Unload Me
```

In the code above we create an instance of the `vcard` class in the Matrix COM Library and fill the class with the information that you collect in the vCard form. After filling the class, call the `MainForm.cSession.UpdateVcard` method and pass in your newly created `vcard` class. The Matrix COM Library then takes the class, changes it to XML, and sends it to the Jabber server. Figure 11-5 shows an example of the vCard form in run mode.

Remember that the first time you access your vCard, the form comes up blank. To see that your code worked correctly, open the Debug window in the OpenIM client that we created in Chapter 8 by selecting Tools ⇨ Debug. You should see something similar to the XML shown in Figure 11-6. You should see one `OUT:` XML and then one `IN:` XML. If you see these blocks of XML, you're ready to enter your vCard information and update your vCard by filling the fields on your vCard information form and clicking the Update button.

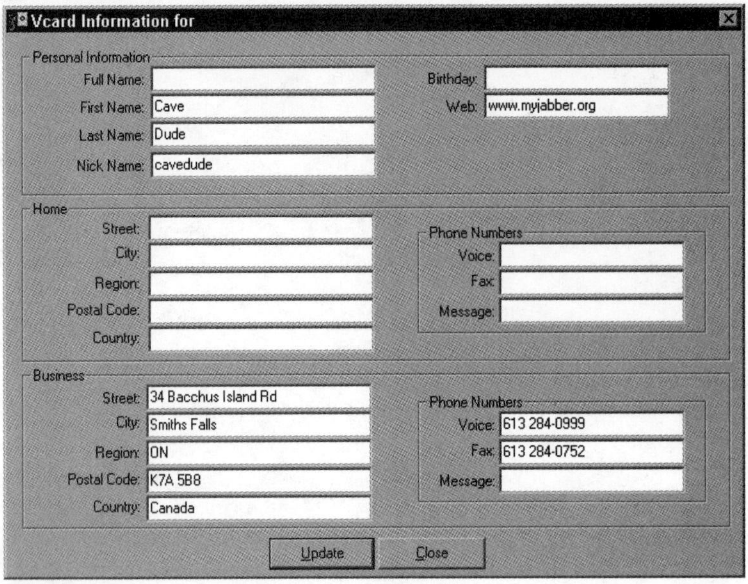

Figure 11-5: Example vCard form

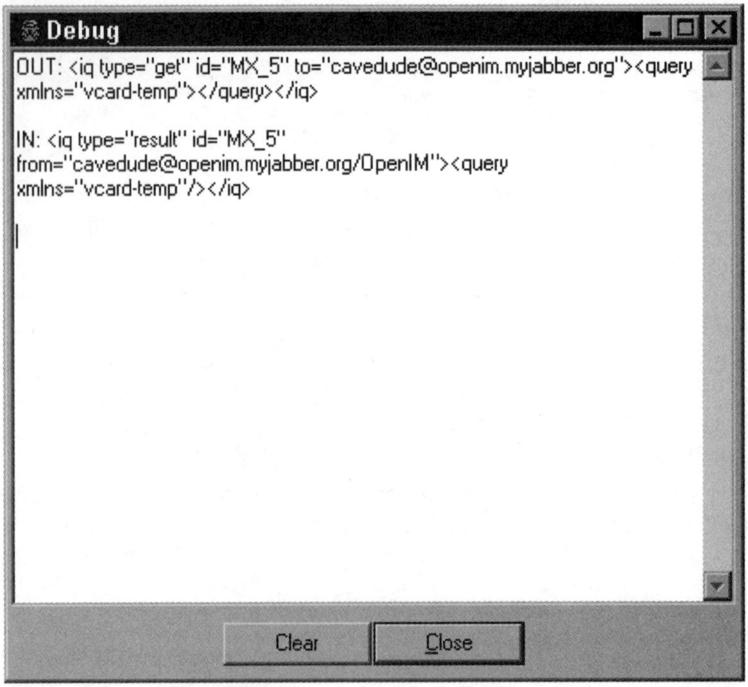

Figure 11-6: Sample vCard XML

You can make this example even more robust with some additional error handling and validation code.

Summary

You can now create and update the client's vCard as well as view vCards for other users. The Matrix COM Library handles all the low-level XML parsing and returns the vCard in a class that your client can easily use.

Chapter 12

Sending and Receiving Chats

In This Chapter

♦ Creating the chat form

♦ Coding for the chat form

Now we'll write the code and design the user interface for a person-to-person (private) chat. After we're done, you'll be able to send and receive chat requests and carry on multiple individual chat sessions.

ON THE CD-ROM You can find the code for this chapter on the CD-ROM in the \openIM\chapter12 folder. This code also includes the code from previous chapters.

When ICQ first came out, instant messaging was a novelty. After several years and several new IM clients, you find that ICQ is one of very few programs that support messaging *and* chat. Most other instant messaging programs around today don't send messages but rather support only person-to-person chat. Some people still like the capability to send a message rather than a chat so that it arrives in an inbox-style format, eliminating the need to keep chat windows open. It is for this reason that myJabber supports both styles of sending messages and that we've included both styles in the OpenIM project. Of course, another reason we are including both in the OpenIM project is that this book is at least partly about creating an instant messaging client.

You can set up your chat window in two different ways. In one, the main text box displays all conversation — as text is entered in the edit window, it appears in the main text box along with that of the other person (see Figure 12-1). The other way uses a split screen, where your text appears in its own window and that of the person you're chatting with appears in another (see Figure 12-2). This second method can prove confusing, however, if your chat continues for a long time, because you must continually glance back and forth between the two windows to read the thread instead of reading the entire chat as you would a book. We prefer to keep the chat all in one window — it's easier to follow the thread of the conversation.

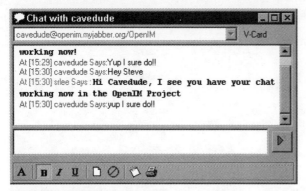

Figure 12-1: myJabber chat window

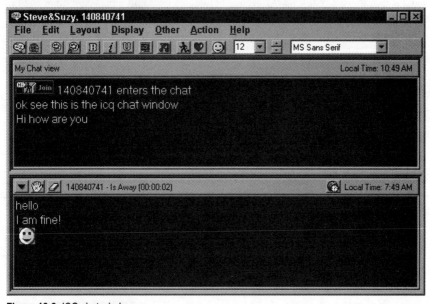

Figure 12-2: ICQ chat window

You don't really find much difference in how you handle the code for a chat window in comparison to that for a message. Look at the following two blocks of code and you see only one difference in the XML that goes to the server.

The following XML sends a message to cavegal from cavedude:

```
<message  id="MX_4" to="cavegal@openim.myjabber.org"         type="normal"
from="cavedude@openim.myjabber.org">
   <body>
      just me saying hi
   </body>
```

```
</message>
```

The following code sends a chat to cavegal from cavedude:

```
<message   id="MX_4" to="cavegal@openim.myjabber.org"        type="chat"
from="cavedude@openim.myjabber.org">
   <body>
       just me saying hi
   </body>
</message>
```

Notice that the only difference is in the `type` attribute of the message tag: You set it to `normal` for a message and to `chat` for a chat. Other than that, the XML code is the same. What this means is that there's really no difference between a chat and a message other than in how the client displays the information. Both require a user to whom to send the message, and both require a message body. myJabber users can even configure it to receive messages in a chat window if they so choose.

Creating the Chat Form

To create the chat form, add a new form to the OpenIM project by following these steps:

1. Set the `(name)` property of the form to `frmChat`, making sure you set the `borderstyle` to `1 - fixed single` (unless you've written the resize code that we keep saying you may want to add!). Set the `caption` of the form to `Chat`.

ON THE CD-ROM We set the icon to the Chat icon that's in the \openIM\Chapter12\graphics directory on the CD.

---

2. You now need to add a new component to your OpenIM project to display a little color in the chat boxes: the Microsoft Rich Textbox Control that ships with Visual Basic. From the Visual Basic menu bar, select Project ⇨ Components. Scroll through the list in the Components dialog box that appears until you find the Microsoft Rich Textbox Control and click the check box to select it. (Figure 12-3 shows what appears on our screen after we select it.) Click the OK button, and you now have the Microsoft Rich Textbox Control in the Visual Basic Toolbox.

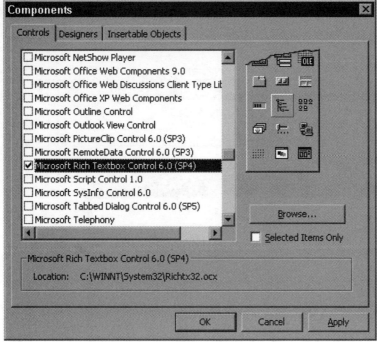

Figure 12-3: Adding the Rich Textbox Control

3. To add a Microsoft Rich Textbox Control to the `frmChat` form and size it so that it fills approximately three-quarters of the chat form, set the `(name)` property of the Microsoft Rich Textbox Control to `rtfChat`; set the `Scrollbars` property to `2 - rtfVertical`; clear the `text` property; and, finally, set the `locked` property to `true` so that the user can't edit the text in the chat window.

4. Create another Microsoft Rich Textbox Control below the first one and fill the remainder of the `frmChat` form with it, leaving enough space on the right-hand side to add a command button. Set the `(name)` property for this Microsoft Rich Textbox Control to `rtfOutPut`; set the `Scrollbars` property to `2 - rtfVertical`; and clear the `text` property. You could add a regular text box here instead of a Microsoft Rich Textbox Control, but in the future, if you want to use different fonts and font colors, that capability is already there for you to use because we have used a Microsoft Rich Textbox Control, which allows the changing of fonts and colors unlike the normal Textbox Control.

CROSS-REFERENCE See the discussion of XHTML in Chapter 10.

5. Add a command button next to the `rtfOutPut` Microsoft Rich Textbox Control, set the `(name)` property to `cmdSend`, and set the `caption` of the button to `&Send`. You use this button to send chat messages. To conserve some space on the form, don't add a Close

button; the user can click the **x** on the title bar of the form to close the window. Very few chat windows include a Close button. In the future, depending on how much functionality you want to add to the chat form, you may decide to add a menu, in which case you can include an Exit menu item.

> **NOTE** The ampersand (&) preceding the captions for buttons and menu items allows for the use of so-called hot keys. If you use `&Send`, for example, the caption of the button will appear as <u>S</u>end, and pressing the Alt key and the S key together will perform the same function as clicking the button.

After you complete these steps, your `frmChat` form should look much like what you see in Figure 12-4.

Figure 12-4: Design view of chat form

Coding for the Chat Form

You now need to add a way to open a new chat from the menu. Follow these steps:

1. Open the Menu Editor in Visual Basic for the `frmMainForm` and, in the Roster Menu of the `frmMainForm`, just below the Send Message item, add a new item; set the `caption` to `Chat` and the `name` property to `mnuRoster_Chat`.

   Make sure that the `frmMainForm` is open and has focus in Visual Basic. Open the Menu Editor and you will see the Menu layout for the `frmMainForm`. (As you are probably aware, each form in your project can have a menu. The Visual Basic Menu Editor acts on the form that currently has the focus.) Just below the Send Message item in the Menu Editor tree, add a new item. Set the `caption` to `Chat` and the `name` property to `mnuRoster_Chat`.

2. As you did for the Message windows, you need to create a collection of chat windows, as you may have more than one chat going simultaneously. In the General Declarations

section of the mOpenIM Module, add the following line of code to declare your collection:

```
Public colChatWindow As New Collection
```

TIP As we've mentioned previously, we suggest you read the Visual Basic Help files on collections if you haven't used them before. You should find that understanding how to use collections is much easier if you take the time to read the Help.

3. You now need to add a new function to the mOpenIM Module to enable you to cycle through the chat form collection to see whether you already have a form open for the JID (Jabber User ID) you're chatting with. Enter the following code in the mOpenIM Module:

```
Public Function CheckForChatWindow(JID As String) As Integer
Dim x As Integer
    ' check to see if chat window is already in use
    ' if so send back the index of the window in the collection
    ' else send back 0
    CheckForChatWindow = 0

    For x = 1 To colChatWindow.Count

        If colChatWindow.item(x).Tag = JID Then
            CheckForChatWindow = x
            Exit For
        End If

    Next

End Function
```

This function checks through the `tag` property of your chat windows collection (which you set as you create the chat window) and returns the index in the collection of the chat window if the user already has a chat window open for this person or returns 0 if it doesn't find the index in the collection. If 0 is returned, then there is not a chat window already open with this tag.

4. In `Private Sub Form_QueryUnload`, add the following code to remove the `frmChatFrm` from the chat window's collection after the user closes the window by clicking the **x** on the title bar:

```
colChatWindow.Remove CheckForChatWindow(Me.Tag)
```

5. In the `mnuRoster_Chat_Click()` event of the `frmMainForm`, enter the following code:

```
Dim myChatFrm As frmChat
Dim iChatWin As Integer
    ' as always check to see we are logged in
    If cSession.Active = True Then
        If Not TreeView1.SelectedItem.Parent Is Nothing Then
            'Make sure the item clicked is a child of the Transport
node
            If TreeView1.SelectedItem.Parent.Text = "OnLine" Or _
                TreeView1.SelectedItem.Parent.Text = "OffLine" Then
                ' check our collection to see if we already have a
window
                ' open with this user
                iChatWin =
CheckForChatWindow(TreeView1.SelectedItem.Key)
                ' no window found create a new one
                If iChatWin = 0 Then
                    Set myChatFrm = New frmChat
                    myChatFrm.Caption = "Chat With " &
TreeView1.SelectedItem.Key
                    myChatFrm.Tag = TreeView1.SelectedItem.Key
                    colChatWindow.Add myChatFrm,
TreeView1.SelectedItem.Key
                Else
                    Set myChatFrm = colChatWindow.item(iChatWin)
                End If
                myChatFrm.Show
            End If 'end online offline check
        End If
    End If ' end active session
```

In this code, you do your normal check to make sure that you have an active connection to the Jabber server; then you check to make sure that the selectedItem of the treeview is a roster item. Trying to send a chat request to one of the transports is pointless, as the transports don't answer anyway. (The transports are just a server component that forwards your messages on to one of the other servers, such as ICQ's, and is not an actual user that you can chat with.) You next call your new CheckForChatWindow function to see whether you're already displaying the chat window; if so, you show it; if not, you create a new chat window and add it to the collection. Notice that, in the code, you're setting the key value and the tag of the chat window to the JID of the user to whom you're talking. Doing so ensures a unique key value and gives you a way to track the JID and the chat window in the collection. (Remember that we keep a collection of chat windows so that we can carry on several chats with different people at the same time.) You also set the caption of the window with the JID so that you can see with whom you're chatting. After this process is complete, you add the chat window to the chat-window collection.

Okay, so this code enables you to start a new chat session with someone in your roster. But what if you receive a chat request? If someone sends you a chat request, the Matrix COM Library fires the `cSession_OnMessage` event.

1. In the `cSession_OnMessage` event, replace the code that you wrote in the preceding chapters with the following code:

```
Dim iChatWin As Integer
Dim sUserName As String
Dim sServer As String

    Select Case MSG.MSG_Type

        Case MSG_Normal
            Dim myReceiveFrm As New frmRecieveMsg
            ' we are receiving a simple message
            'load a new instance of the Receive Message form
            'Load frmRecieveMsg
            With myReceiveFrm
                ' set the tag so we can use it later to reply to the
message
                .Tag = MSG.FromJID
                ' fill the form with the message
                .Caption = "Message From " & MSG.FromJID
                .txtMessage = MSG.Body
                .lblSubject = MSG.Subject
                .Show
            End With
            ' add the form to our collection of Receive forms
            colReceiveMsg.Add myReceiveFrm, Str(myReceiveFrm.hWnd)


        Case MSG_Chat
dim myChatFrm As  frmChat

            'we have recieved a chat message
            ' check our collection to see if we already have a window
            ' open with this user
            iChatWin = CheckForChatWindow(MSG.FromJID)
            ' no window found create a new one
            If iChatWin = 0 Then
```

```
        Set myChatFrm = New frmChat
            myChatFrm.Caption = "Chat With " & MSG.FromJID
            myChatFrm.Tag = MSG.FromJID
            colChatWindow.Add myChatFrm, MSG.FromJID
        Else
            Set myChatFrm = colChatWindow.item(iChatWin)
        End If
        With myChatFrm
            ParseJID MSG.FromJID, sUserName, sServer
            .rtfChat.SelColor = vbBlue
            .rtfChat.SelBold = True
            .rtfChat.SelText = sUserName & " " & "Says:"
            .rtfChat.SelColor = vbBlack
            .rtfChat.SelBold = False
            .rtfChat.SelText = MSG.Body & vbCrLf
            .Show
        End With
    End Select
```

The portion of the code that's of interest right now begins at the MSG_Chat case. Do the same check as after you added the code to the RosterMnu_Chat sub, checking to see whether you already have a chat window open by calling the CheckForChatWindow function. If not, you need to create a new one.

2. Next, you grab the user part of the JID by calling the ParseJID sub procedure that you wrote in Chapter 9 so that you can display it next to the message in the chat window. Set the color for the User says: part of the message to blue and bold so that it stands out a bit and then set the text color back to black and normal. Then output the message. You want to add a carriage return linefeed to the end of the message so that the next message you receive starts on a new line. Then you show the form.

3. Now that you can display a chat window, you must add to the frmChat form the code for sending a chat message back to a roster user. In the rtfOutPut_KeyDown event, add the following code so that pressing Ctrl+Enter on the keyboard sends the message (as opposed to starting a new line in the text field). Remember that, because we have set the multiline property of the Microsoft Rich Textbox Control to true, pressing the Enter key causes a carriage return linefeed. So, don't set the default property of the Send button to true if you want the ability to send multiple lines of text. You must enable Ctrl+Enter so that the user can still use the keyboard to send a message and use the Enter key to start a new line in the outgoing text.

```
Dim CtrlDown As Integer

    CtrlDown = (Shift And vbCtrlMask) > 0
```

```
Select Case KeyCode
    Case vbKeyReturn
        If CtrlDown Then
            ' reset keycode so it doesn't
            ' send a CR to the output window
            KeyCode = 0
            ' call the send button click event to send message
            cmdSend_Click

        End If
End Select
```

The code is pretty straightforward; you check the state of the Ctrl key to see whether it's being pressed and set the `CtrlDown` variable to hold the value. You next do a `select` statement on the `keycode` that is passed in. If the `keycode` is `vbKeyReturn`, then the Enter key on the keyboard was pressed. You check to see whether the Ctrl key is being held down by checking the value of the `CtrlDown` variable and, if the value of `CtrlDown` is `true`, you call the `cmdSend_Click` event. The `cmdSend_Click` event includes the code to send the text of the output text box to the chat window. You must also set the `keycode` to 0 so that the program doesn't send `vbKeyReturn` to the output text box, causing a carriage return linefeed.

> **NOTE** The reason we use a `select` statement is that eventually you'll probably want to check for other keys or key combinations being pressed while typing in the output box, and we find a `select` statement much easier to read and more efficient than an `if elseif` statement.

4. Now you need to add the following code to the `cmdSend_Click` event to add your message to the chat window and send it to the user with whom you're chatting:

```
Dim MSG As cMessage

    'check to make sure we text to send
    If rtfOutPut.Text > "" Then
        If UCase(Left(rtfOutPut.Text, 6)) = "/CLEAR" Then
            rtfChat.Text = ""
        ElseIf UCase(Left(rtfOutPut.Text, 5)) = "/QUIT" Then
            Unload Me
        Else
            If UCase(Left(rtfOutPut.Text, 3)) = "/ME" Then
                rtfOutPut.Text = MainForm.cSession.UserName & " " & _
LTrim(Mid(rtfOutPut.Text, 4, Len(rtfOutPut.Text)))
            End If
```

```
          ' fill the chatwindow with out message
          rtfChat.SelColor = vbBlue
          rtfChat.SelBold = True
          rtfChat.SelText = "I Say:"
          rtfChat.SelColor = vbBlack
          rtfChat.SelBold = False
          rtfChat.SelText = rtfOutPut.Text & vbCrLf

          ' create the message
          Set MSG = MainForm.cSession.CreateMessage

          ' set the message type to a normal message
          MSG.MSG_Type = MSG_Chat
          MSG.ToJID = Me.Tag
          MSG.Body = rtfOutPut.Text
          ' and off it goes!
          MSG.SendMessage

      End If
    'clear the rtfoutput box to start again
    rtfOutPut.Text = ""
    End If
```

The first line of the preceding code checks to make sure that the output textbox is not empty. If it is, we do not execute any code in this module, basically disabling the ability to send. You then see that we check the output text for a couple of different strings; these are actually very common commands in an IRC (Internet Relay Chat) program. We have these and several others in use in the myJabber client, and with almost every release of the myJabber client we add one or two more.

In the code, /CLEAR clears the text from the main chat window; /QUIT closes the chat window; and /ME replaces /ME with the username of the person using the OpenIM client.

5. Next, you add your message to the main chat window, adding I Say in front of the message text so everyone knows that you, and not the person you're chatting with, sent the text.

Remember that you're not going to receive your own message, so that's why you send the message to your own chat window as well as sending the message to the user.

6. You then create a new instance of the MSG object in the Matrix COM Library, setting the MSG_Type to MSG_Chat to indicate that this MSG object will be used to send a chat-style message to the person you are chatting with. You use the tag that you set when you created the chat window as the ToJid of the MSG object; set the Body variable of the MSG object to our outgoing text and then call the SendMessage function to send the message

to the user with whom you're chatting. Figure 12-5 shows an example of the completed chat form in use.

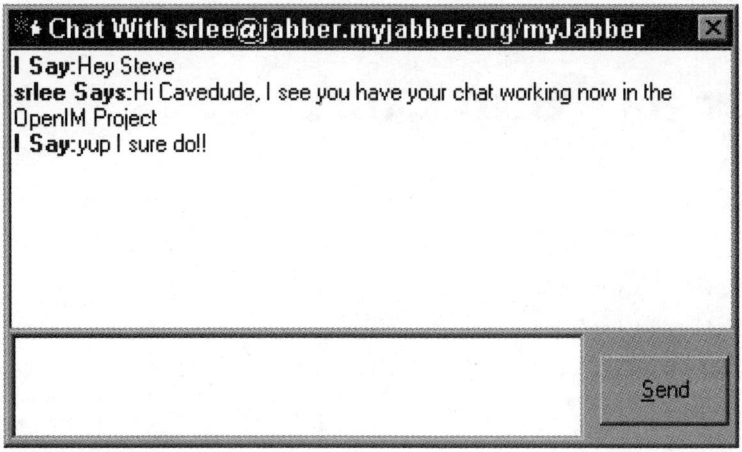

Figure 12-5: Chat session

You can add functionality to the chat windows in many ways: You can add the capability to send formatted text, enabling the user to change fonts in the chat window. You can add a link to the chat window so that you have the capability to call your vCard form (see Chapter 11) for that user. You can add the functionality of printing and/or saving your chat sessions. But again, this book isn't about such topics, so I leave the additional functionality for you to add. Downloading some of the other Jabber clients and reviewing documentation on the Jabber.org site should give you lots of ideas.

Summary

In this chapter, you've created a chat form collection so that you can carry on multiple individual private chats. You've also added a couple of IRC commands to your chat form and sent chat messages.

But what if you want to have a group of friends chat so that everyone can see what everyone else is saying? Never fear. In the next chapter, we add the code to enable you to do group chats!

Chapter 13

Time for a Group Chat

In This Chapter

♦ Creating the Group Chat form

♦ Creating the Group Chat Startup form

♦ Coding the Join Group Chat form

♦ Coding for group chat

In this chapter, we show you how to create the group chat or chat room windows and the code that enables you to chat with a group of people in a single window. After you finish doing so, you can send and receive messages from all your friends or co-workers in a chat room–style format, much as you can by using IRC (Internet Relay Chat).

ON THE CD-ROM You can find the code for this chapter on the CD-ROM in the \openIM\chapter13 folder. This code also includes the code from previous chapters.

Chat rooms predate the Internet, with many BBSs (Bulletin Board Systems) running some form of chat for years. Probably the best-known chat protocol is IRC (Internet Relay Chat); tens of thousands of chat rooms are running in IRC right now, and millions of users participate in them. IRC went online in August 1988 and has since grown to huge proportions. Figure 13-1 shows the popular IRC client mIRC, and Figure 13-2 shows myJabber's group chat window.

TIP You can find a great source of information on IRC (Internet Relay Chat) at www.irc.org. This site includes lots of resources and describes the history of IRC. Another great site is www.irchelp.org, which includes a list of the IRC commands and also some of the lingo that people use in chat rooms.

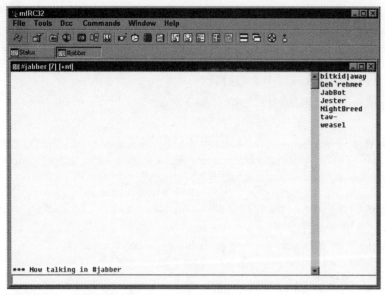

Figure 13-1: mIRC chat window

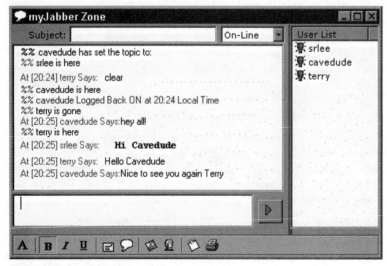

Figure 13-2: A myJabber group chat

Now we have Jabber. Jabber group chat or conferencing is evolving slowly. Several missing pieces in the group chat protocol make it impossible to have a monitor in the rooms to exert any control over the participants' actions. This isn't to say that Jabber won't ever have these features, as like most open-source projects Jabber is evolving and changes are made on a regular basis. It's possible to have private (passworded) chat rooms, user-created chat rooms that vanish after the last person leaves, and permanent chat rooms.

TIP You can find information about conferencing for Jabber at the following URL: `http://docs.jabber` `.org/draft-proto/html/conferencing.html`.

Creating the Group Chat Form

Now let's code your group chat window. Just follow these steps:

1. From the Visual Basic menu bar, select Project ⇨ Add Form, and then click the Open button in the dialog box that appears to create a new blank form. Set the `(name)` property of your new form to `frmGroupChat` and set the `BorderStyle` to `1 - Fixed Single`. Set the `Caption` property to `Group Chat`. We include a new icon in the \OpenIM\ch13\graphics folder on the CD for this chapter, `GroupChat.ico`; set the `icon` property of the form to this graphic.

2. Copy the Image list from the `MainForm` and paste it into the newly created `frmGroupChat` form. Use the same graphics for presence on the Group Chat form as you did in the roster list on the `MainForm`.

3. You now need to add a ListView that displays the people who are in the chat room. Create the ListView and place it on the right side of your Group Chat form, filling about one-quarter to one-third of the window's width and filling it completely from top to bottom. In the properties of the ListView control, set the `view` property to `3 - lvwReport`, the `Label Edit` property to `1 - lvwManual`, and put a check mark next to the `FullRowSelect` property. On the Image List tab of the ListView properties dialog box, set the `normal` and `small` properties to `ImageList 1` and leave every other property at its default value. On the Column Headers tab, click the Insert Column command button, set the `Text` property to `User`, and click OK.

4. Add a Rich Textbox to the `frmGroupChat` form and size it so that it fills approximately three-quarters of the chat form in length and fills the window next to the ListView. Set the `(name)` property of the Rich Textbox to `rtfChat`, set the `ScrollBars` property to `2 - rtfVertical`, clear the `Text` property, and, finally, set the `locked` property to `true` so that the user can't edit the text in the chat window.

5. Create another Rich Textbox below the first one and fill the remainder of the `frmGroupChat` form with it, leaving enough space on the right-hand side to add a small command button. Set the `(name)` property for this Rich Textbox to `rtfOutPut`, set the `ScrollBars` property to `2 - rtfVertical`, and clear the `text` property. You could use a text box here, but as with the chat form, if you want to set different fonts and font colors, the capability is already there for you to use.

6. Add a command button next to the `rtfOutPut` Rich Textbox, set the `(name)` property to `cmdSend`, and set the `Caption` of the button to `>`. You use this button to send your chat messages. To conserve some space on the form, don't add a Close button but rather have the user click the **x** on the title bar of the form to close the window. (Very few group

chat windows include a Close button on the form. In the future, depending on how much functionality you add to the Group Chat form, you will probably want to include a menu, in which case you can add an Exit menu command.)

After you complete these steps, your `frmGoupChat` form should look much like Figure 13-3.

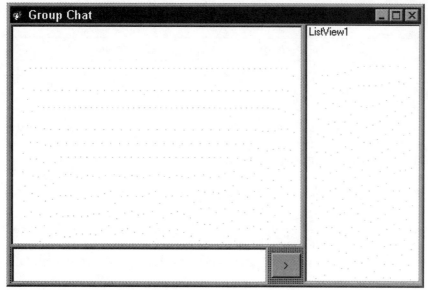

Figure 13-3: Design view of Group Chat form

As with the chat windows you created in Chapter 12, you may want to visit multiple chat rooms at the same time, so you need to create a collection of group chat windows. To do so, add the following code to the General Declarations section of your mOpenIM module:

```
Public colGroupChatWindow As New Collection
```

Creating the Group Chat Startup Form

For users to start a group chat, they must supply a couple of pieces of information, such as the server they want to connect to and the chat room they want to join.

To add the Group Chat Startup form to your project:

1. Add a new form to your OpenIM project, as you do in the steps in the preceding section. Set the (name) property of your new form to `frmJoinGroupChat` and set the `BorderStyle` to `1 - Fixed Single`. Set the `Caption` property to `Join Group Chat` and set the `icon` property of the form to the `groupchat.ico` graphic.

2. Add the labels in the following table to the left side of your `frmJoinGroupChat` form.

Label Index	Alignment	Caption
0	1 - Right Justify	Server Address:
1	1 - Right Justify	Chat Room:
2	1 - Right Justify	Nick Name:
3	1 - Right Justify	Password:
4	1 - Right Justify	Room Name:
5	1 - Left Justify	(Enter a room name only if you want to create a chat room)

1. Create a text box next to each label, setting the (name) property of the text box next to the Server Address: label to txtServerAddress, the one next to Chat Room: to txtChatroom, the one next to the Nick Name: label to txtNickName, and the text box next to the Password: label to txtPassword. Add a text box next to the Room Name: label and set its (name) property to txtRoomName. Make sure you clear the text property of each one.

2. Add two buttons to your form; set the (name) property of the first one to cmdConnect and set the Caption to &Connect. Set the Default property of this button to True. For the second button, set the (name) property to cmdCancel and the Caption to &Cancel.

After you complete these steps, you should have a form that looks like Figure 13-4.

Figure 13-4: Design view of the Join Group Chat form

Coding the Join Group Chat Form

To code the Join Group Chat form, you need to add a menu item to call your new form. Just follow these steps:

1. Open your `MainForm` and, on the Visual Basic menu bar, select Tools ⇨ Menu Editor. Then add a new item to the Tools menu, below the Vcard command. Set the `Caption` to `Join Group Chat` and the `Name` to `mnuTools_JoinGroupChat`.

2. In the `mnuTools_JoinGroupChat_Click` event, add the following code:

```
If cSession.Active Then
        frmJoinGroupChat.Show
  End If
```

This code is pretty straightforward. You just check for an active connection and then show the `frmJoinGroupChat` form.

3. In the Code view of the `frmJoinGroupChat` form, add the following code in the `cmdCancel_Click` event:

```
Unload Me
```

The preceding code is pretty self-explanatory, as you've used it on almost every form that you've created. (If you need the explanation, though, see Chapter 8.)

4. In the `cmdConnect_Click` event, add the following code to send the group chat request:

```
Dim myGC As cGroupChat

    ' create a new groupchat class
    Set myGC = New cGroupChat

    If txtServerAddress.Text > "" And txtChatRoom.Text > "" Then
        'set the info we have gathered to the class
        myGC.JID = txtServerAddress.Text
        myGC.ChatRoom = txtChatRoom.Text
        ' make sure we have a nickname cause it isn't gunna work
        ' without one
        If txtNickName.Text = "" Then
            myGC.NickName = MainForm.cSession.UserName
        Else
            myGC.NickName = txtNickName.Text
        End If
        myGC.Password = txtPassword.Text
        myGC.RoomName = txtRoomName.Text
```

```
        ' Send the Groupchat request to Matrix
        MainForm.cSession.SendGroupChatRequest txtChatRoom.Text & "@" & _
                        txtServerAddress.Text, MX_Available, myGC

        Unload Me
    Else
        MsgBox " You need to have a server address and a chatroom to be
able to connect", vbInformation
    End If
```

After the user enters the information on the `JoinGroupChat` form and hits the Connect button, you create a new instance of the `GroupChat` class and fill it with the information that the user entered. The user must fill in at least the Server Address and Chat Room text boxes or the Jabber server can't attempt a connection to the chat room; if the user leaves the Nick Name text box blank, you fill it with the `Username` from the `cSession` object. The only time you need anything in the Room Name text box is if the user is trying to create a chat room on the server rather than connect to one that already exists.

Once the instance of the `Groupchat` class has been filled with the information , a call is made to the `cSession.SendGroupChatRequest` method to request a connection to the chat room. You pass the JID of the chat room you want to create, which is in the format of *chatroom@theservername*; you send `MX_Available` to tell the server that you want to connect; and finally, you pass the new instance of the `GroupChat` class.

Coding for Group Chat

The Matrix COM Library then sends the necessary XML to the Jabber server from the information that we sent to Matrix in the previous section and waits for a reply. After the Jabber server running the Conference transport responds, Matrix parses out the response and fires the `OnGroupChat` event.

In the `MainForm` code window, find the event `cSession_OnGroupChat` and enter the following code:

```
' send our presence
    cSession.SendGroupChatPresence FromJID, MX_Available
    ' setup a groupchat window
    SetupGCWindow FromJID, GC.RoomName
```

You really don't need to do a lot here. After you know that the conference server has notified Matrix, you send your presence to the JID that Matrix provides and tell it that you are available by sending `MX_Available`. Then you call the `SetupGCWindow` subprocedure.

At this point, you need to create a new code module in which to place the utilities you need for the group chat. Just follow these steps:

1. From the Visual Basic menu bar, choose Project ⇨ Add Module. After the Add Module dialog box appears, click the Open button. In the Properties dialog for the new module, set the (Name) property to mGCUtils.

2. Add the following code to the mGCUtils module:

```
Public Sub SetupGCWindow(JID As String, RoomName As String)
Dim iGCIndex As Integer
Dim myGroupChatFrm As frmGroupChat


    iGCIndex = CheckForGCWindow(JID)

    If iGCIndex = 0 Then
        Set myGroupChatFrm = New frmGroupChat
        myGroupChatFrm.Caption = RoomName
        myGroupChatFrm.Tag = JID
        'store the nickname for later use
myGroupChatFrm.rtfChat.Tag = sNickName            colGroupChatWindow.Add
myGroupChatFrm, JID
    Else
        Set myGroupChatFrm = colGroupChatWindow.Item(iGCIndex)
    End If
    myGroupChatFrm.Show

End Sub
```

3. Add the following code, which you call from the SetupGCWindow subprocedure:

```
 Public Function CheckForGCWindow(JID As String) As Integer
Dim x As Integer

    ' check to see if group chat window is already in use
    For x = 1 To colGroupChatWindow.Count
        If colGroupChatWindow.Item(x).Tag = JID Then
            CheckForGCWindow = x
            Exit For
        End If
    Next

End Function
```

4. Return to the `SetupGCWindow` subprocedure and check to see whether the group chat window is already in your group chat window collection by calling `CheckForGCWindow`. The `CheckForGCWindow` function just cycles through the collection and checks the tag of each group chat window to see whether the JID of the chat room you're joining is already in your list. If it is, the function returns the index of the item; if not, the function returns `0`.

If the index is `0`, the `SetUpGCWindow` subprocedure creates a new instance of the `frmGroupChat` form, sets the `Caption` of the window to the name of the chat room you're joining, sets the tag to the JID of the chat room and your nickname to the tag of the `rtfOutPut` text box, and adds the form to the group chat window collection. You see after you write the code to send messages why you want to store your nickname on the form.

If the index is greater than `0`, set the group chat window to the form from the group chat window collection.

Either way, you display the form onscreen.

After the Matrix Server receives your presence request, it starts to send you `BrowseItems` through the `cSession_OnGroupChatItem` event. The items it sends you are the names of all the users who are in the chat room (including you).

5. In the `cSession_OnGroupChatItem` event of the `MainForm`, enter the following code:

```
Dim bAvailable As Boolean
    If BrowseItem.SubType = "" Then
        bAvailable = True
    Else
        bAvailable = False
    End If
    CheckGCPresence BrowseItem.JID, bAvailable, BrowseItem.Name
```

Check the subtype of `BrowseItem` and, if it's empty, set the `Available` flag to `true`, indicating that the user is available in the chat room. If it's not empty, set the value to `remove`, which indicates that the user is exiting the chat room.

6. Call the `CheckGCPresence` subprocedure. In the `mGCUtils` module, enter the following new code:

```
Public Sub CheckGCPresence(sJID As String, bAvailable As Boolean, Optional
sNickName As String)
Dim iGCIndex As Integer
Dim myGroupChat As frmGroupChat
Dim lvitm As ListItem
Dim lvIndex As Long
Dim lPresItm As Long
```

```
    iGCIndex = CheckForGCWindow(RemoveResource(sJID))
    If iGCIndex > 0 Then
        Set myGroupChat = colGroupChatWindow.Item(iGCIndex)
        lvIndex = FindListviewItem(myGroupChat.ListView1, Right(sJID,
Len(sJID) - InStr(sJID, "/")))
        lPresItm = MainForm.cSession.FindPresence(sJID)
        If lvIndex = 0 Then
            If bAvailable Then
                Set lvitm = myGroupChat.ListView1.ListItems.Add
                If sNickName > "" Then
                    lvitm.Text = sNickName
                End If
                lvitm.Key = Right(sJID, Len(sJID) - InStr(sJID, "/"))
                If lPresItm > 0 Then
                    Select Case
MainForm.cSession.Presence(lPresItm).Showtype
                        Case eShowType.MX_Away
                            lvitm.SmallIcon = eIcons.ICON_Away
                        Case eShowType.MX_ExtendedAway
                            lvitm.SmallIcon = eIcons.ICON_Away
                        Case eShowType.MX_DND
                            lvitm.SmallIcon = eIcons.ICON_Away
                        Case Else
                            lvitm.SmallIcon = eIcons.ICON_Online
                    End Select
                Else
                    lvitm.SmallIcon = eIcons.ICON_Online
                End If
            End If
        Else
            If bAvailable Then
                Set lvitm = myGroupChat.ListView1.ListItems.Item(lvIndex)
                If sNickName > "" Then
                    lvitm.Text = sNickName
                End If
                If lPresItm > 0 Then
                    Select Case
MainForm.cSession.Presence(lPresItm).Showtype
                        Case eShowType.MX_Away
                            lvitm.SmallIcon = eIcons.ICON_Away
                        Case eShowType.MX_ExtendedAway
                            lvitm.SmallIcon = eIcons.ICON_Away
```

```
                          Case eShowType.MX_DND
                                lvitm.SmallIcon = eIcons.ICON_Away
                          Case Else
                                lvitm.SmallIcon = eIcons.ICON_Online
                     End Select
                Else
                     lvitm.SmallIcon = eIcons.ICON_Online
                End If
           Else
                myGroupChat.ListView1.ListItems.Remove lvIndex
           End If
      End If
   End If
   DoEvents
End Sub
```

Although a fair amount of code appears here, it's really pretty straightforward.
CheckGCPresence takes two arguments. The first is the JID of the user in the chat room; the
JID is the name of the chat room appended to the conference server name. Finally, a hash value
for the user is added by the conference server. An example of a JID follows:

```
myjabber@conference.myjabber.org/24c476f8fbf3219b86e3bfc8fdb185cca61343e8
```

The code listing above shows that you're connecting to the myJabber room on the myJabber
conference server and then the hash value of the user. Next, the CheckGCPresence
subprocedure takes an Available flag, which really indicates whether the user is leaving or
joining the room, and last, the nickname of the user in the chat room. sNickName is an
optional argument, because you can retrieve the user nickname from the
cSession_OnGroupChatItem subprocedure.

In the subprocedure, look up the chat window you want to deal with. You do so by stripping
the hash value from the JID, which you accomplish by calling the RemoveResource sub.
Then call the CheckGCwindow function that you wrote in Chapter 9. If the index that returns
is greater than 0 — or, in other words, you find the group chat window in your collection —
you set an instance of a Group Chat form to the Group Chat form that you find in the
collection. You can access the Group Chat form in the collection directly, but we find that
writing the code this way makes it much easier to read.

You now need to add a new function to your mUtils module by following these steps:

1. In the mUtils module, enter the following code:

    ```
    Public Function FindListviewItem(myListView As ListView, Item As String) As
    Long
    Dim x As Long
    ```

```
    With myListView
        For x = 1 To .ListItems.Count
            If .ListItems.Item(x).Key = Item Then
                FindListviewItem = x
                Exit Function
            End If
        Next x
    End With

End Function
```

This function searches through a ListView that passes to the function, looking for a matching key value to the item that also passes to the function. This function is a multi-use function, so you put it in the generic `mUtils` module.

2. To return to `CheckGCPresence`, call your new `FindListView` function. If it finds the key, it returns the index in the ListView of the item; if not, it returns `0`. If the index is `0` and the user is available, you need to add him or her to your group chat ListView. You create a new ListView item by calling the `listview.add` method.

3. Set the ListView item's `text` property to the NickName that `BrowseItem` sent in; set the key to the hash value of the user so that you can find the user later; check the presence collection on the Matrix COM Library to see whether you have a presence item for the user and, if so, set the icon to the appropriate one depending on the user's status. If you don't find a presence item, set the icon to the online item.

4. If the ListView index that returns from the `FindListview` item is greater than `0`, set your ListView item to the item that the index that returns indicates. In this case, you need to check only the presence item for the user, as it's already in the list; and you don't need to reset key property, as it should never change for a user during any session. You do, however, need to reset the `text` property, as a user can change his or her nick name during a group chat session.

5. If the `Available` flag is `False`, remove the user from the ListView, as that user has left the chat room.

If a user changes his presence during a chat session, you receive an `onPresence` event from the Matrix server. We list the whole `cSession_OnPresence` event code here so that you can see where to add the code to check for group chat presence:

```
Dim nodx As Node
Dim sJID As String
Dim Item As Long
Dim sOldKey As String
Dim sNickName As String
Dim JIDNoResource As String
```

```
    ' if this is a groupchat item then deal with it
    ' then exit this sub
If PresItem = MX_GroupChatItem Then
    CheckGCPresence JID, Available
    Exit Sub
End If


    ' remove the resource to see if they are in our list
JIDNoResource = RemoveResource(JID)
'look up the JID in our current treeview nodes
Item = FindTreeviewNode(TreeView1, JIDNoResource)
If Item = 0 Then
    Item = FindTreeviewNode(TreeView1, JID)
End If
' also if the node can't be found then we shouldn't be changing
' it anyway
If Item > 0 Then
    'let's hold onto the Old JID and NickName before removing the
    ' Node
    'sOldKey = TreeView1.Nodes.item(item).Key
    sNickName = TreeView1.Nodes.Item(Item).Text
    TreeView1.Nodes.Remove (Item)
    If Available = True Then
        'we are only interested in transports/agents and rosteritems at
the moment
        Select Case PresItem
            Case MX_RosterItem
                Set nodx = TreeView1.Nodes.Add("OnLine", tvwChild, JID,
sNickName, eIcons.ICON_Online)

            Case MX_AgentItem
                Set nodx = TreeView1.Nodes.Add("Transport", tvwChild,
JID, sNickName, eIcons.ICON_Online)
        End Select
    Else
        'we are only interested in transports/agents and rosteritems at
the moment
        ' take the resource off the jid when storing in the offline
parent node
        ' in case the user logs back in under a different resource
        JIDNoResource = RemoveResource(JID)
```

```
        Select Case PresItem
            Case MX_RosterItem
                Set nodx = TreeView1.Nodes.Add("OffLine", tvwChild,
JIDNoResource, sNickName, eIcons.ICON_Offline)

            Case MX_AgentItem
                Set nodx = TreeView1.Nodes.Add("Transport", tvwChild,
JIDNoResource, sNickName, eIcons.ICON_Offline)


        End Select

    End If
End If
```

The code you're adding to this event follows:

```
' if this is a groupchat item then deal with it
    ' then exit this sub
  If PresItem = MX_GroupChatItem Then
     CheckGCPresence JID, Available
     Exit Sub
  End If
```

All you're doing is checking to see whether `PresItem` is a group chat, and if it is, you call your `CheckGCPresence` subprocedure without passing the nickname.

Now you should be able to see the people who are in the chat room, and if they change their nicknames or presence, your group chat window should reflect that.

1. To see what the users are typing, you need to add the code to receive the messages that others send to the group chat window. To do so, you need to add code to the `cSession_OnMessage` event in the `MainForm`. Again, we list the complete code here so that you can see where to add the new code:

```
Dim iChatWin As Integer
Dim sUserName As String
Dim sServer As String
Dim iGCIndex As Integer
Dim ilvItem As Integer

    Select Case MSG.MSG_Type
        Case MSG_Normal
            Dim myReceiveFrm As New frmRecieveMsg
            ' we are receiving a simple message
```

```
                    'load a new instance of the Receive Message form
                    'Load frmRecieveMsg
                    With myReceiveFrm
                        ' set the tag so we can use it later to reply to the
message
                        .Tag = MSG.FromJID
                        ' fill the form with the message
                        .Caption = "Message From " & MSG.FromJID
                        .txtMessage = MSG.Body
                        .lblSubject = MSG.Subject
                        .Show
                    End With
                    ' add the form to our collection of Receive forms
                    colReceiveMsg.Add myReceiveFrm, Str(myReceiveFrm.hWnd)


                Case MSG_Chat
                    Dim myChatFrm As frmChat
                    'we have recieved a chat message
                    ' check our collection to see if we already have a window
                    ' open with this user
                    iChatWin = CheckForChatWindow(MSG.FromJID)
                    ' no window found create a new one
                    If iChatWin = 0 Then
                        Set myChatFrm = New frmChat
                        myChatFrm.Caption = "Chat With " & MSG.FromJID
                        myChatFrm.Tag = MSG.FromJID
                        colChatWindow.Add myChatFrm, MSG.FromJID
                    Else
                        Set myChatFrm = colChatWindow.Item(iChatWin)
                    End If
                    With myChatFrm
                        ParseJID MSG.FromJID, sUserName, sServer
                        .rtfChat.SelColor = vbBlue
                        .rtfChat.SelBold = True
                        .rtfChat.SelText = sUserName & " " & "Says:"
                        .rtfChat.SelColor = vbBlack
                        .rtfChat.SelBold = False
                        .rtfChat.SelText = MSG.Body & vbCrLf
                        .Show
                    End With


                Case MSG_GroupChat
                    Dim myGroupChatFrm As frmGroupChat
```

```
        iGCIndex = CheckForGCWindow(RemoveResource(MSG.FromJID))
    If iGCIndex > 0 Then
        Set myGroupChatFrm = colGroupChatWindow.Item(iGCIndex)
        With myGroupChatFrm
            ilvItem = FindListviewItem(.ListView1,
Right(MSG.FromJID, Len(MSG.FromJID) - InStr(MSG.FromJID, "/")))

            If InStr(MSG.FromJID, "/") = 0 Or MSG.subject > ""Then
                sUserName = "%% "
            Else
                sUserName = .ListView1.ListItems(ilvItem).Text
                sUserName = sUserName & " " & "Says: "
            End If
            .rtfChat.SelColor = vbBlue
            .rtfChat.SelBold = True
            .rtfChat.SelText = sUserName
            .rtfChat.SelColor = vbBlack
            .rtfChat.SelBold = False
            .rtfChat.SelText = MSG.Body & vbCrLf
            .Show
        End With

    End If
End Select
```

The portion of the code that's of interest here starts at the case MSG_Groupchat. You again need to check through the group chat window collection to find the group chat that's receiving the message. If you find the index (which you should, unless you receive a message at the same instant you close the group chat window), next check to see whether the message is from the conference server — which is indicated by the lack of a hash value on the end of the FromJID — or whether someone is setting the topic for the chat room — which is indicated by the Subject of the message not being empty. If it's from the conference server or is a topic change, set the Username variable to %%, which you use to indicate that the message isn't from a user.

2. If a hash value is on the end of the JID, search through the ListView to find the user who sent the message, using your FindListview function, and set the UserName to the text value of the ListView item. The text value of the ListView is the nickname the user picked when joining the room or the nickname he or she changed to during the group chat session.

3. Add the user name to the chat box on the Group Chat form, using a blue font and adding bold to it. Next to the user name, output the message that was sent and add a carriage-return linefeed to end the message. Then display the form, in case it's been minimized by

the user during a group chat session. That way, the user is notified of a new message arriving.

Figure 13-5 shows an example of a group chat window in use.

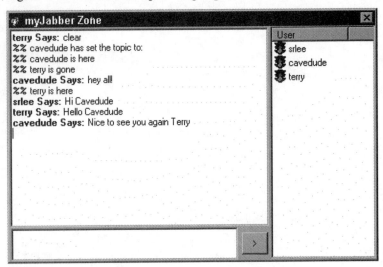

Figure 13-5: Group chat window

Now you need the capability to reply to the messages people are sending you and to add a couple of features to the Group Chat form. Just follow these steps:

1. Add the same code in `rtfOutPut_KeyDown` as you added to the Chat form in Chapter 12.

```
Dim CtrlDown As Integer

    CtrlDown = (Shift And vbCtrlMask) > 0

    Select Case KeyCode
        Case vbKeyReturn
            If CtrlDown Then
                ' reset keycode so it doesn't
                ' send a CR to the output window
                KeyCode = 0
                ' call the send button click event to send message
                cmdSend_Click

            End If
    End Select
```

As in the chat form, you capture the Ctrl+Enter key combination for a keyboard command to send your message. (You probably noticed that we tried to name the controls the same on both the Chat form and the Group Chat form. Doing so makes maintaining the code easier in the future.)

2. To add the code to the Send button, add the following code to the `cmdSend_Click` event of the Group Chat form:

```
Dim MSG As cMessage
Dim lEnd As Long


    'check to make sure we text to send
    If rtfOutPut.Text > "" Then
        If UCase(Left(rtfOutPut.Text, 6)) = "/CLEAR" Then
            rtfChat.Text = ""

        ElseIf UCase(Left(rtfOutPut.Text, 5)) = "/QUIT" Then
            Unload Me

        ElseIf UCase(Left(rtfOutPut.Text, 5)) = "/NICK" Then
                lEnd = InStr(7, rtfOutPut.Text, " ")
                If lEnd = 0 Then lEnd = Len(rtfOutPut.Text) + 1
                rtfChat.Tag = Mid(rtfOutPut.Text, 7, lEnd - 1)
                MainForm.cSession.ChangeGCNickName Me.Tag, rtfChat.Tag

        ElseIf UCase(Left(rtfOutPut.Text, 6)) = "/TOPIC" Then
            ' create the message
            Set MSG = MainForm.cSession.CreateMessage
            ' set the message type to a GroupChat message
            MSG.MSG_Type = MSG_GroupChat
            MSG.ToJID = Me.Tag
            'set the subject to the string after /topic
            MSG.subject = Mid(rtfOutPut.Text, 8, Len(rtfOutPut.Text) + 1)
            MSG.body = rtfChat.Tag & " has changed the subject to: " &
MSG.subject
            ' and off it goes!
            MSG.SendMessage

        Else
            If UCase(Left(rtfOutPut.Text, 3)) = "/ME" Then
                rtfOutPut.Text = rtfChat.Tag & " " &
LTrim(Mid(rtfOutPut.Text, 4, Len(rtfOutPut.Text)))
            End If
```

```
        ' create the message
        Set MSG = MainForm.cSession.CreateMessage

        ' set the message type to a GroupChat message
        MSG.MSG_Type = MSG_GroupChat
        MSG.ToJID = Me.Tag
        MSG.body = rtfOutPut.Text
        ' and off it goes!
        MSG.SendMessage

    End If
'clear the rtfoutput box to start again
rtfOutPut.Text = ""
End If
```

You may notice that a lot of the code here looks very similar to the code that you added to the chat form Send button.

First, check to make sure you have some text in the Output Richtext box to deal with; if not, don't do anything. If you do have text to work with, check for a few of the IRC-style commands listed in the following table.

IRC-Style Command	Description
/CLEAR	Clears the `rtfChat` Rich Textbox of all text
/QUIT	Closes the current group chat window
/NICK	Changes your nickname from the current to a new value; an example would be /NICK joe. This command would change your nickname to joe.
/TOPIC	Changes the topic for the chat room; the topic or subject describes the current conversation. Example: /TOPIC what do you think of OpenIM?

If during the parsing you discover that the user wants to change his or her nickname, parse the text next to the /NICK command and call the MainForm.cSession.ChangeGCNickName function to make the Matrix COM Library send a request to the conference server to update the nickname. MainForm.cSession.ChangeGCNickName takes two arguments. The first is the group chat room JID, and the second is the new nickname. Figure 13-6 shows cavedude about to change his name to joe, and Figure 13-7 shows the window after his nickname changes.

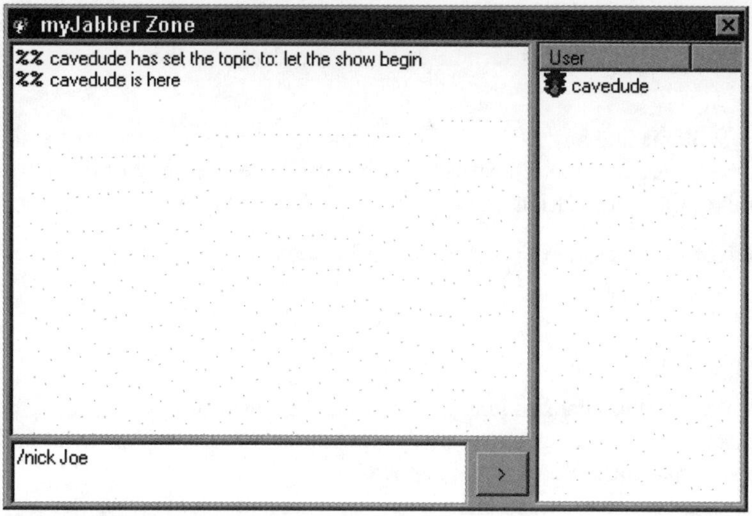

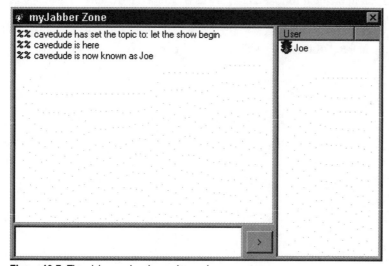

Figure 13-6: Cavedude is about to change his nickname.

Figure 13-7: The nickname has been changed.

If you find the /TOPIC IRC-style command, create a new message instance in the Matrix COM Library, set the subject of the message to the text next to the /TOPIC command, and set the body of the message to a string indicating that you're changing the topic. Set the ToJID to the JID of the group chat and then send the message off to the Matrix COM Library for forwarding to the conference server.

If you find the /ME command, parse off the /ME and replace it with your nickname, which you stored (earlier in this section) in the tag property of the rtfOutPut Rich Textbox.

Finally, if you don't find any IRC-style commands, create a new instance of a message and fill in the ToJID, as you did earlier in this section. Set the body of the message to the text in the rtfOutPut Rich Textbox and send the message off to the server.

In any case, always clear the rtfOutPut Rich Textbox so that it's ready to accept more input.

Summary

You can now conduct group chat sessions with others, see who's online in a group chat room, and send and receive messages in a group chat room. You can add a ton of different things to the group chat that we don't get into here.

You should have enough functionality and background to add new features to your group chat window. You can add another text box to display the topic of the group chat or enable a user to change his or her presence to an away status and then back to online again. As with all messaging, you can implement formatted text by using the XHTML spec. You can enable users to send private chat messages to others in the ListView by using the chat form that you created in Chapter 12. These examples are only a few of the features you can add, and you're probably already thinking of others as well.

Chapter 14

Adding Options

In This Chapter

- ♦ Getting a roster user's local time
- ♦ Replying to a time request
- ♦ Getting a roster user's client version
- ♦ Replying to a version request
- ♦ Getting the time the roster user was last online

In this closing chapter, we show you how to add options to your OpenIM client. You can add many such options, such as events for the `iq:jabber:events` namespace (see `http://docs.jabber.org/draft-proto/html/events.html`). This includes being able to see when others are replying to your message and when your message has been displayed to them. For the purposes of illustration, we're going to show you how to send and receive requests for the version of client that someone else is using and the user's local time as well as check to determine when the roster user was last online. During the development process of myJabber, we found it useful to have the capability to check the version of software and the OS version the roster user is running.

ON THE CD-ROM You can find the code for this chapter on the CD-ROM in the \openIM\chapter14 folder. This code also includes the code from previous chapters.

Getting a Roster User's Local Time

If you want to know the time where the roster user you're chatting with is located, a simple call to the Matrix server can tell you.

You need to add a menu item to the `MainForm` to send your request. To do so, just follow these steps:

1. Open the Menu Editor and add a new menu item to the Roster menu, placing it just above the Presence menu item; give it a `caption` of `CTCP Requests` and set the `name` to

`MnuRoster_CTCP`. Then, as a subitem of `MnuRoster_CTCP`, add a new entry and set the caption to `Get Time` and the name to `mnuRoster_CTCP_GetTime`.

2. In the `mnuRoster_CTCP_GetVersion_Click` event of the `MainForm`, add the following code:

```
If cSession.Active Then
    With TreeView1
        ' make sure the selected Item has a parent then we know
        ' that it is a roster item or transport
        If Not .SelectedItem.Parent Is Nothing Then
            If .SelectedItem.Parent.Text = "OnLine" Then
                ' send the gt time request
                cSession.SendTimeRequest .SelectedItem.Key
            End If
        End If
    End With
End If
```

As in all calls to the Matrix COM Library, you first need to make sure that you have an active connection. Then check to see whether the user is online by checking the parent node of the treeview. For you to check the user's time, that user must be online.

3. Call the `SendTimeRequest` function in the Matrix COM Library, sending it the JID of the roster user from whom you want to retrieve the time. The Matrix COM Library then sends the XML request to the Jabber server and waits for a reply. After the Jabber server replies (if it replies at all — some clients don't support the time request), the Matrix COM Library fires the `OnTimeResult` event in the OpenIM client.

In `cSession_OnTimeResult`, you need to add the code to display the information that the Matrix COM Library returns. `cSession_OnTimeResult` returns the JID that sends you the reply, as well as the UTC-formatted time as a string. (UTC is Coordinated Universal Time, which was formerly known as Greenwich Mean Time.)

4. You use the message form that you created in Chapter 10 to display the information. In `cSession_OnTimeResult`, add the following code:

```
Dim myReceiveFrm As New frmRecieveMsg


    'load a new instance of the Receive Message form
    With myReceiveFrm
        ' set the tag so we can use it later to reply to the message
        .Tag = FromJID
        ' fill the form with the message
        .Caption = "Message From " & FromJID
```

```
        .txtMessage = "Time: " & Local_DateTime & vbCrLf
        .lblSubject = "Time Response from " & FromJID
        .Show
    End With
    ' add the form to our collection of Receive forms
    colReceiveMsg.Add myReceiveFrm, Str(myReceiveFrm.hWnd)
```

CROSS-REFERENCE For the details of this function, see Chapter 10.

Figure 14-1 shows a time response.

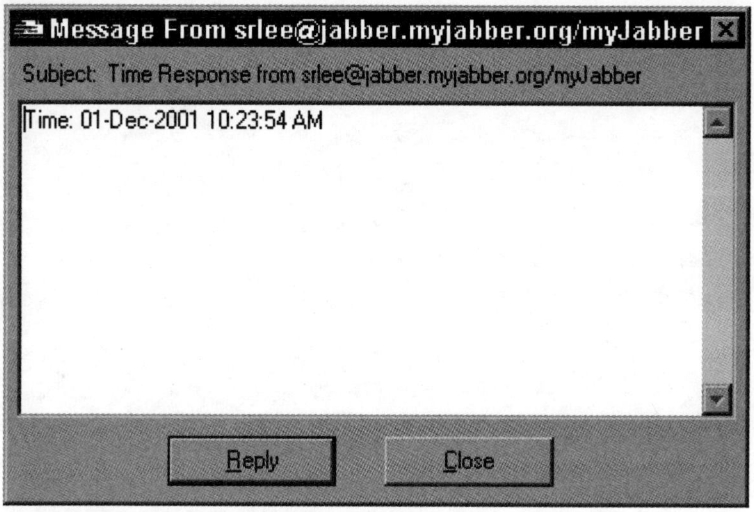

Figure 14-1: Example of a time response

Replying to a Time Request

We've haven't made any API calls up to this point, but in this case, we use them to return the time zone of the client. If you're using API calls, you must declare them in your module.

To reply to a time request, follow these steps:

1. Open the `mUtils` module and, in the General Declarations area, enter the following code:

```
'/******************** Time Zone information declares
********************/

Private Type SYSTEMTIME
    wYear As Integer
    wMonth As Integer
    wDayOfWeek As Integer
```

```
      wDay As Integer
      wHour As Integer
      wMinute As Integer
      wSecond As Integer
      wMilliseconds As Integer
End Type


Private Type TIME_ZONE_INFORMATION
   Bias As Long
   StandardName(0 To 63) As Byte ' used to accommodate Unicode strings
   StandardDate As SYSTEMTIME
   StandardBias As Long
   DaylightName(0 To 63) As Byte ' used to accommodate Unicode strings
   DaylightDate As SYSTEMTIME
   DaylightBias As Long
End Type


Private Const TIME_ZONE_ID_INVALID = &HFFFFFFFF
Private Const TIME_ZONE_ID_UNKNOWN = 0
Private Const TIME_ZONE_ID_STANDARD = 1
Private Const TIME_ZONE_ID_DAYLIGHT = 2


Private Declare Function GetTimeZoneInformation Lib "kernel32" _
(lpTimeZoneInformation As TIME_ZONE_INFORMATION) As Long
```

> **NOTE** We generated these declarations by using the API text viewer utility that ships with Visual Basic.

2. Add the following function to the `mUtils` module:

```
Public Function GetTimeZone() As String
Dim TZ As TIME_ZONE_INFORMATION
Dim lRetVal As Long
Dim lLength As Long


    lRetVal = GetTimeZoneInformation(TZ)
    lLength = InStr(1, TZ.StandardName, Chr$(0))
    GetTimeZone = Left(TZ.StandardName, lLength - 1)


End Function
```

TIP We very highly recommend that you review the documentation on making Win API calls within Visual Basic. Although they're not difficult, you do need to follow certain rules, but those rules are beyond the scope of this book. The one thing we do point out is that you need to allocate all strings to the right length before sending them into an API call.

3. Now, after someone sends a request to you to get your local time, the Matrix COM Library fires the `cSession_OnTimeRequest` event. In that event of the `MainForm`, enter the following code:

```
Dim sUTC As String
Dim sTZ As String
Dim sDisplay As String

    ' set up return fields
    sUTC = Format(Now, "YYYYDDMM") & "T" & Format(Now, "hh:mm:ss")
    sTZ = Trim(GetTimeZone())
    sDisplay = Format(Now, "Short Date") & " " & Format(Now, "Long
time")

    ' send response
    cSession.SendTimeResponse FromJID, sUTC, sTZ, sDisplay
```

The `cSession_OnTimeRequest` event sends in the JID of the user requesting the data and, as do almost all the events that the Matrix fires, it also returns the full XML data.

You reply to the message by formatting a string with the UTC time and another string with your time zone. You can get your time zone by calling the wrapper function `GetTimeZone()` that you created in `mUtils` and, finally, you create a string that displays your date and time in a readable format.

4. Call the `SendTimeResponse` function in the Matrix COM Library, passing in the `FromJID` and the strings that you just created. Figure 14-2 shows an example of the information we sent this way in the myJabber client.

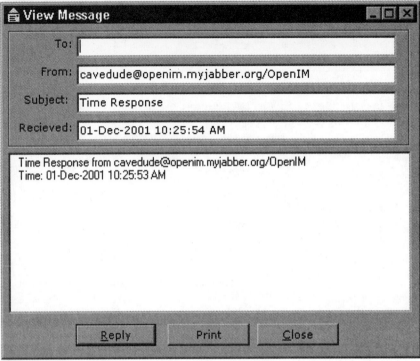

Figure 14-2: Example of myJabber receiving our Time Response

Getting a Roster User's Client Version

In this section, we show you how to send a request to a roster user to find out what client the user is running. Just follow these steps:

1. Open the Menu Editor again and, under the CTCP menu item, add a subitem, as you did with the Get Time menu item in the "Getting a Roster User's Local Time" section of this chapter. Set the caption to Get Version and the name property to mnuRoster_CTCP_GetVersion.

2. In the mnuRoster_CTCP_GetVersion_Click event of the MainForm, add the following code:

```
If cSession.Active Then
        With TreeView1
                ' make sure the selected Item has a parent then we know
                ' that it is a roster item or transport
                If Not .SelectedItem.Parent Is Nothing Then
                    If .SelectedItem.Parent.Text = "OnLine" Then
```

```
                    ' send the gt time request
                cSession.SendVersionRequest .SelectedItem.Key
            End If
        End If
    End With
End If
```

This code is almost exactly the same as that of the `GetTime_Click` event, but you call `cSession.SendVersionRequest` instead of `cSession.SendTimeRequest`. Again, the user must be online for you to retrieve the version of client that user is running. As it does with the `SendTimeRequest` method, the Matrix COM Library sends the XML to the server and, after it receives a reply, fires the `cSession_OnVersionResult` event.

In `cSession_OnVersionResult`, you need to add the code to display the information that returns. `cSession_OnVersionResult` sends in the JID that sent you the reply, the application name and version number of the client that the roster user is running, and the operating system version that the roster user is using.

3. In the `cSession_OnVersionResult` event of the `MainForm`, add the following code to produce a message, the same as you did for `cSession_OnTimeResult`:

```
Dim myReceiveFrm As New frmRecieveMsg
Dim sMsg As String

    ' build the message string
    sMsg = "Application Name: " & AppName & vbCrLf
    sMsg = sMsg & "Application Version: " & AppVer & vbCrLf
    sMsg = sMsg & "Operating System: " & OS

    'load a new instance of the Receive Message form
    With myReceiveFrm
        ' set the tag so we can use it later to reply to the message
        .Tag = FromJID
        ' fill the form with the message
        .Caption = "Message From " & FromJID
        .txtMessage = sMsg
        .lblSubject = "Version Response from " & FromJID
        .Show
    End With
    ' add the form to our collection of Receive forms
    colReceiveMsg.Add myReceiveFrm, Str(myReceiveFrm.hWnd)
```

The only difference here is that the body of the message contains the results of the version request. Other than that, the Message form is created the same way, as it is everywhere else you use it in the program. Figure 14-3 shows a version response appearing in a Message form.

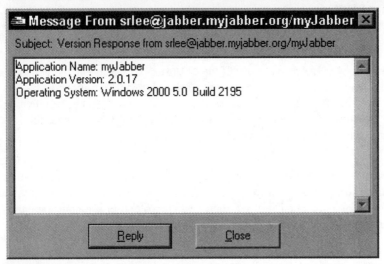

Figure 14-3: Example of a version response

Replying to a Version Request

You need another API call to return the OS version of the client, so follow these steps:

1. Open the mUtils module again and, in the General Declarations section, add the following declarations:

```
'/******** GET OS Version Info ****************/
Public Type OSVERSIONINFO
    dwOSVersionInfoSize As Long
    dwMajorVersion As Long
    dwMinorVersion As Long
    dwBuildNumber As Long
    dwPlatformId As Long
    szCSDVersion As String * 128       '  Maintenance string for PSS
usage
End Type


Public Const VER_PLATFORM_WIN32s = 0
Public Const VER_PLATFORM_WIN32_WINDOWS = 1
Public Const VER_PLATFORM_WIN32_NT = 2
```

```
Public Declare Function GetVersionEx Lib "kernel32" Alias
"GetVersionExA" (lpVersionInformation As OSVERSIONINFO) As Long
```

TIP Don't let the use of API calls intimidate you. Making API calls is no different from calling a normal DLL or COM object. A little time spent with API calls can make a tremendous difference in the performance and user friendliness of your application.

2. Add the following code for the new `GetOSVersion` function:

```
Public Function GetOSVersion() As String
Dim OS As OSVERSIONINFO
Dim result As Long

    OS.dwOSVersionInfoSize = Len(OS)
    result = GetVersionEx(OS)

    Select Case OS.dwPlatformId
        Case VER_PLATFORM_WIN32_NT
            If OS.dwMajorVersion <= 4 Then
                GetOSVersion = "Windows NT "
            End If
            If OS.dwMajorVersion = 5 Then
                GetOSVersion = "Windows 2000 "
            End If

        Case VER_PLATFORM_WIN32_WINDOWS
            If OS.dwMajorVersion > 4 Or (OS.dwMajorVersion = 4 And
OS.dwMinorVersion > 0) Then
                GetOSVersion = "Windows 98 "
            Else
                GetOSVersion = "Windows 95 "
            End If
    End Select

    GetOSVersion = GetOSVersion & OS.dwMajorVersion & "." &
OS.dwMinorVersion & "  Build " & OS.dwBuildNumber

End Function
```

NOTE You can access the documentation for the entire API in the API Reference on MSDN at the following URL: `http://msdn.microsoft.com/library/`.

After someone sends a request to you to get your client version, the Matrix COM Library fires the `cSession_OnVersionRequest` event. The following code returns the information to the client requesting the information:

```
Dim sAppName As String
Dim sAppVersion As String
Dim sOS As String

    sAppName = App.ProductName
    sAppVersion = App.Major & "." & App.Minor & "." & App.Revision
    sOS = GetOSVersion()
    cSession.SendVersionResponse FromJID, sAppName, sAppVersion, sOS
```

You may notice that we use the `App` object in Visual Basic to return the requested information. Doing so saves us from having to update this code every time we release a new version. We then call our new `GetOSVersion` function to return the operating system that we're using and, finally, call the `SendVersionResponse` method of the Matrix server, passing the information we've gathered. `cSession_OnVersionRequest` again sends in the JID of the client asking for the response, and we use it to deliver the information back to them. Figure 14-4 shows an example of the myJabber client receiving our Version Response.

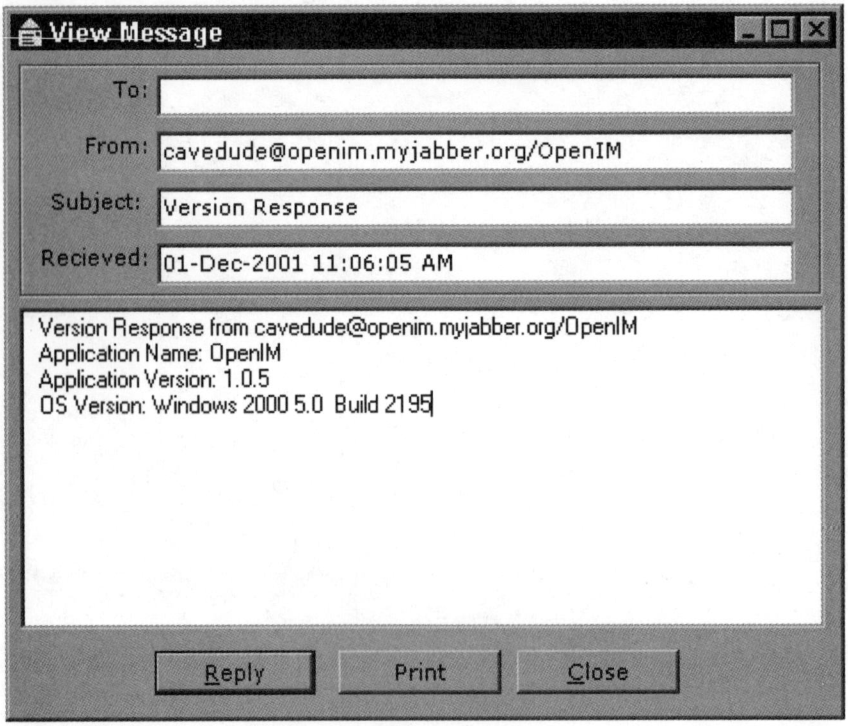

Figure 14-4: Example of myJabber receiving a version response

Getting the Time the Roster User Was Last Online

If you're looking for a particular roster user and wonder when that person was last online, it's no problem with Jabber! Just make a simple call to the `SendLastSeenRequest` event of the Matrix server, and you can find out. Follow these steps:

1. Open the Visual Basic Menu Editor and on the Roster menu, just below the Presence subitem, add a new item. Set the `caption` to `Last Seen` and the name to `MnuRoster_LastSeen`.

2. In the `MnuRoster_LastSeen_Click` event of the `MainForm` code window, enter the following code:

```
If cSession.Active Then
    With TreeView1
        ' make sure the selected Item has a parent then we know
        ' that it is a roster item or transport
        If Not .SelectedItem.Parent Is Nothing Then
            ' send the gt time request
            cSession.SendLastSeenRequest .SelectedItem.Key
        End If
    End With
End If
```

Notice that, this time, you don't check to determine whether the roster user is online; obviously, you don't need the roster user online for this event. The Jabber server is actually what responds to this event and not the client program. So all you do is call the `cSession.SendLastSeenRequest` method of the Matrix COM Library, passing the JID that you're querying.

3. After the Jabber server responds, the Matrix COM Library fires the `cSession_OnLastSeenResult` event. In `cSession_OnLastSeenResult`, enter the following code:

```
Dim myReceiveFrm As New frmRecieveMsg
    'load a new instance of the Receive Message form
    With myReceiveFrm
        ' set the tag so we can use it later to reply to the message
        .Tag = FromJID
        ' fill the form with the message
        .Caption = "Message From " & FromJID
        .txtMessage = FromJID & " Was last seen " &
SecondsToDate(Seconds) & " ago"
        .lblSubject = "Last Seen Response from " & FromJID
        .Show
    End With
```

```
' add the form to our collection of Receive forms
colReceiveMsg.Add myReceiveFrm, Str(myReceiveFrm.hWnd)
```

As before, you're going to display the result in a Message window. Notice that the `cSession_OnLastSeenResult` event returns the last time that the user was online, in seconds. To make the result more readable, you can convert the seconds to days, hours, minutes, and seconds. The following code shows you how to do this.

In the `mUtils` module, create the following new function:

```
Public Function SecondsToDate(lSeconds As Long) As String
Dim iDays As Long
Dim iHours As Long
Dim iMinutes As Long
Dim iSeconds As Long

    SecondsToDate = ""
    If lSeconds > 0 Then
        iDays = Int(lSeconds / 86400)
        iHours = Int((lSeconds - (iDays * 86400)) / 3600)
        iMinutes = Int((lSeconds - (iDays * 86400) - (iHours * 3600)) /
60)
        iSeconds = Int((lSeconds - (iDays * 86400) - (iHours * 3600) -
(iMinutes * 60)))
        If iDays > 0 Then
            SecondsToDate = iDays & " Day(s) "
        End If
        If iHours > 0 Then
            SecondsToDate = SecondsToDate & iHours & " Hours(s) "
        End If
        If iMinutes > 0 Then
            SecondsToDate = SecondsToDate & iMinutes & " Minutes(s) "
        End If
        If SecondsToDate > "" Then
            SecondsToDate = SecondsToDate & " and " & iSeconds & "
seconds "
        End If
    End If

End Function
```

This function converts the seconds into a readable string. Figure 14-5 shows an example of the Message window after it receives a last seen result.

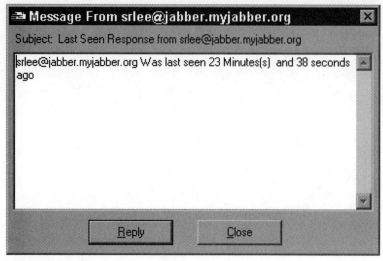

Figure 14-5: Example of a last seen result

Summary

You now can retrieve a roster user's client version and operating system as well as the user's current time and the last time that the user was online. You can also reply to the same requests from a roster user. This should give you enough insight to be able to add other options to the client based on what you see in other Jabber clients and from reading information at `www.jabber.org`.

You now have an instant messaging client that you can use. As we mention several times throughout the book, this program is only a basic client, but it's usable, and you can now give it to your friends to help you find all the little bugs and such that you missed. One of the biggest things that you probably want to do is to add much more error-handling capabilities to the package. We avoided adding it to this code so that it didn't interfere with the Jabber code we were trying to show you.

Appendix A

What's on the CD-ROM

This appendix provides you with information on the contents of the CD that accompanies this book. (For the latest and greatest information, please refer to the ReadMe file that you find at the root of the CD.) The following list describes what you find in this appendix:

♦ System requirements
♦ Using the CD with Windows, Linux, and Macintosh
♦ What's on the CD
♦ Troubleshooting

System Requirements

Make sure that your computer meets the minimum system requirements that we list in this section. If your computer doesn't match most of these requirements, you may experience a problem using the contents of the CD.

For Windows 9x, Windows 2000, Windows NT4 (with SP 4 or later), Windows Me, or Windows XP, you need the following:

♦ PC with a Pentium processor running at 120 Mhz or faster
♦ At least 32 MB of total RAM; for best performance, we recommend at least 64 MB
♦ Ethernet network interface card (NIC) or modem with a speed of at least 28,800 bps
♦ A CD-ROM drive

For Linux, you need the following:

♦ PC with a Pentium processor running at 120 Mhz or faster
♦ At least 32 MB of total RAM; for best performance, we recommend at least 64 MB
♦ Ethernet network interface card (NIC) or modem with a speed of at least 28,800 bps

◆ A CD-ROM drive

For Macintosh, you need the following:

◆ Mac OS computer with a 68040 or faster processor running OS 7.6 or later; for JabberFOX, you need OS X

◆ At least 32 MB of total RAM; for best performance, we recommend at least 64 MB

Using the CD with Windows

To install the items from the CD to your hard drive, follow these steps:

1. Insert the CD into your computer's CD-ROM drive.

2. A window appears displaying the following options: Install, Explore, eBook, Links, and Exit. The following list describes these options:

   ◆ **Install:** Enables you to install the supplied software and/or the author-created samples on the CD-ROM.

   ◆ **Explore:** Enables you to view the contents of the CD-ROM in its directory structure.

   ◆ **eBook:** Enables you to view an electronic version of the book.

   ◆ **Links:** Opens a hyperlinked page of Web sites.

   ◆ **Exit:** Closes the autorun window.

If you don't have autorun enabled or if the autorun window doesn't appear, follow these steps to access the CD:

1. Click Start ⇨ Run.

2. In the dialog box that appears, type d:\\setup.exe, where d is the letter of your CD-ROM drive. This action opens the autorun window that we describe in the preceding steps.

3. Choose the Install, Explore, eBook, Links, or Exit option from the menu. (See Step 2 in the preceding list for a description of these options.)

Using the CD with Linux

To install the items from the CD to your hard drive, follow these steps:

1. Log in as root.

2. Insert the CD into your computer's CD-ROM drive.

3. If Auto-Mount is enabled on your computer , wait for the CD to mount. Otherwise, follow these steps:

Command-line instructions: At the command prompt, type the following command:

```
mount /dev/cdrom /mnt/cdrom
```

(This command mounts the cdrom device to the mnt/cdrom directory. If your device has a different name, exchange cdrom with that device name — for example, cdrom1.)

Graphical instructions: Right-click the CD-ROM icon on the desktop and choose Mount CD-ROM from the pop-up menu. This command mounts your CD-ROM.

4. Browse the CD and follow the individual installation instructions for the products that we list in the section "What's on the CD," later in this appendix.

5. To remove the CD from your CD-ROM drive, follow these steps:

Command-line instructions: At the command prompt, type the following command:

```
umount /mnt/cdrom
```

Graphical instructions: Right-click the CD-ROM icon on the desktop and choose UMount CD-ROM from the pop-up menu. This command mounts your CD-ROM.

Using the CD with the Mac OS

To install the items from the CD to your hard drive, follow these steps:

1. Insert the CD into your CD-ROM drive.

2. Double-click the icon for the CD after it appears on the desktop.

3. Most programs come with installers; for those, simply open the program's folder on the CD and double-click the Install or Installer icon. *Note:* To install some programs, just drag the program's folder from the CD window and drop it on your hard drive icon.

What's on the CD

The following sections provide a summary of the software and other materials that you find on the CD.

Author-created materials

All author-created material from the book, including code listings and samples, are on the CD in the \\OpenIM folder.

Applications

The following applications are on the CD:

♦ **Adobe Acrobat:** Adobe® Acrobat® Reader® is free software that enables you to view and print Adobe Portable Document Format (PDF) files on all major computer platforms, as well as fill in and submit Adobe PDF forms online. An expanded version of Acrobat Reader for Windows offers additional functionality, including support for the visually impaired and the capability to search a collection of Adobe PDF files.

♦ **Gabber:** Gabber is a free and open-source GNOME client for the Jabber instant messaging system. Jabber is a free and open-source-distributed system. It doesn't rely on a single server, and the protocol is well documented. Jabber enables communication with many different instant messaging systems, including ICQ and AIM. Several different Jabber clients are already available, but no other GNOME clients as of this writing.

♦ **Jabber:** We include the Jabber server; the AIM transport for connecting to the AOL instant messaging service; the ICQ transport for connecting to the ICQ instant messaging service; the MSN transport for connecting to the MSN messaging service; the Yahoo transport for connecting to the Yahoo! chat services; JUD, the Jabber User Directory, Conference; the Jabber Conference or group-chat server; JOSL, the Jabber Open Source License and (GPL); and the GNU General Public License.

♦ **JabberFOX:** JabberFOX is a Jabber client for the Mac OS X; the name stands for "Jabber *For OS X*." Jabber is an open-source instant messaging system fully based on XML. Thanks to the server-side Jabber agents, Jabber clients can communicate with users of other instant messaging systems, such as AIM, ICQ, Yahoo! Messenger, MSN Messenger, and IRC. JabberFOX is written in Objective-C, using Apple's Cocoa API, and tries to make full use of Aqua, Apple's cool new user-interface system. It aims at implementing all the standard Jabber features, including chat, group chat, messages, the roster (list of contacts), and agents. Eventually, we hope to incorporate all the features of the Jabber protocol, including browsing, strong encryption, and the new conferencing protocol.

♦ **Jabbernaut:** Jabbernaut is a client for the Jabber instant messaging system. It's different from other IM systems such as AIM and ICQ in that you not only can send Jabber messages, but you can also use a Jabber client to talk with other IM systems!

♦ **Jarl:** Jarl is a Perl/Tk application that enables you to access a Jabber account and gain full access to the Jabber IM system. It runs on any platform that supports Perl and Tk, which at this time is most of them. Jarl will eventually be a full-featured Jabber client that supports all the features that the Jabber IM offers.

♦ **Matrix:** Matrix is the name for our COM library, the library that the OpenIM client uses to communicate with the Jabber server. Matrix is written in Visual Basic by sltsCommunications and, at the time of this writing, isn't open source. This situation may change in the future. The Matrix COM Library focus is to enable a client to communicate with a Jabber server as easily as possible. Matrix is written as a set of classes, starting with a base Socket class. The design of Matrix enables you to add or change functionality very quickly.

♦ **Matrix Programmer's Guide:** The latest version available at the time of the release of this book. This guide changes frequently, and we recommend that you check `http://openIM.myjabber.org` for the most recent version.

♦ **myJabber:** myJabber is your gateway to the world of dependable, easy-to-use instant messaging and group conferencing. Lightweight, configurable, and very user friendly, myJabber has quickly become the top choice of users everywhere.

Designed for both the individual user and the corporate sector, myJabber contains many features that users of instant messaging want. Part of the worldwide Jabber community, myJabber interacts with AIM, ICQ, MSN Messenger, Yahoo! Messenger, and IRC, plus it can communicate with the unique Jabber group-chat and person-to-person chat rooms. myJabber contains customizable sound cues, supports person-to-person file transfers, and accepts "headline" broadcasts from MSN, Hotmail, and Yahoo!.

myJabber runs on Windows 95/98, NT, Me, XP, and Windows 2000. myJabber uses fewer system resources than other clients, displays a simple and friendly interface, and has fewer quirks to learn than other clients.

The sltsCommunications team tests each and every release by using these releases *every day*, at home and in the office. Couple myJabber with the Jabber networks that are springing up all around the world, and we believe that you're not going to find a more suitable instant messaging/conferencing system on the planet.

The myJabber home site at `www.myjabber.net` offers the latest releases, Jabber community news, and other information from the world of computers and open-source development.

♦ **OpenSSL:** The OpenSSL Project is a collaborative effort to develop a robust, commercial-grade, full-featured, open-source toolkit implementing the Secure Sockets Layer (SSL v2/v3) and Transport Layer Security (TLS v1) protocols, as well as a full-strength general-purpose cryptography library. A worldwide community of volunteers manages the project, and members use the Internet to communicate, plan, and develop the OpenSSL toolkit and its related documentation.

♦ **Phat Linux v3.3:** In late 1998, Phat Linux created a simple, easy-to-use Linux operating system that ran on a Windows 95/98 partition. Since then, many have tried to replicate what Phat Linux has done. It remains the leading Linux distribution that runs on a Windows partition, however, because of its support for and dedication to the Linux OS.

Phat Linux enables Windows users to run Linux while preserving their Windows partition. Phat Linux v3.3 comes with lots of popular software, including KDE 2.0, XFree86 3.3.6, Netscape, and much more.

♦ **PuTTY:** PuTTY is a free SSH, Telnet, and Rlogin client for 32-bit Windows systems.

♦ **WinRar (shareware):** WinRar is a Win32 archiving program with support for multimedia files. The WinRAR GUI runs on Windows 9*x*/ME/NT/2000/XP and is available in many languages. Rar command-line (console mode) versions run on Linux, BeOS, DOS, OS/2, and various flavors of Unix.

♦ **WinZip (shareware):** WinZip, a Win32 archiving program, brings the convenience of Windows to the use of zip files and other compression formats. The optional wizard interface makes zipping and unzipping easier than ever. WinZip features built-in support for CAB files and for popular Internet file formats such as TAR, gzip, UUencode, BinHex, and MIME. ARJ, LZH, and ARC files are supported via external programs. WinZip interfaces to most virus scanners.

Shareware programs are fully functional, trial versions of copyrighted programs. If you like particular programs, register with their authors for a nominal fee and receive licenses, enhanced versions, and technical support. *Freeware programs* are copyrighted games, applications, and utilities that are free for personal use. Unlike shareware, these programs don't require a fee or provide technical support. *GNU software* is governed by its own license, which we include inside the folder of the GNU product. See the GNU license for more details.

Trial, demo, or evaluation versions are usually limited either by time or functionality (such as no capability to save projects). Some trial versions are very sensitive to system date changes. If you alter your computer's date, the programs "times out" and is no longer functional.

eBook version of *Jabber™ Programming*

The complete text of this book is on the CD in Adobe's Portable Document Format (PDF). You can read and search through the file with the Adobe Acrobat Reader (also included on the CD). You should find this extremely handy while working on the source code that we include in the book.

Troubleshooting

If you have difficulty installing or using any of the materials on the companion CD, try the following solutions:

♦ **Turn off any anti-virus software that you may have running.** Installers sometimes mimic virus activity and can make your computer incorrectly believe that a virus is infecting it. (Make sure that you turn the anti-virus software back on later.)

♦ **Close all running programs.** The more programs that you're running, the less memory is available to other programs. Installers also typically update files and programs; if you keep other programs running, installation may not work correctly.

♦ **Reference the ReadMe.** Please refer to the ReadMe file that you find at the root of the CD-ROM for the latest product information at the time of publication.

If you still experience trouble with the CD, please call the Hungry Minds Customer Care phone number: (800) 762-2974. Outside the United States, call 1 (317) 572-3994. You can also contact Hungry Minds Customer Service by e-mail at `techsupdum@hungryminds.com`. Hungry Minds provides technical support only for installation and other general quality-control items; for technical support on the applications themselves, consult the program's vendor or author.

jabber.xml and the Transport XML Files

In this appendix, we provide the complete, actual `jabber.xml` and transport XML files that you use on the `openIM.myJabber.org` server. These are the completed files excerpts of which are shown in the earlier chapters. Included here are comments from the original `jabber.xml` file as well as comments that we added. These files are also available on the CD.

First is the `jabber.xml` file:

```
<jabber>

<!--
This is the Jabber server configuration file. The file is
broken into different sections based on the services being
managed by jabberd, the server daemon. Most of the important
sections have comments and are easy to modify. You can find
full instructions in the server howto, which is available at
http://docs.jabber.org/. Note that when you see a tag like
"jabberd:cmdline", it's automatically replaced on startup
with the command line flag passed in to jabberd. This enables
you to override parameters set in this configuration file if
necessary or desired. Also note as you comment things in and
out that jabberd does not like comments within comments, so
be careful with your XML. :)
-->


<!--
The following <service/> section is for the session manager,
the most important component within the server. This section
contains the following types of information:

    * the server's hostname
    * other basic server information
    * the location of the session log file
    * email addresses for server administrators
```

```
      * the location of the server that provides update information
      * registration instructions for new users
      * a welcome message for new users
      * a list of agents with which users can register
      * load rules for the modules within the session manager

  -->

  <service id="sessions">

    <!--
  Change hostname below to something other than "localhost",
      i.e., to the hostname or IP address of your Jabber server.
      Multiple <host/> entries are allowed - each one is for a
      separate virtual server. Note that each host entry must
      be on one line, the server doesn't like it otherwise! :)
      -->

    <host><jabberd:cmdline
  flag="h">openim.myjabber.org</jabberd:cmdline></host>

    <!--
    This is the custom configuration section for the
    Jabber session manager, a.k.a. "JSM".
    -->

    <jsm xmlns="jabber:config:jsm">

      <!--
      The <filter/> section below determines settings
      for mod_filter, a server-side module built into
      JSM that enables users to set delivery rules for
      messages they receive (not yet supported by all
      clients. The <allow/> subsection specifies which
      conditions and actions to enable. High-level
      descriptions of each setting can be found below
      (see docs.jabber.org for full details):

      * <default/> - a user cannot delete this one, it's
        the default rule for delivering messages
      * <max_size/> - the maximum number of rules in a
        user's rule set (we don't want to overdo it!)
      * conditions...
        * <ns/> - matches the query xmlns attrib on an iq packet
        * <unavailable/> - matches when user is unavailable
        * <from/> - matches the sender of the message
        * <resource/> - matches the receiver's resource
        * <subject/> - matches the subject of the message
```

```
        * <body/> - matches the body of the message
        * <show/> - matches the show tag on the receiver's presence
        * <type/> - matches the type of the message
        * <roster/> - matches if the sender is in your roster
        * <group/> - matches if the sender is in the specified group




* actions...
        * <error/> - replies with an error
        * <offline/> - stores the messages offline
        * <forward/> - forwards the message to another jid
        * <reply/> - sends a reply to the sender of the message
        * <continue/> - continues processing of the rules
        * <settype/> - changes the type of the message
    -->
    <filter>
        <default/>
        <max_size>100</max_size>
        <allow>
            <conditions>
                <ns/>
                <unavailable/>
                <from/>
                <resource/>
                <subject/>
                <body/>
                <show/>
                <type/>
                <roster/>
                <group/>
            </conditions>
            <actions>
                <error/>
                <offline/>
                <forward/>
                <reply/>
                <continue/>
                <settype/>
            </actions>
        </allow>
    </filter>

    <!-- The server vCard -->

    <vCard>
      <FN>Open-IM at myjabber</FN>
```

```
        <DESC>A Development Server</DESC>
        <URL>http://openim.myjabber.org/</URL>
    </vCard>



<!--
    Registration instructions and required fields. The
    notify attribute will send the server administrator(s)
    a message after each valid registration if it is set
    to "yes".
-->

    <register notify="yes">
      <instructions>Choose a username and password to register with
this server.</instructions>
      <name/>
      <email/>
    </register>

    <!--
    A welcome note that is sent to every new user who registers
    with your server. Comment it out to disable this function.
    -->

    <welcome>
      <subject>Welcome!</subject>
      <body>Welcome to the Jabber server at openim.myjabber.org -- we
hope you enjoy this experience! For information about how to use Jabber,
refer to your Jabber programming book from Hungry Minds Inc or the CD
provided with the book/</body>
    </welcome>

    <!--
    IDs with admin access - these people will receive admin
    messages (any message to="yourhostname" is an admin
    message).  These addresses must be local ids; they cannot
    be remote addresses.

    Note that they can also send announcements to all
    users of the server, or to all online users. To use
    the announcement feature, you need to send raw xml and be
    logged in as one of the admin users. Here is the syntax
    for sending an announcement to online users:

      <message to="yourhostname/announce/online">
        <body>announcement here</body>
      </message>
```

```
       <message to="yourhostname/announce/motd">
          <body>message (of the day) that is sent only once to all users
that are logged in and additionally to new ones as they log in</body>
       </message>

     Sending to /announce/motd/delete will remove any existing
     motd, and to /announce/motd/update will only update the motd
     without re-announcing to all logged in users.

     The <reply> will be the message that is automatically
     sent in response to any admin messages.
     -->


     <admin>
        <read>tsmelser@openim.myjabber.org</read>
        <write>tsmelser@openim.myjabber.org</write>
  <write>srlee@openim.myjabber.org</write>
  <write>cavedude@openim.myjabber.org</write>
        <reply>
           <subject>CaveDude Reply</subject>
           <body>This is a special administrative address. Your message
was received and forwarded to server administrators.</body>
        </reply>
     </admin>
     <!-- The above section (admin) has to be uncommented in the
default
          xml file. This section is not needed for the server to run.
TS
     -->


     <!--
     This is the resource that checks for updated versions
     of the Jabber server software. Note that you don't lose
     any functionality if you comment this out. Removing the
     <update/> config is especially a good strategy if your
     server is behind a firewall. If you want to use this
     feature, change 'localhost' to the hostname or IP address
     of your server, making sure that it is the same as your
     entry for <host/> above.
     -->
     <!--
     <update><jabberd:cmdline
flag="h">localhost</jabberd:cmdline></update>
     -->

     <!-- The update section should be commented out as it has been
causing
```

```
        problems for most admins and there are better ways of updating the
server.
        TS
    -->


    <!--
    This enables the server to automatically update the
    user directory when a vCard is edited.  The update is
    only sent to the first listed jud service below.  It is
    safe to remove this flag if you do not want any users
    automatically added to the directory.
    -->


    <vcard2jud/>

    <!--
    The <browse/> section identifies the transports and other
    services that are available from this server. Note that each
    entity identified here must exist elsewhere or be further
    defined in its own <service/> section below. These services
    will appear in the user interface of Jabber clients that
    connect to your server.
    -->

    <browse>

        <!--
        This is the default agent for the master Jabber User
        Directory, a.k.a. "JUD", which is located at jabber.org.
        You can add separate <service/> sections for additional
        directories, e.g., one for a company intranet.
        -->
<!--
        <service type="jud" jid="users.jabber.org" name="Jabber User
Directory">
            <ns>jabber:iq:search</ns>
            <ns>jabber:iq:register</ns>
        </service>

-->

        <service type="jud" jid="jud.openim.myjabber.org" name="OpenIM
User Directory">
            <ns>jabber:iq:search</ns>
            <ns>jabber:iq:register</ns>
        </service>
```

```
<!--
 For the sake of example I will start adding my services here and leave
 the examples alone to be used as reference.
 -->
<conference type="public" jid="conference.openim.myjabber.org"
name="Conferencing"/>

<service type="icq" jid="icq.openim.myjabber.org" name="ICQ Transport">
            <ns>jabber:iq:gateway</ns>
            <ns>jabber:iq:register</ns>
  <ns>jabber:iq:search</ns>
      </service>

      <service type="msn" jid="msn.openim.myjabber.org" name="MSN
Transport">
        <ns>jabber:iq:gateway</ns>
        <ns>jabber:iq:register</ns>
      </service>

      <service type="yahoo" jid="yahoo.openim.myjabber.org"
name="Yahoo! Transport">
        <ns>jabber:iq:gateway</ns>
        <ns>jabber:iq:register</ns>
      </service>


      <service type="aim" jid="aim.openim.myjabber.org" name="AIM
Transport">
        <ns>jabber:iq:gateway</ns>
        <ns>jabber:iq:register</ns>
      </service>

    </browse>

  </jsm>

  <!--
  The following section dynamically loads the individual
  modules that make up the session manager. Remove or
  comment out modules to disable them. Note that the order
  of modules is important, since packets are delivered
  based on the following order!!
  -->

  <load main="jsm">
    <jsm>./jsm/jsm.so</jsm>
    <mod_echo>./jsm/jsm.so</mod_echo>
    <mod_roster>./jsm/jsm.so</mod_roster>
    <mod_time>./jsm/jsm.so</mod_time>
```

```
      <mod_vcard>./jsm/jsm.so</mod_vcard>
      <mod_last>./jsm/jsm.so</mod_last>
      <mod_version>./jsm/jsm.so</mod_version>
      <mod_announce>./jsm/jsm.so</mod_announce>
      <mod_agents>./jsm/jsm.so</mod_agents>
      <mod_browse>./jsm/jsm.so</mod_browse>
      <mod_admin>./jsm/jsm.so</mod_admin>
      <mod_filter>./jsm/jsm.so</mod_filter>
      <mod_offline>./jsm/jsm.so</mod_offline>
      <mod_presence>./jsm/jsm.so</mod_presence>
      <mod_auth_plain>./jsm/jsm.so</mod_auth_plain>
      <mod_auth_digest>./jsm/jsm.so</mod_auth_digest>
      <mod_auth_0k>./jsm/jsm.so</mod_auth_0k>
      <mod_log>./jsm/jsm.so</mod_log>
      <mod_register>./jsm/jsm.so</mod_register>
      <mod_xml>./jsm/jsm.so</mod_xml>
    </load>

</service>

<!-- OK, we've finished defining the Jabber Session Manager. -->

<!-- The <xdb/> component handles all data storage, using the
filesystem. -->

<xdb id="xdb">
  <host/>
  <load>
    <xdb_file>./xdb_file/xdb_file.so</xdb_file>
  </load>
  <xdb_file xmlns="jabber:config:xdb_file">
    <spool><jabberd:cmdline flag='s'>./spool</jabberd:cmdline></spool>
  </xdb_file>
</xdb>

<!--
The following service manages incoming client socket connections.
There are several items you can set here to optimize performance:

  * authtime - default is unlimited, but you can set this to
    limit the amount of time allowed for authentication to be
    completed, e.g., <authtime>10</authtime> for 10 seconds

  * karma - this is an input/output rate limiting system that
    the Jabber team came up with to prevent bandwidth hogging.
    For details about karma, read the io section at the bottom
    and/or see docs.jabber.org. These are the low settings and
    apply per connection/socket and can be changed as desired.
-->
```

```
<service id="c2s">
  <load>
    <pthsock_client>./pthsock/pthsock_client.so</pthsock_client>
  </load>
  <pthcsock xmlns='jabber:config:pth-csock'>
    <authtime/>
    <karma>
      <init>10</init>
      <max>10</max>
      <inc>1</inc>
      <dec>1</dec>
      <penalty>-6</penalty>
      <restore>10</restore>
    </karma>

    <!--
    Use these to listen on particular addresses and/or ports.
    <ip port="5222">127.0.0.1</ip>
    -->
    <ip port="5222"/>

    <!--
    The <ssl/> tag acts pretty much like the <ip/> tag,
    except it defines that SSL is to be used on the
    ports and IP addresses specified. You must specify
    an IP address here, or the connections will fail.
    <ssl port='5223'>127.0.0.1</ssl>
    <ssl port='5224'>192.168.1.100</ssl>
    -->

  </pthcsock>
</service>

<!--
This is the default server error logging component,
which copies to a file and to STDERR.
-->

<log id='elogger'>
  <host/>
  <logtype/>
  <format>%d: [%t] (%h): %s</format>
  <file>error.log</file>
  <stderr/>
</log>

<!--
This is the default server record logging component,
```

```
which logs general statistical/tracking data.
-->

<log id='rlogger'>
  <host/>
  <logtype>record</logtype>
  <format>%d %h %s</format>
  <file>record.log</file>
</log>

<!-- The following two services are for handling server-to-server
traffic. -->

<!-- External asychronous DNS resolver -->

<service id="dnsrv">
  <host/>
  <load>
    <dnsrv>./dnsrv/dnsrv.so</dnsrv>
  </load>
  <dnsrv xmlns="jabber:config:dnsrv">
   <resend service="_jabber._tcp">s2s</resend> <!-- for supporting SRV
records -->
   <resend>s2s</resend>
  </dnsrv>
</service>

<!--
The following 's2s' config handles server connections and
dialback hostname verification.  The <legacy/> element is
here to enable communication with old 1.0 servers. The
karma settings are a little higher here to handle the
higher traffic of server-to-server connections (read
the io section below for more details, medium settings).
-->

<service id="s2s">
  <load>
    <dialback>./dialback/dialback.so</dialback>
  </load>
  <dialback xmlns='jabber:config:dialback'>
    <legacy/>
    <!-- Use these to listen on particular addresses and/or ports.
    <ip port="7000"/>
    <ip port="5269">127.0.0.1</ip>
    -->
    <ip port="5269"/>
    <karma>
      <init>50</init>
```

```
            <max>50</max>
            <inc>4</inc>
            <dec>1</dec>
            <penalty>-5</penalty>
            <restore>50</restore>
        </karma>
    </dialback>
 </service>

 <service id ="conference.openim.myjabber.org">
  <load><conference>./conference/conference.so</conference></load>
  <conference xmlns="jabber:config:conference">
<public/>
    <vCard>
    <FN>Conference Server</FN>
    <DESC>This is your Conference Server</DESC>
    <URL>Http://openim.myjabber.org</URL>
    </vCard>
  <history>20</history>
  <notice>
  <join> just got here</join>
  <leave> has run away</leave>
  <rename> has changed names to </rename>
  </notice>
  </conference>
  </service>

  <service id="jud">
    <host>jud.openim.myjabber.org</host>
    <load><jud>./jud/jud.so</jud></load>
    <jud xmlns="jabber:config:jud">
      <vCard>
        <FN>User Directory on OpenIM</FN>
        <DESC>This service provides a simple user directory
service</DESC>
        <URL>http://openim.myjabber.org</URL>
      </vCard>
    </jud>
  </service>

  <service id="icq_linker">
    <host>icq.openim.myjabber.org</host>
    <accept>
      <ip>xxx.xxx.xxx.xxx</ip>
      <port>7001</port>
      <secret>k7asfon</secret>
    </accept>
  </service>
```

```xml
  <service id="msn_linker">
    <host>msn.openim.myjabber.org</host>
    <accept>
      <ip>xxx.xxx.xxx.xxx</ip>
      <port>9001</port>
      <secret>k7asfon</secret>
    </accept>
  </service>

  <service id="yahoo_linker">
    <host>yahoo.openim.myjabber.org</host>
    <accept>
      <ip>xxx.xxx.xxx.xxx</ip>
      <port>6001</port>
      <secret>k7asfon</secret>
    </accept>
  </service>

<service id="aim_linker">
    <host>aim.openim.myjabber.org</host>
    <accept>
      <ip>xxx.xxx.xxx.xxx</ip>
      <port>8001</port>
      <secret>k7asfon</secret>
    </accept>
  </service>


<!-- ICQ Transport Starts Here -->
<!--
 <service id="icq.openim.myjabber.org">
 <icqtrans xmlns="jabber:config:icqtrans">
 <instructions>Please enter your ICQ number (in the "username"
field),nickname, and password. Leave the "username" field blank to
create a new ICQ number.</instructions>
 <search>Search for ICQ users</search>
 <vCard>
  <FN>ICQ Transport</FN>
  <DESC>This is the ICQ Transport</DESC>
  <URL>http://openim.myjabber.org/</URL>
 </vCard>
 <prime>37</prime>
 <ports>
 <min>2000</min>
 <max>3000</max>
 </ports>
 <server>
        <ip>xxx.xxx.xxx.xxx</ip>
        </server>
```

```
</icqtrans>
    <load>
<icqtrans>./icq-transport/icqtrans.so</icqtrans>
    </load>
    </service>
-->



<!--
If you identified additional agents in the main <service/>
section (see examples above), you'll need to define each
of them here using a separate <service/> section for each
<agent/> you identified. Note that the <agent/> sections
determine what gets shown to clients that connect to your
server, whereas the following <service/> sections define
these services within the server itself. The following are
examples only, you will need to create/modify them to get
them working on your Jabber server. See the README files
for each agent and/or the server howto for further
information/instructions.
-->

<!-- we're commenting these out, of course :)  I always leave these
examples in place to use as a reference when I get lost. TS

<service id="conference">
  <load>
    <groupchat>/path/to/groupchat.so</groupchat>
  </load>
  <host>conference.localhost</host>
</service>

<service id="irc">
  <host>irc.localhost</host>
</service>

<service id="aim.localhost">
  <accept>
    <ip/>
    <port>7009</port>
    <secret>jabber-rocks</secret>
  </accept>
</service>

<service id="yahoo.localhost">
  <accept>
    <ip/>
    <port>9001</port>
```

```
      <secret>jabber-rocks</secret>
   </accept>
</service>

end of <service/> examples -->

<!--
The following <io/> config initializes the top-level
I/O, otherwise known as MIO (Managed Input/Output).
-->

<io>

   <!-- Set the default karma for *all* sockets -->
   <!-- definition of terms:

     * Avg. Throughput - The number of bytes you can
       send every second without incurring any penalty.

     * Burst Allowed - The maximum number of bytes you
       can send in 2 seconds without incurring any penalty.

     * Max Sustained Rate - If you send data as fast as
       you can, you will hit penalty, and will not be
       able to send for 10 seconds; the max sustained
       rate is the average rate you can dump data when
       you are dumping as much data as you can, as fast
       as you can.

     * Seconds to Recover from Burst - The amount of time
       it will take to reach Avg. Throughput capability
       after sending a max burst of data.

     * Penalty Length - The length of your penalty is
       determined according to this formula:
              abs(penalty) * Heartbeat seconds
       E.g., a penalty of -5 and heartbeat of 2 will
       cause your penalty length to be 10 seconds.
       Note that a penalty CANNOT be less than -100,
       otherwise strange things might happen.

   -->
   <!-- Example of Low Karma Limits
       Avg. Throughput: 1k-2k/s
       Burst Allowed To: 5.5k/s
       Max Sustained Rate: 485b/s
       Seconds to Recover from Burst: 20
       Penalty Length: 12 seconds
   <karma>
```

```
  <heartbeat>2</heartbeat>
  <init>10</init>
  <max>10</max>
  <inc>1</inc>
  <dec>1</dec>
  <penalty>-6</penalty>
  <restore>10</restore>
</karma>
-->

<!-- Example of Medium Karma Limits
     Avg. Throughput: 5k-10k/s
     Burst Allowed: 125.5k/s
     Max Sustained Rate: 12.6k/s
     Seconds to Recover From Burst: 25
     Penalty Length: 10 seconds
<karma>
  <heartbeat>2</heartbeat>
  <init>50</init>
  <max>50</max>
  <inc>4</inc>
  <dec>1</dec>
  <penalty>-5</penalty>
  <restore>50</restore>
</karma>
-->

<!-- Example of High Karma Limits
     Avg. Throughput: 5k-10k/s
     Burst Allowed: 206k/s
     Max Sustained Rate: 34.3k/s
     Seconds to Recover from Burst: 21
     Penalty Length: 6 seconds
<karma>
  <heartbeat>2</heartbeat>
  <init>64</init>
  <max>64</max>
  <inc>6</inc>
  <dec>1</dec>
  <penalty>-3</penalty>
  <restore>64</restore>
</karma>
-->

<!--
Set rate limits to monitor the number of connection
attempts from a single IP, any more than [points]
within [time] will engage the limit.  This setting
applies to all incoming connections to any service,
```

```
    unless otherwise overridden by that service.
    -->

    <rate points="5" time="25"/>

<!--A word on "Karma". The Default settings placed in this server are
quite useable for almost all applications that I have used it for, Feel
free to experiment, but be careful with your settings, you could have a
server that runs, but will not allow  connections or traffic. TS -->

    <!--
    The following section initializes SSL for top-level I/O.  This works
only when the server is compiled with openssl Get the files for OpenSSl
at http://www.openssl.org.  And see the howto on setting this
up for jabber, included in this book in Appendix C.
    -->
    <!--
    <ssl>
      <key ip='192.168.1.1'>/path/to/cert_and_key.pem</key>
      <key ip='192.168.1.100'>/path/to/other/cert_and_key.pem</key>
    </ssl>
    -->

    <!--
    The following section is used to allow or deny
    communications from specified IP networks or
    addresses. If there is no <allow/> section,
    then *all* IPs will be allowed to connect. If
    you allow one block, then only that block may
    connect. Note that <allow/> is checked before
    <deny/>, so if a specific address is allowed
    but the network for that address is denied,
    then that address will still be denied. This can be used to create a
simple "closed" network.
    -->

    <!--
    <allow><ip>127.0.0.0</ip><mask>255.255.255.0</mask></allow>
    <allow><ip>12.34.56.78</ip></allow>
    <deny><ip>22.11.44.0</ip><mask>255.255.255.0</mask></deny>
    -->

  </io>

    <!--
    This specifies the file to store the pid of the process in. This will
store the File in the same directory  with the jabber.xml file, if you
want the pid file stored  someplace else then you must specify the
location here. TS
```

```
  -->
  <pidfile>./jabber.pid</pidfile>


</jabber>
```

Next is the `msntrans.xml` file:

```
<jabber>

<!-- this is the transport xml file used to run the MSN transport in
it's own separate process. -->


  <service id="msn_linker">
    <uplink/>
    <connect>
      <ip>xxx.xxx.xxx.xxx</ip>
      <port>9001</port>
      <secret>k7asfon</secret>
    </connect>
  </service>

  <service id="msn.openim.myjabber.org">

    <msntrans xmlns="jabber:config:msntrans">

    <vCard>
        <FN>MSN Transport</FN>
        <DESC>myJabber MSN Transport</DESC>
        <URL>http://openim.myjabber.org</URL>
    </vCard>

    </msntrans>

    <load>
      <msntrans>./msn-transport/msntrans.so</msntrans>
    </load>

  </service>

</jabber>
```

Here is the `yahootrans.xml` file:

```
<!-- this is the transport xml file used to run the Yahoo transport in
it's own separate process. -->
```

```
<jabber>

  <service id="yahoo_linker">
    <uplink/>
    <connect>
      <ip>xxx.xxx.xxx.xxx</ip>
      <port>6001</port>
      <secret>k7asfon</secret>
    </connect>
  </service>

  <service id="yahoo.openim.myjabber.org">

    <yahootrans xmlns="jabber:config:yahootrans">
      <instructions> Enter your Yahoo Account and
Password.</instructions>
      <search>Search for Yahoo! users</search>

      <vCard>
        <FN>Yahoo! Transport</FN>
        <DESC>openim Yahoo! Transport</DESC>
        <URL>http://openim.myjabber.org</URL>
      </vCard>
        <disable-tcp/>

    </yahootrans>

    <load>
      <yahoo_transport>./yahoo-
transport/src/yahootrans.so</yahoo_transport>
    </load>

  </service>

</jabber>
```

Here is the `aimtrans.xml` file:

```
<jabber>


<!-- this is the transport xml file used to run the AIM transport in
it's own separate process. -->

  <service id="aim_linker">
    <uplink/>
    <connect>
```

```
        <ip>xxx.xxx.xxx.xxx</ip>
        <port>8001</port>
        <secret>k7asfon</secret>
    </connect>
  </service>

  <service id="aim.openim.myjabber.org">

    <aimtrans xmlns="jabber:config:aimtrans">
        <instructions> Enter your AIM Account and
Password.</instructions>
        <search>Search for AIM users</search>

<!-- Remember that the AIM Program file  must be located by this file,
the following lines point to it -->
        <aimbinarydir>/usr/local/jabber/jabber2/aimprogram</aimbinarydir>
        <vCard>
          <FN>AIM Transport</FN>
          <DESC>openim AIM Transport</DESC>
          <URL>http://openim.myjabber.org</URL>
        </vCard>
        <disable-tcp/>

    </aimtrans>

    <load>
        <aim_transport>./aim-transport/src/aimtrans.so</aim_transport>
    </load>

  </service>

</jabber>
```

Here is the `icqtrans.xml` file:

```
<jabber>
<!-- this is the transport xml file used to run the ICQ transport in
it's own separate process. -->

  <service id="icqlinker">
    <uplink/>
    <connect>
      <ip>xxx.xxx.xxx.xxx</ip>
      <port>7001</port>
      <secret>k7asfon</secret>
    </connect>
  </service>
```

```
   <service id="icq.openim.myjabber.org">

     <icqtrans xmlns="jabber:config:icqtrans">

       <instructions>Please enter your ICQ number (in the "username"
field),
                    nickname, and password.  Leave the "username" field
blank
                    to create a new ICQ number.</instructions>

       <search>Search for ICQ users</search>

       <vCard>
         <FN>ICQ Transport</FN>
         <DESC>This is ICQ Transport</DESC>
         <URL>http://openim.myjabber.org/</URL>
       </vCard>
       <prime>501</prime>
       <ports>
         <min>2000</min>
         <max>3000</max>
       </ports>
       <server>
         <ip>xxx.xxx.xxx.xxx</ip>
       </server>
     </icqtrans>

     <load>
       <icqtrans>./icq-transport/icqtrans.so</icqtrans>
     </load>

   </service>
</jabber>
```

Appendix C

Matrix Programmer's Guide

cSession

This is the main object that allows you to communicate to the Jabber server. The `Session` object handles all the socket functionality so the developer using Matrix does not have to worry about any socket programming. Also included in the `Session` object is most of the XML parsing and raising of events to make GUI programming much easier by passing common data used for specific events but at the same time always exposing a Matrix XML node in case the developer needs to further parse the XML or handle anything specific that Matrix does not support.

Properties

- `Active` [Boolean — Read Only] — Returns `True` if the Jabber `Session` is active.
- `Available` [Boolean — Read Only] — Returns `True` if your `Session` is available and able to receive presence from `RosterItems`.
- `AuthType` [eAuthType] — Setting to contain `auth` type used to authorize on the Jabber server; by default this is `auto` and will use the most secure method common to the server and Matrix.
- `UseSSL` [Boolean] — Define if you wish to use SSL to secure the Jabber session.
- `ServerAddress` [String] — Contains the string of the server address to connect to.
- `Port` [Integer] — Contains the port number to use to connect to the server.
- `UserName` [String] — Contains the username you wish to log in as on the Jabber server.
- `Resource` [String] — Contains the resource to use for the session.
- `Password` [String] — Contains the password you wish to use to log in to the Jabber server.
- `Priority` [Integer] — The priority you wish to use for this connection (1–10).
- `LocalIP` [String — Read Only] — Returns the local IP of the interface used to connect to the Jabber server.

Members

- `Roster` [Collection] — Contains a collection of all the `RosterItems` in your

Jabber session.
- `Agents` [Collection] — Contains a collection of all the `AgentItems` in your Jabber session.

Methods

Method Name	Passing Arguments	Returned	Description
`Connect`	None	None	Initiates the process of connecting the Jabber session and beginning the `auth` process.
`Disconnect`	None	None	Disconnects the Jabber session.
`SendPresence`	JID (String), SubType (eSubType)	None	Used to send presence to a specific JID or to the server to update your presence.

Passing Arguments:
- [`JID`] — Represents the JID of the item you wish to send presence to, such as a server, a group chat, or a specific person.
- [`SubType`] — Represents the type of presence/subscription you wish to send, such as a subscribe or available presence.

`SendGroupChatPresence`	JID (String), SubType (eSubType), Optional Nickname (String)	None	Used to send presence to a conference room, passing the JID as the JID of the conference room.

Passing Arguments:
- [`JID`] — Represents the JID of the group chat you wish to send presence to.
- [`SubType`] — Represents the subscription/presence type you wish to send as the presence, such as `available`, `unavailable`.
- [`Optional Nickname`] — This is an optional argument, should be used only when initially entering a group chat. When changing presence in a room, omit this argument.

`CreateMessage`	None	`cMessage`	Pass an empty instance of `cMessage` to this function and it will initialize your message.

Returned:
- This function returns type `cMessage`, used in an assignment statement — for example, `myMessage = cSession.CreateMessage()`.

FetchAgents	None	None	Used to tell the session to begin the process of fetching all the agents off the server.
FetchRoster	None	None	Used to tell the session to begin the process of fetching all the roster items in your roster.
FindAgent	JID (String)	Integer	Used to search the AgentCollection for that specific JID and returns its reference number in the collection.

Passing Arguments:
- [JID] — Represents the JID of the agent you wish to search for; if an agent with a matching JID is found it will return the reference number it is located at in the Agents Collection.

SendVCardRequest	JID (String)	None	Used to send a request to the server for a user's vCard information.

Passing Arguments:
- [JID] — Represents the JID you wish to request a vCard from, such as a JID of someone in your roster.

SendLastSeenRequest	JID (String)	None	Used to send a request to the server for the last-seen date of a user.

Passing Arguments:
- [JID] — Represents the JID you wish to request the last-seen time of, such as a JID of someone in your roster.

SendTimeRequest	JID (String)	None	Used to send a request to a user for his or her current local time.

Passing Arguments:
- [JID] — Represents the JID you wish to request the time from, such as the JID from someone in your roster.

SendVersionRequest	JID (String)	None	Used to send a request to a user for his or her client

			version.

Passing Arguments:
- [JID] — Represents the JID you wish to request the client version from, such as a JID from someone in your roster.

GetCurrentID	None	String	Used to get the current ID used for the last server request.
GetNextID	None	String	Used to get the next ID used for the next server request if you need to make your own request manually.
SendXML	XML (String)	None	Used if you need to send raw XML to the server manually.

Events

Event Name	Passed Arguments	Description
OnAuthorized	None	Triggers when the session has been accepted and authorized.
OnError	FromJID (String), ErrorCode (Integer), ErrorDescription (String), XML_Node (cXML_Node)	Triggers when an error has occurred and passes the XML node with the error XML embedded.

Passed Arguments:
- [FromJID] — Represents the JID of the client that sent back the error.
- [ErrorCode] — Represents the error code that represents the error.
- [ErrorDescription] — Represents the description of the error that occurred.
- [XML_Node] — The XML node that contains the raw XML sent for the error, used incase you need further parsing capabilities.

| OnIQError | FromJID (String), ErrorCode (Integer), ErrorDescription (String), XML_Node (cXML_Node) | Triggers when an error on a IQ request has happened, passing the XML node with the error XML embedded. |

Passed Arguments: • [FromJID] — Represents the JID of the client that sent back the error. • [ErrorCode] — Represents the error code that represents the error. • [ErrorDescription] — Represents the description of the error that occurred. • [XML_Node] — The XML node that contains the raw XML sent for the error, used in case you need further parsing capabilities.		
OnIncomingXML	XML_Node (cXML_Node)	Triggers when any XML from the server is received before any parsing is done.
Passed Arguments: • [XML_Node] — This is the XML node containing the raw XML that was received and can be used to manually parse the XML if needed, or just used to output to a debug window using the XML_Node.XML property.		
OnOutGoingXML	XML_Node (cXML_Node)	Triggers when any XML has been sent to the server.
Passed Arguments: • [XML_Node] — The XML node containing the raw XML that has been sent to the server. It cannot be used to change the XML before it goes out, but it can be used to keep track or use in a debug window using the XML_Node.XML property.		
OnMessage	MSG (cMessage)	Triggers when an incoming message has been received.
Passed Arguments: • [MSG] — Represents an instance of cMessage containing the incoming message. Can be used to extract the message details.		
OnPresence	JID (String), PresItem (eItemType), Available (Boolean), Status (String), XML_Node (cXML_Node)	Triggers when a presence has been sent to the session.
Passed Arguments: • [JID] — Represents the JID that has sent you presence. This could be from a person, agent, group chat etc.. • [PresItem] — Represents the item the presence is from, such as if presence is from an agent, group chat, person, or unknown. • [Available] — Represents if the JID is sending an available presence or unavailable presence. • [Status] — Represents a more specific status of the JID sending the presence. • [XML_Node] — Contains the raw XML in the presence sent. This can be used to further parse or view the XML contained.		
OnIQ	XML_Node (cXML_Node)	Triggered when a response to an IQ request is returned from the server.

Passed Arguments:		
• [XML_Node] — Contains the Raw XML received from an IQ query sent. Since IQ Queries contained varied data use this XML node to parse the data you need from the results.		
OnSubscriptionRequest	JID (String), SubType (eSubType)	Triggered when a subscription request has been sent to your session.

Passed Arguments:
- [JID] — Represents the JID of the person who is sending you the subscription request.
- [XML_Node] — Contains the raw XML received from a subscription request. This can be used to further parse the XML to extract anything you need.

OnSubscriptionAccept	JID (String), Status (String)	Triggered when a subscription request you sent has been accepted.

Passed Arguments:
- [JID] — Represents the JID of the person who is sending you the notice that a subscription request you sent has been accepted.
- [Status] — Represents the status of the subscription request that has been accepted.

OnSubscriptionDenied	JID (String), Status (String)	Triggered when a subscription request you sent has been denied.

Passed Arguments:
- [JID] — Represents the JID of the person who is sending you a notice that a subscription request you sent has been denied.
- [Status] — Represents the status of the subscription request that has been denied.

OnAgentBegin	None	Triggered when the agent list is just about to be received from the server.
OnAgentItem	Agent (cAgentItem), XML_Node (cXML_Node)	Triggered when an agent item is being received.

Passed Arguments:
- [Agent] — Represents the agent being passed and its information. Agent is an instance of cAgentItem so you can use cAgent's properties and functions to get or set what you require.
- [XML_Node] — Contains the raw XML from the agent. This can be used to further parse or retrieve what you require that may not be contained inside the AgentItem.

OnAgentEnd	None	Triggered when the list of agents being received is done.

OnRosterBegin	None	Triggered when the roster list is just about to be received from the server.
OnRosterItem	RosterItem (cRosterItem), XML_Node (cXML_Node)	Triggered when a RosterItem is being received.
Passed Arguments: • [RosterItem] — Represents an instance of cRosterItem containing all the roster information from that item, such as nickname, JID, and subscription type you have with the RosterItem. • [XML_Node] — Contains the raw XML from the incoming RosterItem for use in further XML parsing if needed.		
OnRosterEnd	None	Triggered when the list of roster items being received is over.
OnVCardResult	FromJID (String), Vcard (cVcard), XML_Node (cXML_Node)	Triggered when you have sent a vCard request and it has returned a result.
Passed Arguments: • [XML_Node] — Contains the raw XML from the result of a vCard request you have sent. Use this to parse and retrieve from the vCard the data you need.		
OnLastSeenResult	XML_Node (cXML_Node)	Triggered when you have sent a last-seen request and it has returned a result.
Passed Arguments: • [XML_Node] — Contains the raw XML from the result of a last-seen request you have sent. Use this to parse and retrieve the data you need.		
OnTimeRequest	FromJID (String), XML_Node (cXML_Node)	Triggered when another user requests your current time.
Passed Arguments: • [FromJID] — Represents the JID of the person who is making a time request. • [XML_Node] — Contains the raw XML from the time request. Use this to parse and retrieve the data you need.		
OnTimeResult	FromJID (String), UTC (String), TimeZone (String), Local_DateTime(String) XML_Node (cXML_Node)	Triggered when you have sent a request for the time from a user and the user has provided a response.

Passed Arguments:

- [FromJID] — Represents the JID of the person who is sending you the response from a time request you have sent.
- [UTC] — Contains the UTC time returned from the person from whom you requested from the time.
- [TimeZone] — Contains the time zone returned from the person from whom you requested the time.
- [Local_DateTime] — Contains the local date and time of the person from whom you requested time.
- [XML_Node] — Contains the raw XML from the time result. Use this to further parse or retrieve data you require.

OnVersionRequest	FromJID (String), XML_Node (cXML_Node)	Triggered when someone has requested your client version.

Passed Arguments:

- [FromJID] — Represents the JID of the person who has requested your client version.
- [XML_Node] — Contains the raw XML from the version request. Use this to parse or retrieve data you require.

OnVersionResult	FromJID (String), AppName (String), AppVer (String), OS (String), XML_Node (cXML_Node)	Triggered when you have requested the client version from another user and the user has provided the response.

Passed Arguments:

- [FromJID] — Represents the JID of the person who is responding to a version request you have sent.
- [AppName] — Represents the application name returned from the version request.
- [AppVer] — Represents the application version returned from the version request.
- [OS] — Represents the operating system name/version returned from the version request.
- [XML_Node] — Contains the raw XML from the version result. Use this to further parse or retrieve data you require.

OnGroupChat	FromJID (String), GC (cGroupChat), XML_Node (cXML_Node)	Triggered when a reply is received in response to sending the server a groupchat request.

Passed Arguments:		
• [FromJID] — Represents the JID of the conference room. • [GC] — Represents a Groupchat Object. • [XML_Node] — Contains the raw XML . Use this to further parse or retrieve data you require.		
OnGroupChatItem	FromJID (String), BrowseItem (cBrowseItem), XML_Node (cXML_Node)	Triggered when the server begins sending The list of users in the Chat room.
Passed Arguments:		
• [FromJID] — Represents the JID of the conference room. • [BrowseItem] — Represents a BrowseItem Object. • [XML_Node] — Contains the raw XML. Use this to further parse or retrieve data you require.		

cAgentItem

This is the AgentItem object that contains all information in regard to that specific agent along with methods for updating and deleting information contained in the AgentItem.

Properties

- JID [String — Read Only] — Get the JID of the agent.
- Name [String — Read Only] — Get the name of the agent.
- Service [String — Read Only] — Get the service of the agent.
- Search [Boolean — Read Only] — Get whether the agent has search capabilities.
- Registered [Boolean — Read Only] — Get whether the session is registered on this agent.
- XML [String — Read Only] — Get the raw XML contained in the XML node of the agent.

Members

- Fields [Collection] — Collection of cAgentField objects.
- Attribs [Collection] — Collection of cAgentAttrib objects.
- XML_Node (cXML_Node) — XML node containing the raw XML from the agent.

Methods

Method Name	Passing Arguments	Returned	Description
Update	None	None	Submits the updated information on the AgentItem to the server.
Delete	None	None	Submits a request to the server to delete the agent.

AddField	FieldName (String), FieldValue (String)	None	This method will add a field to the agent with the name of `FieldName` and a value in the field of `FieldValue`.

Passed Arguments:
- [`FieldName`] — Represents the name you want the new field to be.
- [`FieldValue`] — Represents the value you wish the new field to contain.

AddAttrib	AttribName (String), AttribValue (String)	None	This method will add an `attrib` to the agent with the name of `AttribName` and the value in the field of `AttribValue`.

Passed Arguments:
- [`AttribName`] — Represents the name of the new attribute you wish to add.
- [`AttribValue`] — Represents the value to be contained in the new attribute.

FindField	FieldName (String)	Integer	This method will search for a field located in the agent with the name passed and will return the number of its reference in the `Fields` collection.

Passed Arguments:
- [`FieldName`] — Represents the field name you wish to locate.

Returned:
- [`Integer`] — Represents the reference number in the fields collection where the field you requested is located, 0 if it was not located.

FindAttrib	AttribName (String)	Integer	This method will search for an `attrib` located in the agent with the name passed and will return the number of its reference in the `Attribs` collection.

Passed Arguments:
- [`AttribName`] — Represents the attribute name you wish to locate.

Returned:
- [`Integer`] — Represents the reference number in the field collection where the field you requested is located, 0 if it was not located.

GetField	FieldName (String)	String	This method will search the fields collection for the passed `FieldName` and will return the value of the field.

Passed Arguments:
- [`FieldName`] — Represents the field name whose value you wish to retrieve.

Returned:
- [`String`] — Represents the returned string value captured from the fields collection. Returns an empty string if not found.

GetAttrib	AttribName	String	This method will search the `Attribs`

	(String)		collection for the passed `AttribName` and will return the value of the `attrib`.

Passed Arguments:
- [`AttribName`] — Represents the attribute name whose value you wish to retrieve.

Returned:
- [`String`] — Represents the returned string value captured from the attributes collection. Returns an empty string if not found.

`SetField`	FieldName (String), FieldValue (String)	None	This method will search the field collection for the passed `FieldName` and if found it will update the value with the one specified in `FieldValue`.

Passed Arguments:
- [`FieldName`] — Represents the field name whose value you wish to set.
- [`FieldValue`] — Represents the value you wish to set the field with.

`SetAttrib`	AttribName (String), AttribValue (String)	None	This method will search the `Attribs` collection for the passed `AttribName` and if found it will update the value with the one specified in `AttribValue`.

Passed Arguments:
- [`AttribName`] — Represents the attribute name whose value you wish to set.
- [`AttribValue`] — Represents the value you wish to set the attribute with.

cAgentField

This is the `AgentField` object which represents a single field that's located in the agents properties in the raw XML. `AgentField`s are accessible via the fields collection in the `AgentItem` object.

Properties

- `Name` [String — Read Only] — Get the name of that specific field.
- `Value` [String — Read Only] — Get the value of that specific field.

cAgentAttrib

This is the `AgentAttrib` object which represents a single attribute that's located in the agents properties in the raw XML. `AgentAttrib`s are accessible via the `Attribs` collection in the `AgentItem` object.

Properties

- `Name` [String — Read Only] — Get the name of that specific field.
- `Value` [String — Read Only] — Get the value of that specific field.

cRosterItem

This is the `RosterItem` object. This object is a representation of one contact in your roster. `RosterItem`s are accessible via the roster collection in the `cSession` object.

Properties

- `JID` [String — Read Only] — Get the JID of the `RosterItem`.
- `Nickname` [String — Read Only] — Set/get the nickname of the `RosterItem`.
- `Subscription` [String — Read Only] — Get the subscription of the `RosterItem`.

Methods

Method Name	Passing Arguments	Returned	Description
`Update`	None	None	This method will submit the changed data in the `RosterItem` to the server for updating.

CGroupChat

This is the `GroupChat` object. It holds a list of the chatrooms that you are currently participating in.

Properties

- `JID` [String] — The JID of the group chat room.
- `RoomName` [String] — The display name of the chat room.
- `NickName` [String] — The users name in the chat room.
- `Password` [String] — Password to enter group chat if required
- `NeedPassword` [Boolean] — `True` if chat room requires a password to enter, otherwise `False`.

CBrowseItem

This is the Browse object.It holds a list of the current participants in a chatroom. (Note: This will be expanded to hold *all* Browse Items from a Jabber server.)

Properties

- JID [String] — The JID of the BrowseItem.
- Name [String] — The name of the BrowseItem.
- SubType [String] — The SubType of the object.

CPresence

This is the Presence object. Presence tracks the presence information for roster users and transports. This is updated by Matrix every time a presence is sent to the Matrix COM Library.

Properties

- JID [String — Read Only] — The JID of the item for which we are storing the presence.
- Status [String — Read Only] — The description of the status (for example, "Out to lunch right now").
- ShowType [eShowType — ReadOnly] — is a constant of MX_None, MX_Chat, MX_Away, MX_ExtendedAway, MX_DND.

Methods

Method Name	Passing Arguments	Returned	Description
FindPresence	JID	Index of Presence Item or 0 if not found	This method checks the presence collection for the specified JID.

Passing Arguments:
- [JID] — Represents the JID for which you want to find the presence information.

cMessage

This is the Message object. The Message object can handle many types of messages, such as normal, chat, group chat, and headline messages. This object is used during the receipt of a message and can also be used to create/send a message.

Properties

- `FromJID` [String — Read Only] — Get the `From` JID of the message.
- `ToJID` [String] — Get/set the `ToJID`
- `MSG_Type` [eMsgType] — Get/set the type of message this object is (normal/chat, etc.).
- `Body` [String] — Get/set the body of the message.
- `HasCC` [String] — Get if the current message has `CC` JIDs listed.
- `XML` [String] — Get XML contained in `XML_Node`.

Members

- `XML_Node` [cXML_Node] — Contains the raw XML from the message.

Methods

Method Name	Passing Arguments	Returned	Description
SendMessage	None	None	This method will send the current message to the server where it will be directed to the `ToJID`. This method also will handle if any `CC`s have been specified to ensure they are also sent the message.
AddCC	JID	None	This method will add the JID passed to the list of `CC`s for the message.

Passing Arguments:
- [JID] — Represents the JID you wish to add to the `CC` list of the message. Each `CC` will be sent a copy of the message along with the list of the other `CC`s and who is originally in the To field of the message.

CVcard

This is the `Vcard` object. It holds a vCard returned for a `RosterItem`.

Properties

- `FullName` [String]
- `FirstName` [String]
- `LastName` [String]
- `NickName` [String]
- `BirthDate` [String]
- `WebPage` [String]
- `HomeStreet` [String]
- `HomeCity` [String]
- `HomeRegion` [String]
- `HomePostalCode` [String]

- HomeCountry [String]
- HomePhone [String]
- HomeFax [String]
- HomeMessage [String]
- BusinessStreet [String]
- BusinessCity [String]
- BusinessRegion [String]
- BusinessPostalCode [String]
- BusinessCountry [String]
- BusinessPhone [String]
- BusinessFax [String]
- BusinessMessage [String]

cXML_Node

This is the XML_Node object used in many different places in Matrix. This object is mostly used as a member of other objects in case you need further XML parsing capability that isn't already provided in easy-to-use methods and properties. XML_Node is also passed to some events that get triggered on the Session object.

Properties

- XML [String] — Get XML contained in XMLObj (see below).

Members

- XMLObj [MSXML 3.0 DOM Object] — XML_Node is a super-set of the MSXML DOM object, making it easier to add/set/get tags and attributes while still exposing the DOM object itself as part of XML_Node in case the developer requires even more capabilities.

Methods

Method Name	Passing Arguments	Returned	Description
AddAttrib	AttribName (String), ParentName (String), Value (String) ** Optional argument should not be used, is for internal use only.	None	This method is used to add an attribute to a tag. It searches for a tag with the name of ParentName and adds the attribute to it if found.

Passing Arguments:
- [AttribName] — Represents the name of the attribute you wish to add.
- [ParentName] — Represents the name of the tag to which you want to add this new attribute.
- [Value] — Represents the value you wish to place in the new attribute.

GetAttrib	AttribName (String) ** Optional argument should not be used, is for internal use only.	String	This method is used to retrieve the value of the attribute specified with the string AttribName.

Passing Arguments:
- [AttribName] — Represents the attribute name whose value you wish to retrieve.

Returned:
- [String] — Represents the value of the attribute you wish to retrieve. If not found it will return a blank string.

SetAttrib	AttribName (String), Value (String) ** Optional argument should not be used, is for internal use only.	None	This method will locate the attribute with the name provided in AttribName. If found it will set the value to the value specified in Value.

Passing Arguments:
- [AttribName] — Represents the attribute name whose value you wish to set.
- [Value] — Represents the value to which you wish to set the attribute.

FindAttrib	AttribName (String) ** Optional argument should not be used, is for internal use only.	Boolean	This method will search for the attribute specified in AttribName. If it is found it will return True; if it is not found it will return False.

Passing Arguments:
- [AttribName] — Represents the name of the attribute you wish to find.

Returned:
- [Boolean] — Returns True if attribute of the name specified is found, otherwise returns False.

GetTag	TagName (String) ** Optional argument should not be used,	String	This method will search for the tag with the name provided in TagName and will return the value.

	is for internal use only.		

Passing Arguments:
- [TagName] — Represents the name of the tag whose value you wish to retrieve.

Returned:
- [String] — Represents the value of the tag you requested to retrieve. Returns an empty string if not found.

AddTag	TagName (String), TagParentName (String), Value (String) ** Optional argument should not be used, is for internal use only.	None	This method will search for a tag with the name TagParentName and will add a child tag to it with the name TagName and the value of Value.

Passing Arguments:
- [TagName] — Represents the name of the new tag to be added.
- [TagParentName] — Represents the name of the tag to which you wish to add the new tag.
- [Value] — Represents the value you wish to be contained inside the new tag.

SetTag	TagName (String), Value (String) ** Optional argument should not be used, is for internal use only.	None	This method will search for a tag with the name TagName and will insert the value of Value in the tag.

Passing Arguments:
- [TagName] — Represents the name of the tag whose value you wish to change.
- [Value] — Represents the new value you want the tag to contain.

FindTag	TagName (String) ** Optional argument should not be used, is for internal use only.	Boolean	This method will search for a tag with the name TagName. If found it will return True, if not found it will return False.

Passing Arguments:
- [TagName] — Represents the name of the tag you wish to search for.

Returned:
- [Boolean] — Returns True if found, otherwise False.

SaveXML_ToFile	Path (String)	None	This method will save the raw

			XML from the XML node to a file with the path specified.

Passing Arguments:
- [Path] — Represents the path where you wish to save the XML contained inside the XML node.

LoadXML_FromFile	Path (String)	None	This method will load the raw XML from the file specified in the path into the XML node. Only qualified XML that follows the XML specifications will load successfully.

Passing Arguments:
- [Path] — Represents the path (filename included) you wish to load into the XML node.

eAuthType

This is the Authorization Type enum structure. It allows the programmer when passing values to functions or properties to restrict to passing only valid arguments. This enum is used during the authorization process explained in cSession.AuthType.

Enums

- MX_AutoAuth — When used, AutoAuth will detect the most secure method available of auth on the server and utilize it to ensure that the Jabber session is as secure as possible.
- MX_Digest — This is currently the highest auth type available with Matrix. Using Digest will work only if the server supports it. If it does not, it will not let you log in. AutoAuth is recommended as it will drop to the next level of auth until it reaches a connection.
- MX_PlainAuth — This is currently supported on all Jabber servers. Not recommended because it sends your username/password in plain text over the Internet; however, good for early development when working with the auth process.

eSubType

This is the Subscription Type enum structure. It allows the programmer when passing values to functions or properties to restrict to passing only valid arguments. This enum is used to describe what type of `Subscription Type` the current subscription is. When sending a presence or receiving a subscription this type is used to easily identify the type of subscription it is.

Enums

- `MX_Available` — Used when one wants to send presence to someone/server/transport that you're available.
- `MX_UnAvailable` — Used when one wants to send presence to someone/server/transport that you're unavailable.
- `MX_Subscribe` — Used when you want to send a subscription request to someone.
- `MX_UnSubscribe` — Used to unsubscribe someone from your roster.
- `MX_Subscribe_Accept` — Used to accept a subscription request.
- `MX_Subscribe_Deny` — Used to deny a subscription request.

eItemType

This is the `Item Type` enum structure. It allows the programmer when passing values to functions or properties to restrict to passing only valid arguments. This enum is used to describe what type of item you're dealing with so you can quickly decide what you need to do with it. This enum is mainly used in the `OnPresence` event of `cSession`. This allows you to quickly determine if the presence being sent is from an agent, someone in your roster, or a group chat and then take the appropriate action.

Enums

- `MX_RosterItem` — Used to identify the item as someone in your roster.
- `MX_AgentItem` — Used to identify the item as an agent.
- `MX_GroupChat` — Used to identify the item as being from a group chat.
- `MX_Unknown` — Used to identify the item as not within your roster, agents list, or a group chat you are located in.

eShowType

This is the `Show Type` enum structure. The enums are used to indicate the presence type of a user.

Enums

- `MX_None` — Indicates a normal online presence.
- `MX_Chat` — Indicates that user is free for a chat.

- `MX_Away` — Indicates that user is away for a few minutes.
- `MX_ExtendedAway` — Indicates that user is away for an extended period of time.
- `MX_DND` — User does not want to be disturbed.

eSubscriptionType

This is the `SubscriptionType` enum structure. The enums are used to indicate the subscription type for an object.

Enums

- `MX_Empty`
- `MX_To`
- `MX_From`
- `MX_Both`
- `MX_Remove`

Appendix D

Related Jabber Web Sites

The following is a list of Jabber Web sites that you may find of benefit when working with Jabber:

- ◆ www.sltscommunications.net: sltsCommunications is a developer of custom clients and server solutions for personal and corporate communications. With several custom clients already on board, sltsCommunications has a team of dedicated, knowledgeable developers to help solve your communications needs. On this home site for sltsCommunications, you can find the latest news on custom Jabber clients and server news.

- ◆ www.jabbercentral.com: As Jabber instant messaging expands and grows to reach destinations as yet unknown, the JabberCentral Web site is a good resource for end users. Through relevant news items, unique feature articles, support documents, and a complete client database, JabberCentral aims at becoming the ultimate destination for all end users of the Jabber platform. Led by dedicated members of the Jabber.org project, JabberCentral contains content originating from experienced users and developers — voices whom end users can trust. Feature articles are written to give unique perspectives and information to both advanced and regular users.

- ◆ www.jabber.org: The official Jabber open-source project site. Content is geared toward developers and server adminstrators.

- ◆ www.jabber.com: Jabber, Inc., is a commercial developer of open software for real-time communications and instant messaging (IM). The company delivers a highly scalable, XML-based communications and presence-management platform to Telecom and Internet service providers, technology developers, and enterprises. Jabber's strength lies in its capability to embed streaming XML data into other applications, devices, and services, thus extending the benefit of real-time communications beyond simple IM. Through the Jabber open-source project, Jabber, Inc., takes an active role in promoting and standardizing the Jabber open protocol.

- ◆ http://openim.myjabber.org: The home site for the open-source OpenIM client that we provide in this book. The site offeres the latest source code available for OpenIM and news and views on Jabber and the OpenIM project.

◆ `www.myjabber.org`: myJabber is your gateway to the world of dependable, easy-to-use instant messaging and group conferencing. Lightweight, configurable, and very user friendly, myJabber has quickly become the top choice of users everywhere. The myJabber site offers the latest releases, Jabber community news, and other information from the world of computer and open-source development.

◆ `www.rivalmessenger.com`: Rival Messenger is being developed as an easy-to-use and stable ICQ-style Windows IM client. It currently features messaging, chats, group chats, and more. Built for beginners, Rival Messenger "takes instant communications one step closer to the end user."

◆ `http://gabber.sourceforge.net`: Gabber is a free and open-source GNOME client for Jabber. Several different Jabber clients are already available but no other GNOME clients as of this writing.

◆ `http://winjab.sourceforge.net`: WinJab is a Jabber client designed to run in any 32-bit Windows environment.

◆ `www.jabber.com/products/clients.shtml#jim`: Jabber Instant Messenger, known as JIM, is the Jabber, Inc., client for Microsoft Windows. Available at no cost for download and usage with JCP (Jabber Communications Platform), JIM is a full-featured package matching the most advanced IM, text conference, roster, and presence features on the JCP server.

◆ `http://jabberfox.sourceforge.net/`: JabberFOX, a client for Mac OS X, is written in Objective-C, using Apple's Cocoa API, and tries to make full use of Aqua, Apple's cool new user-interface system. It aims at implementing all the standard Jabber features, including chat, group chat, messages, the roster (list of contacts), and agents.

◆ `http://Jarl.sourceforge.net`: Jarl is a full-featured cross-platform Perl/Tk-based Jabber client.

◆ `http://jabberapplet.sourceforge.net`: The concept of JabberApplet is to provide a very small, useful Jabber-based instant messaging Java applet that you can use as an enterprise solution to provide users with chat capability within their desired browsers.

◆ `http://Gaim.sourceforge.net`: Gaim was originally designed for AIM, but thanks to Protocol Plugins it's capable of functioning as a Jabber client. It is compatible with IRC, ICQ, Yahoo! Messenger, MSN Messenger, Napster, and Zephyr.

Many Jabber-related Web sites are out there on the Web; we just list some of the more popular ones here. Many sites spring up each month, so naming them all here is almost impossible. (We've also tried to weed out some of the older sites that seem to have abandoned the projects they were working on.) If we missed your site, we apologize.

Appendix E

SSL and mySQL

In the beginning was Jabber, and Jabber spoke unto Chris and said "Bring forth your lieutenants and let us bring light to the darkness of IM." Okay, that's corny, even for me (Terry). Chris McDonald is a friend of mine and is my direct supervisor at the time of this writing. We became interested in Jabber in the fall of 2000 when we, as did millions of others, became frustrated keeping four or five different IM clients open on our desktops just to talk to different people.

IM was in use inside the company that Chris works for to communicate between departments and to share information among members of the various technical and service teams of the kind that you typically find in large corporations. Although the company had an "official" client, it wasn't the best; it was *very* unsecured; and, for the most part, we didn't like it. So we used what we wanted to use, causing even more confusion. Then someone introduced Chris to Jabber. After taking a look at it, he showed it to a few of his friends and co-workers. (We've vowed to get even with him for it.) His attitude was "Awww, come on, guys! This program is just exactly what we need in here — we can get rid of all these other clients and still access them. Plus it's more secure."

In the past year of experimenting with and cursing at Jabber, Chris has easily become one of the most skilled Jabber server developers that I can think of. He managed to get his company interested in the project, and in the course of meeting the security and functionality requirements set out by management, he has really excelled.

He's written the following How-To's, covering the use of Secure Socket Layers (SSL) and the use of mySQL as a backend database (storing user information in a mySQL database as opposed to using the spool directories in Jabber). These How-To's have helped me many times in setting up the various commercial servers that Stephen Lee and I run in our business.

SSL Server Installation

To install the SSL Server, you need the following files:

♦ `jabber-1.4.1.tar.gz` (which you get from `http://download .jabber.org/dist`)

◆ `openssl-0.9.6a.tar.gz` (which you get from `www.openssl.org`)

◆ `ssl-keygen.sh` script (which we include in this How-To)

To install OpenSSL, use the following code:

```
tar -xzf openssl-0.9.6a.tar.gz
cd openssl-0.9.6a
./config
make
su
make install
exit
```

To install, Jabber, use the following code:

```
tar -xzf jabber-1.4.1.tar.gz
cd jabber-1.4.1
./configure --enable-ssl
make
```

To test the server, follow these steps:

1. Open the `jabber.xml` file in a text editor and modify only the following two lines for your server:

```
        <host><jabberd:cmdline
flag="h">your.server.net</jabberd:cmdline></host>
```

and

```
        <update><jabberd:cmdline
flag="h">your.server.net</jabberd:cmdline></update>
```

2. Execute `./jabberd -D` from the /jabberd directory to make sure that the server starts.

3. After you know that you have a funtioning server, you can proceed.

To generate your SSL `Key.pem` file, follow these steps:

1. Open your favorite text editor and create the following text file (called `keygen.sh`) by copying the following into the text editor and saving:

```
        #!/bin/sh


        ######
        #
        # Generate a certificate and key with no passphrase.
        #
        ######
```

```
# change to the correct path of your openssl command
OPENSSL=/usr/bin/openssl
#OPENSSL=/usr/bin/openssl

## This generates the cert and key
$OPENSSL req -new -x509 -newkey rsa:1024 -keyout
privkey.pem -out key.pem
## This will remove the passphrase
$OPENSSL rsa -in privkey.pem -out privkey.pem
## Put it all together
cat privkey.pem >> key.pem
## Cleanup
rm privkey.pem
```

2. Save this file and make it executable by using the chmod command (chmod +x
   keygen.sh).

3. Now execute keygen.sh by using the following command:

```
./keygen.sh
```

4. Complete the fields to fill out the form, and after you finish, you have a file called
   key.pem in the directory from which you executed keygen.sh.

To add SSL to the jabber.xml file, follow these steps:

1. Find the commented SSL section of the jabber.xml file, in the <pthcsock> section,
   and add the following values as necessary. (One line for each IP address your server may
   be listening on.)

```
<ssl port='5223'>127.0.0.1</ssl>
<ssl port='5224'>192.168.1.100</ssl>
<ssl port='5223'>209.86.206.99</ssl>
```

2. At the bottom of the jabber.xml file, you find an additional <ssl> section. Yours
   should look something like the following after you finish editing for your server:

```
<ssl>
<key ip='127.0.0.1'>/usr/local/jabber-
1.4.1/key.pem</key>
<key ip='192.168.1.100'>/usr/local/jabber-
1.4.1/key.pem</key>
<key ip='209.86.206.99'>/usr/local/jabber-
1.4.1/key.pem</key>
</ssl>
```

3. Save the `jabber.xml` file and start the server.

If the server starts correctly, you can proceed with testing it.

Open another terminal window and execute the following command:

```
openssl s_client -connect 127.0.0.1:5223
```

The output should appear something like that of the following example:

```
openssl s_client -connect 209.86.206.99:5223
CONNECTED(00000003)
depth=0
/C=US/ST=Arizona/L=Phoenix/O=organization/OU=Jabber/CN=contact
name/Email=email address
verify error:num=18:self signed certificate
verify return:1
depth=0
/C=US/ST=Arizona/L=Phoenix/O=organization/OU=Jabber/CN=contact
name/Email=email address
verify return:1
---
Certificate chain
0
s:/C=US/ST=Arizona/L=Phoenix/O=organization/OU=Jabber/CN=contact
name/Email=email address

i:/C=US/ST=Arizona/L=Phoenix/O=organization/OU=Jabber/CN=contact
name/Email=email address
---
Server certificate
-----BEGIN CERTIFICATE-----
```

MIIDdDCCAt2gAwIBAgIBADANBgkqhkiG9w0BAQQFADCBiTELMAkGA1UEBhMCVVMx

EDAOBgNVBAgTB0FyaXpvbmExEDAOBgNVBAcTB1Bob2VuaXgxETAPBgNVBAoTCERJ

TExJR0FGMQ8wDQYDVQQLEwZKYWJiZXIxFzAVBgNVBAMTDkNocmlzIE1jRG9uYWxk

MRkwFwYJKoZIhvcNAQkBFgpwaHgtamFiYmVyMB4XDTAxMDYwNjAxNTMwNloXDTAx

MDcwNjAxNTMwNlowgYkxCzAJBgNVBAYTAlVTMRAwDgYDVQQIEwdBcml6b25hMRAw

DgYDVQQHEwdQaG9lbml4MREwDwYDVQQKEwhESUxxMSUdBRjEPMA0GA1UECxMGSmFi

YmVyMRcwFQYDVQQDEw5DaHJpcyBNY0RvbmFsZDEZMBcGCSqGSIb3DQEJARYKcGh4

LWphYmJlcjCBnzANBgkqhkiG9w0BAQEFAAOBjQAwgYkCgYEArbyosgcyf9VNpPZc

```
+nU6yKdfAsOSpBu/n/MkChis5POuLkXo62WEoiYuDYF6bmd6XYaVC7ZwItcCwTIv

OqdErh4u82E2qeArN0j9eq6EX+MMrYBSkv2nzwabNkkWPCS9VaOsVWx+kvRw598p

ACyANf52liFhfDGISIoTlBOn+ysCAwEAAaOB6TCB5jAdBgNVHQ4EFgQUv9mxa1Yj

o7Um9ZK0OSW0phiG23AwgbYGA1UdIwSBrjCBq4AUv9mxa1Yjo7Um9ZK0OSW0phiG

23ChgY+kgYwwgYkxCzAJBgNVBAYTAlVTMRAwDgYDVQQIEwdBcml6b25hMRAwDgYD

VQQHEwdQaG9lbml4MREwDwYDVQQKEwhESUxxMSUdBRjEPMA0GA1UECxMGSmFiYmVy

MRcwFQYDVQQDEw5DaHJpcyBNY0RvbmFsZDEZMBcGCSqGSIb3DQEJARYKcGh4LWph

YmJlcoIBADAMBgNVHRMEBTADAQH/MA0GCSqGSIb3DQEBBAUAA4GBAGzAwYHlBY+P

ioqT8O4t4o30MkIDR7Q9Wqc0Uv1dUXViOKDzkzHXV/gB89yOmFVf6qNg7GB4rexs

0/fMmlSOkvXJPRCvmX05J9c5JpvcprkTjp7ECHPNZgaGsdNT+lilJ2f83uTvpJgM
                KoQY9OKbV4NnkxDM8lxCjvIvGvrbvnkR
                -----END CERTIFICATE-----
```

```
subject=/C=US/ST=Arizona/L=Phoenix/O=organization/OU=Jabber/CN=contact
name/Email=email address

issuer=/C=US/ST=Arizona/L=Phoenix/O=organization/OU=Jabber/CN=contact
name/Email=email address
                ---
                No client certificate CA names sent
                ---
                SSL handshake has read 1042 bytes and written 320 bytes
                ---
                New, TLSv1/SSLv3, Cipher is DES-CBC3-SHA
                Server public key is 1024 bit
                SSL-Session:
                Protocol  : TLSv1
                Cipher    : DES-CBC3-SHA
                Session-ID:
A23C1FB04F635EC09F92CBD722DAB8BB1503B54D4A0E9C61B3708CB33D6ED372
                Session-ID-ctx:
                Master-Key:
C8C25C17D5B4312E1440DBC956FF5738829C50E16E8E704010B84B1A8D33C405995D8B7F
B02E06988890C7ED400ACF32
                Key-Arg   : None
                Start Time: 991792771
                Timeout   : 300 (sec)
                Verify return code: 0 (ok)
                ---
```

If you get the kind of output that you see in the preceding example, it means that you can connect to the server via SSL.

At this point, you can now test connectivity with an actual client. To do so, you need a client that's SSL enabled.

Right now, available SSL-enabled clients include Gabber, Jarl, WinJab, JabberIM, and, soon, myJabber as well. (At the time of this writing, myJabber is close to releasing a new client with SSL support built in.)

AUTHOR'S NOTE Parts of this document are a bit outdated, and in fact myJabber now does support the use of SSL.

Configuring a Jabber Server to Use mySQL as a Backend Database

This section assumes that you already have a functioning Jabber server running the 1.4.1 server code (available from www.jabber.org), a functioning install of mySQL (available from www.mysql.org), and a functioning installation of Perl (available from www.perl.org).

First, get the following files:

- http://download.jabber.org/contrib/xdb_sql-1.0.tar.gz
- http://download.jabber.org/contrib/xdb_sql.README

Additionally, you need the following:

- MySQL-bench
- MySQL-devel

(I used versions 3.23.36-2mdk of both these files.)

The other libs that I used to install this are listed with their locations on the Web, as follows:

- http://download.jabber.org/cvs/xmlstream.tgz
- http://download.jabber.org/cvs/netjabber.tgz (at least version 1.0019 is needed)
- ftp://rpmfind.net/linux/Mandrake/8.0/i586/Mandrake/RPMS/perl-Digest-MD5-2.12-1mdk.i586.rpm
- ftp://rpmfind.net/linux/conectiva/6.0/cd2/conectiva/RPMS/perl-Unicode-String-2.05-10cl.i386.rpm

- ◆ `ftp://speakeasy.rpmfind.net/linux/Mandrake/8.0/SRPMS/perl-MIME-Base64-2.12-1mdk.src.rpm`

- ◆ `ftp://rpmfind.net/linux/Mandrake-devel/cookfire/i586/Mandrake/RPMS/perl-XML-Parser-2.30-1mdk.i586.rpm`

Extract the `xdb_sql-1.0.tar.gz` file into your /jabber-1.4.1 or /jabber2 directory. I ran `make` in the /xdb_sql directory and had to add libs until I had everything that it wanted. I've tried to include a complete list of them here, but I may have missed one or two. If I have, please let me know and I'll add them.

After you can run `make` and it completes with no errors, you can begin to configure your server. Start by executing one of the sample database files in the /xdb_sql directory. `sample_database.sql` is for mySQL, and `sample_database.pg.sql` is for Postgresql. I'm running mySQL, so I base everything that I've documented on that.

I took the `sample_database.sql` script, opened it in an editor, copied/pasted it into mySQL, and then executed it. I'm not going to go into how to execute a script in mySQL because it's outside the scope of this How-To. Personally, I did this by using Webmin (at `www.webmin.com`) only because I think that it's easy to use and very powerful. I use whatever works for me.

After you execute the script, you can query your mySQL Server and find a database called Jabber that contains various tables. Assuming that you make it this far, you're doing fine. Now you need to set the permissions for a user. Again, I did so by using Webmin; you can do this at the mySQL command line if you're familiar with its use. I set the permissions for the same user who executes Jabber just to keep things neat in my mind. Set a user, the password, and the domain from which that user is connecting. For the sake of this exercise, use the following settings:

- ◆ User: `jabber`
- ◆ Password: *`password`*
- ◆ Domain: *`your.servername.com`*
- ◆ Permissions: `all`

For the purposes of this exercise, I'm not going to go into each individual permission in mySQL. After this is done, you can move on to the server configuration for Jabber.

First, open your `jabber.xml` file and add the following section to the `<xdb>` entry. You can leave the information about `xdb_file` because the ./spool directory needs to handle some things that this version of `xdb_sql` doesn't do. So after the starting `<xdb id="xdb">` tag, enter the following information:

```
      <host/>
            <ns>jabber:iq:roster</ns>
            <ns>jabber:x:offline</ns>
            <ns>jabber:iq:filter</ns>
            <ns>jabber:iq:last</ns>
            <ns>jabber:iq:auth</ns>
            <ns>jabber:iq:auth:0k</ns>
            <ns>jabber:iq:register</ns>
            <ns>vcard-temp</ns>
      <load>
            <xdb_sql>./xdb_sql/xdb_sql.so</xdb_sql>
      </load>
      <jabberd:include>./xdb_sql/xdb_sql.xml</jabberd:include>
```

After modification, your <xdb> section looks as follows:

```
      <xdb id="xdb">
      <host/>
      <ns>jabber:iq:roster</ns>
      <ns>jabber:x:offline</ns>
      <ns>jabber:iq:filter</ns>
      <ns>jabber:iq:last</ns>
      <ns>jabber:iq:auth</ns>
      <ns>jabber:iq:auth:0k</ns>
      <ns>jabber:iq:register</ns>
      <ns>vcard-temp</ns>
      <load>
      <xdb_sql>/path/to/xdb_sql.so</xdb_sql>
      </load>
      <jabberd:include>/path/to/xdb_sql.xml</jabberd:include>
      <load>
      <xdb_file>./xdb_file/xdb_file.so</xdb_file>
      </load>
      <xdb_file xmlns="jabber:config:xdb_file">
      <spool><jabberd:cmdline
flag='s'>./spool</jabberd:cmdline></spool>
      </xdb_file>
      </xdb>
```

If you intend to install transports in addition to Jabber, you need to configure this slightly differently. You actually need two separate <xdb> entries and make use of the <host> tags to define which functions which database handles. The following example shows what my <xdb> section now looks like:

```
      <xdb id="xdb_sql">
      <host>your.servername.com</host>
      <ns>jabber:iq:roster</ns>
      <ns>jabber:x:offline</ns>
      <ns>jabber:iq:filter</ns>
```

```
        <ns>jabber:iq:last</ns>
        <ns>jabber:iq:auth</ns>
        <ns>jabber:iq:auth:0k</ns>
        <ns>jabber:iq:register</ns>
        <ns>vcard-temp</ns>
        <load>
        <xdb_sql>/path/to/xdb_sql.so</xdb_sql>
        </load>
        <jabberd:include>/path/to/xdb_sql.xml</jabberd:include>
        </xdb>

        <xdb id="xdb_file">


  <host>msn.your.servername.com</host>
        <host>yahoo.your.servername.com</host>
        <host>icq.your.servername.com</host>
        <host>irc.your.servername.com</host>
        <host>aim.your.servername.com</host>
        <host>jud.your.servername.com</host>
        <ns>jabber:iq:roster</ns>
        <ns>jabber:x:offline</ns>
        <ns>jabber:iq:filter</ns>
        <ns>jabber:iq:last</ns>
        <ns>jabber:iq:auth</ns>
        <ns>jabber:iq:auth:0k</ns>
        <ns>jabber:iq:register</ns>
        <ns>vcard-temp</ns>
        <load>
        <xdb_file>./xdb_file/xdb_file.so</xdb_file>
        </load>
        <xdb_file xmlns="jabber:config:xdb_file">
        <spool><jabberd:cmdline
flag='s'>./spool</jabberd:cmdline></spool>
        </xdb_file>
        </xdb>
```

After that is complete, you need to modify the `xdb_sql.xml` file that's in the /xdbsql directory. You need to change only the top of the file, so that's all I'm including here. Yours should look something like the following example after you're done with it:

```
        <xdb_sql xmlns="jabberd:xdb_sql:config">
        <!-- Backend to use -->
        <backend>mysql</backend>

        <!-- Configure information about the SQL connection -->
        <connection>
```

```
<host>your.servername.com</host>
<db>jabber</db>
<user>jabber</user>
<pass>password</pass>
</connection>
```

You should now be ready to test your brand-new database. The only problems that I encountered in installing this related to libs that I didn't install, and after I installed them, everything went pretty smoothly.

Index

GNU General Public License

Version 2, June 1991

Preamble

The licenses for most software are designed to take away your freedom to share and change it. By contrast, the GNU General Public License is intended to guarantee your freedom to share and change free software — to make sure the software is free for all its users. This General Public License applies to most of the Free Software Foundation's software and to any other program whose authors commit to using it. (Some other Free Software Foundation software is covered by the GNU Library General Public License instead.) You can apply it to your programs, too.

When we speak of free software, we are referring to freedom, not price. Our General Public Licenses are designed to make sure that you have the freedom to distribute copies of free software (and charge for this service if you wish), that you receive source code or can get it if you want it, that you can change the software or use pieces of it in new free programs; and that you know you can do these things.

To protect your rights, we need to make restrictions that forbid anyone to deny you these rights or to ask you to surrender the rights. These restrictions translate to certain responsibilities for you if you distribute copies of the software, or if you modify it.

For example, if you distribute copies of such a program, whether gratis or for a fee, you must give the recipients all the rights that you have. You must make sure that they, too, receive or can get the source code. And you must show them these terms so they know their rights.

We protect your rights with two steps: (1) copyright the software, and (2) offer you this license which gives you legal permission to copy, distribute and/or modify the software.

Also, for each author's protection and ours, we want to make certain that everyone understands that there is no warranty for this free software. If the software is modified by someone else and passed on, we want its recipients to know that what they have is not the original, so that any problems introduced by others will not reflect on the original authors' reputations.

Finally, any free program is threatened constantly by software patents. We wish to avoid the danger that redistributors of a free program will individually obtain patent licenses, in effect making the program proprietary. To prevent this, we have made it clear that any patent must be licensed for everyone's free use or not licensed at all.

The precise terms and conditions for copying, distribution and modification follow.

Terms and Conditions for Copying, Distribution, and Modification

1. This License applies to any program or other work which contains a notice placed by the copyright holder saying it may be distributed under the terms of this General Public License. The "Program", below, refers to any such program or work, and a "work based on the Program" means either the Program or any derivative work under copyright law: that is to say, a work containing the Program or a portion of it, either verbatim or with modifications and/or translated into another language. (Hereinafter, translation is included without limitation in the term "modification".) Each licensee is addressed as "you".

   Activities other than copying, distribution and modification are not covered by this License; they are outside its scope. The act of running the Program is not restricted, and the output from the Program is covered only if its contents constitute a work based on the Program (independent of having been made by running the Program). Whether that is true depends on what the Program does.

2. You may copy and distribute verbatim copies of the Program's source code as you receive it, in any medium, provided that you conspicuously and appropriately publish on each copy an appropriate copyright notice and disclaimer of warranty; keep intact all the notices that refer to this License and to the absence of any warranty; and give any other recipients of the Program a copy of this License along with the Program.

   You may charge a fee for the physical act of transferring a copy, and you may at your option offer warranty protection in exchange for a fee.

3. You may modify your copy or copies of the Program or any portion of it, thus forming a work based on the Program, and copy and distribute such modifications or work under the terms of Section 1 above, provided that you also meet all of these conditions:

   a) You must cause the modified files to carry prominent notices stating that you changed the files and the date of any change.

b) You must cause any work that you distribute or publish, that in whole or in part contains or is derived from the Program or any part thereof, to be licensed as a whole at no charge to all third parties under the terms of this License.

c) If the modified program normally reads commands interactively when run, you must cause it, when started running for such interactive use in the most ordinary way, to print or display an announcement including an appropriate copyright notice and a notice that there is no warranty (or else, saying that you provide a warranty) and that users may redistribute the program under these conditions, and telling the user how to view a copy of this License. (Exception: if the Program itself is interactive but does not normally print such an announcement, your work based on the Program is not required to print an announcement.)

These requirements apply to the modified work as a whole. If identifiable sections of that work are not derived from the Program, and can be reasonably considered independent and separate works in themselves, then this License, and its terms, do not apply to those sections when you distribute them as separate works. But when you distribute the same sections as part of a whole which is a work based on the Program, the distribution of the whole must be on the terms of this License, whose permissions for other licensees extend to the entire whole, and thus to each and every part regardless of who wrote it.

Thus, it is not the intent of this section to claim rights or contest your rights to work written entirely by you; rather, the intent is to exercise the right to control the distribution of derivative or collective works based on the Program.

In addition, mere aggregation of another work not based on the Program with the Program (or with a work based on the Program) on a volume of a storage or distribution medium does not bring the other work under the scope of this License.

4. You may copy and distribute the Program (or a work based on it, under Section 2) in object code or executable form under the terms of Sections 1 and 2 above provided that you also do one of the following:

a) Accompany it with the complete corresponding machine-readable source code, which must be distributed under the terms of Sections 1 and 2 above on a medium customarily used for software interchange; or,

b) Accompany it with a written offer, valid for at least three years, to give any third party, for a charge no more than your cost of physically performing source distribution, a complete machine-readable copy of the corresponding source code, to be distributed under the terms of Sections 1 and 2 above on a medium customarily used for software interchange; or,

c) Accompany it with the information you received as to the offer to distribute corresponding source code. (This alternative is allowed only for noncommercial distribution and only if you received the program in object code or executable form with such an offer, in accord with Subsection b above.)

The source code for a work means the preferred form of the work for making modifications to it. For an executable work, complete source code means all the source code for all modules it contains, plus any associated interface definition files, plus the scripts used to control compilation and installation of the executable. However, as a special exception, the source code distributed need not include anything that is normally distributed (in either source or binary form) with the major components (compiler, kernel, and so on) of the operating system on which the executable runs, unless that component itself accompanies the executable.

If distribution of executable or object code is made by offering access to copy from a designated place, then offering equivalent access to copy the source code from the same place counts as distribution of the source code, even though third parties are not compelled to copy the source along with the object code.

5. You may not copy, modify, sublicense, or distribute the Program except as expressly provided under this License. Any attempt otherwise to copy, modify, sublicense or distribute the Program is void, and will automatically terminate your rights under this License. However, parties who have received copies, or rights, from you under this License will not have their licenses terminated so long as such parties remain in full compliance.

6. You are not required to accept this License, since you have not signed it. However, nothing else grants you permission to modify or distribute the Program or its derivative works. These actions are prohibited by law if you do not accept this License. Therefore, by modifying or distributing the Program (or any work based on the Program), you indicate your acceptance of this License to do so, and all its terms and conditions for copying, distributing or modifying the Program or works based on it.

7. Each time you redistribute the Program (or any work based on the Program), the recipient automatically receives a license from the original licensor to copy, distribute or modify the Program subject to these terms and conditions. You may not impose any further restrictions on the recipients' exercise of the rights granted herein. You are not responsible for enforcing compliance by third parties to this License.

8. If, as a consequence of a court judgment or allegation of patent infringement or for any other reason (not limited to patent issues), conditions are imposed on you (whether by court order, agreement or otherwise) that contradict the conditions of this License, they do not excuse you from the conditions of this License. If you cannot distribute so as to satisfy simultaneously your obligations under this License and any other pertinent obligations, then as a consequence you may not distribute the Program at all. For example, if a patent license would not permit royalty-free redistribution of the Program by all those who receive copies directly or indirectly through you, then the only way you could satisfy both it and this License would be to refrain entirely from distribution of the Program.

If any portion of this section is held invalid or unenforceable under any particular circumstance, the balance of the section is intended to apply and the section as a whole is intended to apply in other circumstances.

It is not the purpose of this section to induce you to infringe any patents or other property right claims or to contest validity of any such claims; this section has the sole purpose of protecting the integrity of the free software distribution system, which is implemented by public license practices. Many people have made generous contributions to the wide range of software distributed through that system in reliance on consistent application of that system; it is up to the author/donor to decide if he or she is willing to distribute software through any other system and a licensee cannot impose that choice.

This section is intended to make thoroughly clear what is believed to be a consequence of the rest of this License.

9. If the distribution and/or use of the Program is restricted in certain countries either by patents or by copyrighted interfaces, the original copyright holder who places the Program under this License may add an explicit geographical distribution limitation excluding those countries, so that distribution is permitted only in or among countries not thus excluded. In such case, this License incorporates the limitation as if written in the body of this License.

10. The Free Software Foundation may publish revised and/or new versions of the General Public License from time to time. Such new versions will be similar in spirit to the present version, but may differ in detail to address new problems or concerns.

    Each version is given a distinguishing version number. If the Program specifies a version number of this License which applies to it and "any later version", you have the option of following the terms and conditions either of that version or of any later version published by the Free Software Foundation. If the Program does not specify a version number of this License, you may choose any version ever published by the Free Software Foundation.

11. If you wish to incorporate parts of the Program into other free programs whose distribution conditions are different, write to the author to ask for permission. For software which is copyrighted by the Free Software Foundation, write to the Free Software Foundation; we sometimes make exceptions for this. Our decision will be guided by the two goals of preserving the free status of all derivatives of our free software and of promoting the sharing and reuse of software generally.

No Warranty

12. BECAUSE THE PROGRAM IS LICENSED FREE OF CHARGE, THERE IS NO WARRANTY FOR THE PROGRAM, TO THE EXTENT PERMITTED BY APPLICABLE LAW. EXCEPT WHEN OTHERWISE STATED IN WRITING THE COPYRIGHT HOLDERS AND/OR OTHER PARTIES PROVIDE THE PROGRAM "AS IS" WITHOUT WARRANTY OF ANY KIND, EITHER EXPRESSED OR IMPLIED, INCLUDING, BUT NOT LIMITED TO, THE IMPLIED WARRANTIES OF

MERCHANTABILITY AND FITNESS FOR A PARTICULAR PURPOSE. THE ENTIRE RISK AS TO THE QUALITY AND PERFORMANCE OF THE PROGRAM IS WITH YOU. SHOULD THE PROGRAM PROVE DEFECTIVE, YOU ASSUME THE COST OF ALL NECESSARY SERVICING, REPAIR OR CORRECTION.

13. IN NO EVENT UNLESS REQUIRED BY APPLICABLE LAW OR AGREED TO IN WRITING WILL ANY COPYRIGHT HOLDER, OR ANY OTHER PARTY WHO MAY MODIFY AND/OR REDISTRIBUTE THE PROGRAM AS PERMITTED ABOVE, BE LIABLE TO YOU FOR DAMAGES, INCLUDING ANY GENERAL, SPECIAL, INCIDENTAL OR CONSEQUENTIAL DAMAGES ARISING OUT OF THE USE OR INABILITY TO USE THE PROGRAM (INCLUDING BUT NOT LIMITED TO LOSS OF DATA OR DATA BEING RENDERED INACCURATE OR LOSSES SUSTAINED BY YOU OR THIRD PARTIES OR A FAILURE OF THE PROGRAM TO OPERATE WITH ANY OTHER PROGRAMS), EVEN IF SUCH HOLDER OR OTHER PARTY HAS BEEN ADVISED OF THE POSSIBILITY OF SUCH DAMAGES.

End Of Terms And Conditions